I0828063

Nomos Universitätsschriften

Recht

Band 986

Ryan Kraski

Pay-to-Play

How the United States' Collective Patrimony Has Been Locked in an Ivory Tower, Beyond a Paywall

Nomos

The Deutsche Nationalbibliothek lists this publication in the Deutsche Nationalbibliografie; detailed bibliographic data are available on the Internet at http://dnb.d-nb.de

a.t.: Köln, Univ., Diss., 2021

ISBN 978-3-8487-7194-3 (Print)
978-3-7489-1226-2 (ePDF)

British Library Cataloguing-in-Publication Data
A catalogue record for this book is available from the British Library.

ISBN 978-3-8487-7194-3 (Print)
978-3-7489-1226-2 (ePDF)

Library of Congress Cataloging-in-Publication Data
Kraski, Ryan
Pay-to-Play
How the United States' Collective Patrimony Has Been Locked in an Ivory Tower, Beyond a Paywall
Ryan Kraski
278 pp.
Includes bibliographic references.

ISBN 978-3-8487-7194-3 (Print)
978-3-7489-1226-2 (ePDF)

Onlineversion
Nomos eLibrary

1st Edition 2021

Dedicated to the memory of Uncle Frank

Prelude

This dissertation was submitted in 2020 to the Faculty of Law at the University of Cologne and successfully defended on January 7, 2021. All observations, conclusions and citations contained herein are current as of this disputation date and all viewpoints, opinions or conclusions expressed are my own.

While researching on the topic of copyright, I became fascinated with its protection of "authorship," and what this word truly means. In the US legal context, an author is an originator who produces a creative work. Going further, a comparable German term *der Schöpfer*, can be translated into English as "author," "originator," or, in the theological context, "The Creator." Regardless of how mundane or momentous any new work may appear to be, authorship is a profound undertaking. Authorship entails devising new ideas in the immaterial realm, formulating them into words or other means of expression, and fixing the expressions into a tangible medium. When new works are conceived, new worlds are created and unchartered territory is forged. Authorship can be a remarkable gift to others; it gives a grip on the complexities of the world. Using previous works as a springboard, future authors may take hold, engage with, and expand upon them. Along these lines, it is my hope that this thesis will provoke thought on the issues presented, guide subsequent research, and invite new, creative theories by future authors, creators and *Schöpfer*.

Acknowledgments

I look back on the doctoral process with nothing but the warmest feelings. Much of this dissertation was devised and drafted in the early *Kölner* mornings with the sun slowly rising above my courtyard, a family of *Mauersegler* performing their daily airshow outside my window, and always with a freshly brewed cup of coffee within reach.

For their unending support throughout this project, my heartfelt gratitude goes out to:

Paul S. McGrath, Christopher Atzbach, Mayor Matthew Rudzki, Dr. Sezer Dogan and Dr. Joseph DiSarro for their friendship as well as the many amusing, insightful and stimulating conversations.

Past and present colleagues including Marie Pflüger, Michelle Quindeau, P. Matthew Roy, Lukas Plenk, Dr. Leopold Thon and Yvonne Siebenhaar for their immense amount of support, which makes the adventure of living in a foreign country a continuous pleasure, along with their guidance that makes every day a learning experience.

My fellow Doktoranden Saskia Münster, Dr. Marek Prityi, Dr. Ricardo Kerkhof, Dr. Jakob Bünemann and Deginet Wotango Doyiso for being a source of inspiration, making writing labs and seminars enjoyable, and the many Thanksgivings and 4th of Julys celebrated together.

Prof. Kirk W. Junker for his extensive guidance as my doctoral supervisor, engagement with my work, feedback, and mentorship.

Mom, Dad, my brothers, and the rest of my family, from whom the pandemic has kept me away for over a year; I am extremely privileged to have always had their unconditional support and interest in all my endeavors.

And, finally, this work would not have been possible without the companionship and support of Mareike Plenk, who brightens all my days.

Table of Contents

List of Abbreviations

AAU	The Association of American Universities
CC	Creative Commons
DMCA	Digital Millennium Copyright Act of 1998
FIRE	The Foundation for Individual Rights in Education
GST	General Systems Theory
HEA	Higher Education Act of 1965
IP	Intellectual property
IRC	Internal Revenue Code
IRS	Internal Revenue Service
MOOCs	Massive open online courses
NCAA	National Collegiate Athletic Association
NDEA	National Defense Education Act of 1958
Sallie Mae	Student Loan Marketing Association
TEACH Act	The Technology, Education and Copyright Harmonization Act
TRIPs	The Agreement on Trade-Related Aspects of Intellectual Property Rights
UBIT	Unrelated Business Income Tax
US	United States
WCT	The World Intellectual Property Organization Copyright Treaty

Introduction

In an 1899 letter to the Smithsonian Institution, Wilbur Wright mentioned that he was "about to begin a systematic study of the subject in preparation for practical work," and that he "wish[ed] to avail [himself] of all that is already known...."[1] The brothers Orville and Wilbur Wright are now known for their inventions that made manned flight a reality. First taking off in 1903, the brothers, both bicycle mechanics, had not only accomplished something that many other prominent inventors had failed at, but which had also commonly been regarded as impossible. The Wright brothers' amateur curiosity was fueled by the writings of authors such as German engineer Otto Lilienthal, French artist Louis Pierre Mouillard and American astronomer Samuel Pierpont Langley, just to name a few.[2] These pioneering engineers, poets and naturalists that recorded their observations and failed attempts at flight were, in large part, university or technically educated men. Orville and Wilbur Wright were not university educated but were undoubtedly aided by knowledge proliferating systems; universities and early copyright laws facilitated the Wright Brothers' research by providing a pathway from which they could ascend. The outcome of Wilbur Wright's systematic study of the materials sent to him by the Smithsonian Institution amounts to one of the greatest innovative leaps in world history.[3]

Only two centuries prior to the first takeoff, Thomas Hobbes published his observations on the natural condition of humanity, concluding that

1 McCullough, David. *The Wright Brothers*. Simon & Schuster, 2015, pp. 27, 32.

2 *Ibid.* at 28–42 (noting significant influence from others such as the civil engineer Octave Chanute, physician Etienne-Jules Marey, naturalist James Bell Pettigrew, engineer Sir George Cayley, inventor Hiram Maxim, engineer Alexander Graham Bell and Clement Ader).

3 As mentioned above, the Wright Brothers were hardly alone in their curiosity, many brilliant individuals in many disciplines preceded their study of flight. The brothers' implementation of manned flight, though, was a watershed moment that led to a subsequent boom in both scientific study and practical development. *See* Magraner Rullan, Jp, and R. Martinez-Val. "The Birth of Airplane Stability Theory." *Proceedings of the Institution of Mechanical Engineers, Part G: Journal of Aerospace Engineering*, vol. 228, no. 9, 2013, p. 1498.

life was "solitary, poor, nasty, brutish, and short."[4] Human nature was plagued by war, leaving "no place for industry," no culture, no navigation, no building, no knowledge of the world, "no account of time, no arts, no letters, no society" and "continual fear and danger of violent death."[5] Modern observers paint a much different picture.[6] Life is no longer *solitary*; technology and globalization promote the spread of knowledge and prosperity throughout the world. Life is not nearly as *poor* as it once was; extreme poverty has been essentially eradicated in developed countries and the UN has set a realistic goal to put an end to extreme poverty by 2030.[7] Advances in medical technology, nutrition and sanitation and their corresponding reduction of suffering have reduced *nastiness*.[8] Vaccinations and other treatments have eradicated polio and smallpox while decimating the death tolls from AIDS, measles and malaria.[9] The last fifty years have also demonstrated a less *brutish* human condition; there has been a precipitous drop-off in war, battle deaths and genocide.[10] Finally, life is not as *short* as it once was; due to lower infant and child mortality rates, improved medical science and increased access to healthcare, the world's average

---

4 Hobbes, Thomas. *Leviathan, or, the Matter, Forme and Power of a Commonwealth Ecclesiasticall and Civill*. Green Dragon in St. Paul's Churchyard, 1651, p. 97.

5 *Ibid*. at 96–97.

6 *See* Pinker, Steven. *Enlightenment Now the Case for Reason, Science, Humanism, and Progress*. Viking, 2018, p. 364 (describing pre-Enlightenment life as being "darkened by starvation, plagues, superstations, maternal and infant mortality, marauding knight-warlords, sadistic torture-executions, slavery, which hunts, and genocidal crusades, conquests, and wars of religion." Life today is "longer, healthier, richer, safer, happier, freer, smarter, deeper, and more interesting.").

7 "Goal 1: End Poverty in All Its Forms Everywhere – United Nations Sustainable Development." *United Nations*, https://www.un.org/sustainabledevelopment/poverty/; *see also* Pinker, *supra* note 6, at 79, 89, 117 (noting that the rate of extreme poverty has plummeted over the last two hundred years from ninety to ten percent worldwide, with most of the progress occurring over the last thirty-five years. Further, nearly all US households below the poverty line have the most basic amenities and, outside of the US, the poor in developed countries are exponentially more likely to suffer from the effects of obesity than starvation).

8 Greenwood, Brian. "The Contribution of Vaccination to Global Health: Past, Present and Future." *Philosophical Transactions: Biological Sciences*, vol. 369, no. 1645, 19 June 2014, pp. 1–9.

9 *Ibid*.

10 Pinker, *supra* note 6, at 159–62; *but see* Dwyer, Philip. "Whitewashing History." *Historical Reflections/Réflexions Historiques*, vol. 44, no. 1, 1 Mar. 2018, p. 63 (concurring that there has been an overall decrease in violence but calling into question the direct causality between Enlightenment ideals and reduced violence).

life expectancy increased by over forty years, since the mid-eighteenth century.[11]

The improved human condition, characterized by interconnectivity, increased peace and improved health and wealth, can be causally linked to the economic improvements resulting from the Enlightenment, Scientific Revolution and industrialization.[12] Although the surge of industrialization was certainly accelerated by technological creation and innovation, we "know remarkably little about the kind of [systems] that foster and stimulate technological progress and more widely, intellectual innovation."[13] Respect for property rights, enforceable contracts, and checks on government are just a few of the "favorable [systems]" associated with economic growth, whereas systems promoting free expression, intellectual property (hereinafter, IP) and higher education are a few of those that are thought to promote technology and innovation.[14] Of these systems, this dissertation will take an extensive look at the individual incentives created by copyright law and the role of private, nonprofit universities with regard to the creation and dispersion of knowledge. These systems exist to educate people and advance the boundaries of existing knowledge, thereby leading to a less solitary, poor, nasty and brutish world.

Whether they be independent amateurs, private experts or university researchers, people have always had ideas, passed them on to others, expanded upon them and opened the door to many new areas of curiosity. Knowledge is not just a final product, but, rather, a system in which basic ideas, facts and concepts are processed and refined to expand the boundaries of our understanding. In the quest to facilitate knowledge production, several systems have been engrained in the United States' (hereinafter, US) legal tradition to ensure that knowledge production is more than a mere temporary advancement. As knowledge centers, univer-

---

11 Roser, Max, et al. "Life Expectancy." *Our World in Data*, Oct 2019, https://ourworldindata.org/life-expectancy#citation.

12 Crow, Michael M., and William B. Dabars. *Designing the New American University*. Johns Hopkins University Press, 2015, p. 155 (citing to Mokyr, Joel. *The Gifts of Athena: Historical Origins of the Knowledge Economy*. Princeton University Press, 2004, pp. 1–8). Suggesting here that there is causality between improvements in the human condition, industrialization and the underlying knowledge systems is by no means meant to dismiss some of the simultaneously occurring negative outcomes such as environmental degradation or the creation of weapons of mass destruction.

13 Mokyr, Joel. *A Culture of Growth: the Origins of the Modern Economy*. Princeton University Press, 2017, p. 6.

14 *Ibid.* at 6–7, 267.

sities share a parallel innovation track with the outside world, leading to increased overall innovation. Such innovation would not be possible without the many written, copyrighted works that provide future innovaters a basis of knowledge. This systematization of knowledge is meant to produce a society in which ideas can flourish, and, consequently, a flourishing society, which can be passed on to future generations.

A. Exigence

Today with content streaming, all types of works made for entertainment are more abundant and affordable than ever before. Video, music and audiobook streaming platforms all make millions of titles cheaply and instantly available. On the other hand, an expansive body of academic, educational and scientific works continues to grow, but remains locked away behind for-profit paywalls. Accessing academic works, in contrast to their entertainment counterparts, is astonishingly expensive. Hardly any individuals can afford full access, while thousands of universities are forced to pay millions of dollars per year for institutional access. These monopoly prices are made possible by the stringent protection that is automatically afforded to all copyrighted works. Once accessed, most databases still have extensive technical and contractual limitations, restricting how their content may be used. The costs of accessing academic works are pushed directly on to students and indirectly on to society, which nonetheless continues to pump massive amounts of resources into the university system. University and copyright law systems are aimed specifically at expanding and sharing knowledge, but their promise of democratizing access to knowledge remains presently unfulfilled, hampering the innovation process. This dissertation explores how the public either benefits or fails to benefit from these knowledge systems considering the numerous access issues.

Access is only a precondition to the proliferation of knowledge. As will be discussed below, there are many legal limitations on what one can do with copyrighted knowledge once it is accessed. These limitations, though, are irrelevant if the content is inaccessible. Knowledge is inaccessible when works remain unpublished, difficult or impossible to reproduce, otherwise rare or too expensive. Copyright in the US exists specifically to incentivize authorship and the spread of knowledge but has had the opposite effect regarding academic works. Similarly, numerous university admission hindrances precondition individual access to higher education, as well as a society's pool of expertise and intergenerational intellectual growth. Once access to higher education is realized, only then does the discussion regarding quality, educational goals, proliferation of knowledge and the various university privileges begin.

Technology that enables the dissemination of knowledge has played and continues to play a major role in driving change in copyright law as well as in the universities. It will be shown how pivotal innovations, such as the printing press and Internet, have changed the models of knowledge dispersion. Within the US, the copyright regime has been gradually adapted to these technological changes. Universities have similarly changed their models. Today's technology has lowered most political and geographical boarders. On the global scale, knowledge has not traditionally been dispersed evenly; this has led some authors to distinguish various countries and regions based on their either rich or poor access to knowledge.[15] Whether knowledge can be easily transferred, adopted and implemented is highly dependent on the domestic systems, but there is reason to believe that innovation is possible anywhere, given the right circumstances.[16]

With the flood gates opened by digitalization and the Internet, many of those in countries with traditionally poor access to knowledge today have just as good, if not better access to academic works than their counterparts in lands with traditionally rich access to knowledge. During a discussion with a professor from India, it was disclosed that many academics in India turn to pirating websites, which make electronic versions of almost all conceivable books and journals available.[17] Further candid discussions with academics, lawyers and students from virtually every continent con-

---

15 McSherry, Corynne. *Who Owns Academic Work?: Battling for Control of Intellectual Property*. Harvard University Press, 2001, p. 5.

16 Mokyr, *Gifts of Athena*, *supra* note 12, at 286.

17 There are different cultural norms concerning IP protection in places such as India. During a research visit there, I observed that essentially all book vendors in the streets were openly selling photocopies of books, not to mention the many trademark-dubious KFC chicken stands, Nike shoes with candy-cane shaped "swooshes" and misspelled Puma-brand products that I came across. Many regular bookstores were also selling photocopies. Interview with Professor from India (name withheld) (Nov. 13, 2018); *see also* Pugatch, Meir, et al. "U.S. Chamber International IP Index, 6th Ed." *U.S. Chamber International IP Index, 6th Ed.*, Global Innovation Policy Center, 2018, https://www.uschamber.com/sites/default/files/023331_gipc_ip_index_2018_opt.pdf (ranking fifty countries' IP protection on a number of factors such as financial resources, human capital, competitiveness and creativity. The top five countries listed were the US, UK, Sweden, France and Germany. At the bottom of the list were Argentina, Pakistan, Egypt, Algeria and, ranked last, Venezuela. It was noted that, especially due to increased IP awareness and efforts to enforce IP laws, China ranked in the middle of the pack. India

firmed that they too access pirated materials, even when coming from countries with rich access to knowledge. Such an example is demonstrative of the challenges facing authors, users and regulators. The technological gateways through which information flows, such as search engines, social media platforms, paywalled databases and databases full of pirated content, demonstrate that, for every bit of technological progress within the platforms, a new series of questions arise relating to copyright, free speech, knowledge proliferation and fair use.

The American legal systems that intersect directly with knowledge creation and dispersion were created with the purpose of benefiting society; the law of nonprofits, namely private, nonprofit universities, as well as copyright law share this stated purpose. Both systems, which are at the center of focus in this dissertation, have been drastically adapted in their legal forms and practices over the course of time to keep up with technological changes and other outside factors. When functioning properly, these systems both serve the progress of science by the furtherance of knowledge production, dissemination and, relatedly, through education. More importantly, these knowledge systems and the linkages between them promote the creation and dissemination of knowledge for the public benefit. An example of one of these linkages, which will be explored in-depth below, is that the university system has assumed a patronage role for the creation of academic works, supplanting some of the incentives for authorship created by copyright law. Universities' direct involvement in knowledge creation has the potential to fuel open access publishing, but, thus far, they have fallen short of their potential to make research openly accessible.

I. Definitions

The word "knowledge" is defined in terms of formal methods or procedures, whereby *facts* and *data* can be systematically collected, validated and purposefully organized.[18] Knowledge comes in a number of different forms; for example, *general, basic* or *pure* knowledge can be seen in research on philosophy, mathematics or physics, and *applied* knowledge in many

---

remained towards the bottom of the list due to an incomplete IP legal framework and limited enforcement).

18 Walshok, Mary Lindenstein., and Daniel Yankelovich. *Knowledge without Boundaries: What Americas Research Universities Can Do for the Economy, the Workplace, and the Community*. Jossey-Bass, 1995, p. 7.

consumer products or military hardware. Further, *professional training* provides a class of qualified individuals to facilitate the functioning of civil society. Through extensive research output, universities create troves of knowledge, while sometimes redefining what the parameters of general and applied knowledge are.[19] On the instructional side, universities admit students and pass on all types of knowledge, preparing them to work and compete in the modern economy and to participate in society. Knowledge is useful in collective decision making and innovation processes; the public benefits both directly and indirectly from increased innovation, better services and stable political processes. While universities and copyright laws are meant to be conduits through which knowledge is facilitated and passed on, both systems are currently floundering to meet their goals, and the public is paying the price for it, while being excluded.

Knowledge is at the core of the university mission; therefore, it is no coincidence that many university crests advertise this with references to "truth" or "knowledge."[20] Aristotle regarded learning, virtue and utility as the foundations of society. Eventually it would become the role of the universities to "produce learned men, to educate in virtue, or to satisfy the material needs of society."[21] This approach was apparent during the Renaissance, when many universities provided general *liberal* education, focusing on the humanities, while also venturing to provide professional training.[22] University curricula continued to expand over the centuries, and modern universities retain the traditional goal of encouraging critical thought, organization and communication of ideas. Although, this may be endangered due to profuse university involvement in professional training, costly research, and many extraneous activities that have nothing to do with education.[23] The creation and dissemination of knowledge by univer-

19 Gumport, Patricia J. *Academic Pathfinders: Knowledge Creation and Feminist Scholarship*. Greenwood Press, 2002, p. 24.

20 Haidt, Jonathan. *Coddling of the American Mind: How Good Intentions and Bad Ideas Are Setting up a Generation for Failure*. Penguin Publishing Group, 2018, p. 253 (noting that Harvard uses "Veritas," Yale has "Lux et Veritas" and "even the fictional Faber College in the film *Animal House* had the motto "knowledge is good").

21 Frijhoff, Willem. "Patterns." In *A History of the University in Europe: Volume II, Universities in Early Modern Europe*, edited by Walter Rüegg, Cambridge University Press, 1996, p. 43.

22 *Ibid*. at 43, 67.

23 Best, Joel, and Eric Best. *The Student Loan Mess: How Good Intentions Created a Trillion-Dollar Problem*. University of California Press, 2014, p. 130.

sities and copyright law will be addressed in the first two parts of this dissertation.

The term "university" is used generally throughout this work primarily to refer to private, nonprofit institutions of post-secondary, higher learning, but, when otherwise indicated, it may include other university forms, undergraduate liberal arts colleges, trade schools, community colleges, German *Hochschulen*, just to name a few.[24] Although the focus is ultimately on private nonprofit universities, discussion of both public and for-profit universities is unavoidable, particularly for points of comparison and contrast. Universities are both producers and users of knowledge and copyrighted content; this means that they create and have rights over various copyrighted works and, at the same time, are dependent on other copyright owners for their usage of protected materials.[25] University education inevitably requires access to copyrighted materials for professors, researchers and students.[26] Of the four major forms of IP, copyright, patent, trademark and trade secret, "copyright is the most central to the day-to-day function of higher education."[27] In order to create new copyrighted materials, academics must read and learn from existing knowledge,

24 This usage of the term "university" is admittedly broad. The technical distinction between colleges and universities is that colleges offer bachelor's degrees and universities consist of at least one college in addition to their master and doctoral programs. While using more concise terminology when necessary, the broad usage of "university" is done specifically to avoid confusion. For example, this dissertation speaks about Harvard at various points in time, such as at its founding when it was Harvard College and, today, as the world-class Harvard University. Others were founded as colleges and remained so.

25 In a 2015 survey of 4,664 US institutions, eighty-five percent of all US students were enrolled in universities offering doctoral, associate's and master's degrees. It would be most accurate to describe higher education in the US as a small percentage of institutions enrolling many students, and a large group of other institutions that enroll relatively fewer students. The two largest categories for student enrollment are doctoral universities (thirty-one percent of all student enrollment) and associate's colleges (thirty-two percent). The third-most attended type of institution are master's colleges and universities with twenty-two percent of overall enrollment. The many other institutions offering baccalaureate and special focus degrees, along with tribal institutions, have relatively fewer students. *See* 2015 Update Facts & Figures, Descriptive Highlights, The Carnegie Classification of Institutions of Higher Education (2015), http://carnegieclassifications.iu.edu/downloads/_CCIHE2015-FactsFigures.pdf.

26 Elkin-Koren, Niva. "The New Frontiers of User Rights." *American University International Law Review*, vol. 32, no. 1, 2016, pp. 1, 6.

27 Rooksby, Jacob H. "Copyright in Higher Education: A Review of Modern Scholarship." *Duquesne University Law Review*, vol. 54, no. 1, 2016, p. 197.

make use of its content, be able to rearrange it, change it, create new meanings, engage with its issues and to share their own work; these uses often put universities at the crossroads of copyright, access issues and fair use policy.[28]

While there are many types of copyrighted works, this dissertation sets out to focus on the unique area of creative works that are scholarly, academically, educationally and scientifically oriented. For the purpose of simplicity, the works in this category henceforth will be referred to as "academic works."[29] It is also necessary to define a pair of sub-categories within academic works. The two subdivisions relate to how *available* the works are. Some academic works are scarcer because they are only available at a premium—e.g. scholarly journals, treatises, monographs, and other content found in exclusive databases—I refer to these as "first-class works." Other academic works are much more readily available, but have a different relationship to copyright law—government publications, newspaper articles, websites, podcasts, book snippets, and a broad array of content on Internet streaming platforms—therefore, I will refer to this category as "second-class works."[30] These two categories are not necessarily distinguishing quality, although first-class works are more likely to be written by specialists and peer-reviewed. Nor are they meant to designate importance. Most research begins with readily available second-class works that offer enough information to formulate complex understandings of issues, which could be further substantiated by first-class works. Some government publications, such as Supreme Court decisions, are highly authoritative and, simultaneously, second-class works.

---

28 Elkin-Koren, *supra* note 26, at 1, 5.

29 Instead of using the term "academic works," most authors choose to distinguish between "commercial works" and "noncommercial works," which are, admittedly, truer to the terminology typically used for a fair use analysis. My usage of "academic works" in juxtaposition with "works made for entertainment," allows for me to still incorporate the concept of (non-) commerciality, while being able to further distinguish types of works that are contemplated in the Constitution's Copyright Clause from those that are not.

30 Note that there are other common distinctions such as "primary" and "secondary" sources. I wish to avoid these terms because they refer only to the sources' conceptual proximity to an event, a fact or an observation. The terms "primary" and "secondary" do not refer to the source's availability; all primary legal materials in the US—the Constitution, statutes, cases—are in the public domain and are freely accessible. Because terms such as these fail to denote availability, they are less helpful for a copyright / fair use discussion.

There is a divide in the commentary on copyright law where a large group of mainly academic authors, on one side, argues for the reduced scope and duration of copyright protection against the copyright-industry, on the other side, which tends to caution against this.[31] Those who recommend shorter terms and less protection focus on academic works and those that support longer terms universally refer to works made for entertainment, while it is rare that either side makes such explicit distinctions. These groups are speaking past each other; while their common topic, copyright, is the same, their areas of focus, academic works and works made for entertainment, are governed by substantially different economic incentives. Academia is plagued by the nearly century-long terms of protection under the current copyright regime, which substantially hinder access and limit the uses of works, whereas the entertainment industry is clearly dependent on this strong and lengthy protection.[32] Academic works that promote the public benefit through the progress of science are tied to an engine of innovation that has accelerated so rapidly that it has outpaced copyright terms of protection entirely. Scientific and technological innovation are now measured in single years, not decades, centuries or millennia, as they once were. At the same time, copyright protection is longer and more stringent than ever before. Nonetheless, it is certain that this accelerated innovation was fostered by the university and copyright systems over the past centuries.

II. Why Focus on Universities and Copyright Law?

Universities and copyright are interlinked as systems of knowledge creation and dispersion because of the nature of knowledge. First, knowledge is *cumulative*, meaning that its dispersion protects against knowledge-loss; modern technologies promote rapid copying and the spread of private thought into the public realm drives progress.[33] Second, knowledge is *non-rivalrous*; this means that it loses no value when it is openly accessible.[34]

---

31 *See e.g.*, Kemp, Deborah. "Copyright on Steroids: In Search of an End to over Protection." *McGeorge Law Review*, vol. 41, 2017, p. 835; *but see* Carlisle, Stephen. "Why Reducing Current Copyright Terms Would Be Unwise... And Unconstitutional." *Office of Copyright*, 26 Feb. 2016, http://copyright.nova.edu/copyright-terms/.

32 Kemp, *supra* note 31.

33 Mokyr, *Culture of Growth*, *supra* note 13, at 159–60.

34 *Ibid.* at 42.

Contrary to rivalrous goods, the broad dispersion and critical analysis of any body of knowledge adds value to its underlying theories and its applications can bring great benefits to society.[35] In other words, knowledge is a *common / public good* where the entire society benefits, it is available to anyone who desires it and does not diminish in value once it has been used.[36] One issue, which will be explored later, is that knowledge sprouting from universities and other open sources has "been privatized and [commoditized]."[37] The creation of barriers to the access and usage of knowledge serves as a major limitation to academic communication, knowledge production and circulation of ideas.[38]

Focusing on knowledge systems, it is nearly impossible to determine which contributing conditions were *necessary* and which were *sufficient* for industrialization and modernization. In terms of universities and copyright, they alone were almost certainly not sufficient to ensure progress. For example, it could be shown that trade secret or techniques and procedures held secret by guilds of artisans could have played just as large of a role in progressing the useful arts as published information that we would today consider copyrightable. Some economic historians would go even further to argue that the inventions themselves, such as the steam engine, had an even more considerable role on science than science had on them.[39] Further, universities were always purveyors of knowledge, but the greatest innovators often were and continue to be university outsiders.[40] Copyright

35 Crow & Dabars, *supra* note 12, at 22.

36 Willinsky, John. *The Access Principle: the Case for Open Access to Research and Scholarship*. MIT Press, 2006, p. 9.

37 Fuchs, Christian, and Marisol Sandoval. "The Diamond Model of Open Access Publishing: Why Policy Makers, Scholars, Universities, Libraries, Labour Unions and the Publishing World Need to Take Non-Commercial, Non-Profit Open Access Serious." *TripleC*, 11(2), Sept. 2013, pp. 428, 441.

38 *Ibid.* (stating, "[a] single article is not just an individual creation, it is the creation of the whole academic communication process, into which manifold contributors are involved over many years and ages.").

39 Kerker, Milton. "Science and the Steam Engine." *Technology and Culture*, vol. 2, no. 4, 1961, p. 381.

40 This statement should be qualified. University outsiders, tradesmen in the past and private research labs today, are unparalleled in their output of practical applications, techniques and designs. Following the invention of the printing press and prior to universities taking an active role in research, university outsiders had a tendency to further their practical fields as well as to develop entirely new ones, which the universities did not initially adopt. Up until the Scientific Revolution, universities sought primarily to convey settled knowledge. Eventually, the role of the university expanded to incorporate research, which would lead to

and universities, though, were likely necessary systems for the technological and innovation boom. In order to press forward, promote knowledge creation, its dissemination and protect against knowledge being lost over the course of time, these systems have traditionally provided the necessary structure and incentives.[41]

Since universities and copyright law are only two components of a much larger and more complex knowledge-producing apparatus, why choose private, nonprofit universities and copyright law for this analysis?[42] First, universities have always played a role in knowledge proliferation through their attempts to educate as well as with their involvement in research. The majority of universities in the US are private nonprofits, despite the majority of students attending massive state flagship universities and the recent expansion of for-profit universities.[43] Furthermore, from a cultural aspect, private nonprofit universities are the paradigm for higher education in the US; among their ranks are some of the oldest and most prestigious institutions. These private, nonprofit universities offered quality education for centuries in the US without any "system of

---

the creation of new knowledge. Today's American research universities conduct immense amounts of general research, resulting in many quality publications and relatively few patents, and are left far behind outside research labs, conducting applied research that leads to patentable technologies and processes. One concern brought up in this dissertation is the fact that individuals today who do not have institutional affiliations are locked out of some of the largest paywalled systems for knowledge creation and proliferation; *see* Drake, Stillman. "Early Science and the Printed Book: The Spread of Science beyond the University." *Renaissance and Reformation*, vol. 6, no. 3, 1970, pp. 46–49; *see also* Roche, Mark. *Was Deutsche von der amerikanischen Universität lernen können und was sie vermeiden sollten*. Translated by Christiana Goldmann, Meiner Felix Verlag, 2014, p. 22 (noting that some of the greatest thinkers of the seventeenth and eighteenth centuries, such as "Bacon, Hobbes, Descartes, Spinoza, Locke, Leibniz, Voltaire [and] Rousseau" were also university outsiders).

41 Mokyr, *Culture of Growth*, *supra* note 13, at 340.

42 My research began by generally looking into the IP ownership by nonprofits, but it became clear that both categories, IP and nonprofits, were far too broad and multifaceted to analyze. My initial research indicated that, within these two broad systems, copyright and private, nonprofit universities were most compatible because of their purposes and linkages. Just as one example, the first factor of the fair use analysis, although now weakened, provides a straightforward and explicit nexus between copyright, nonprofit educational organizations and their ability to make fair usage of works. The creation of this factor under the common law demonstrates the clear linkage between the systems.

43 Snyder, Thomas D., et al. "Digest of Education Statistics, 2017." 53rd ed., National Center for Education Statistics, 2019, Table 318.60.

governmental quality regulation" due, in large part, to their institutional form and outside competition.[44] Their tradition of private giving from alumni and other donors to support students and university programs offers an unparalleled degree of independence and fiscal stability, which also promotes longevity.[45] The top private, nonprofit universities have become the envy of the world; their model has been often imitated, but never duplicated.[46] Second, copyright law is a particularly good fit for the analysis of knowledge creation and dissemination because virtually all research today is in a fixed medium and automatically receives stringent copyright protection. Third, despite copyright being the most prevalent form of IP that universities control, the linkages between the university and copyright law systems are understudied.[47] Finally, I have had the privilege of attending private nonprofit universities at both the undergraduate and graduate levels. My personal experiences have stimulated my interest in these types of institutions along with my curiosity for IP.

The university and copyright systems were created and perpetuated for the *public benefit*, but this overarching goal is often paid lip service to and then left behind by courts, legislatures and executive overseers. What is the public benefit? At least in terms of universities and copyright, the public benefit can be determined by the systems' goals and intended outcomes. Statutes, cases, university bylaws, mission statements, academic research and university curricula define universities' goals. Copyright law's goals are ascertainable through statutory law, legislative debates, scholarly commentary as well as through the practice and development of the common law. By first inquiring into the purposes and goals of each system, this dissertation sets out to further analyze private nonprofit universities, copyright law and the many linkages between the two. Modern technology and the immense public subsidization of knowledge centers have the promise of improving our collective body of knowledge as well as our access to it. Thus, this dissertation generally considers if the university and copyright

---

44 Hansmann, Henry B. "The Evolving Economic Structure of Higher Education." *The University of Chicago Law Review*, vol. 79, 2012, pp. 159, 169.

45 Vest, Charles M. *The American Research University from World War II to World Wide Web: Governments, the Private Sector, and the Emerging Meta-University*. University of California Press, 2007, p. 8.

46 Salmi, Jamil. "Paths to a World-Class University." In *Paths to a World-Class University: Lessons from Practices and Experiences*. Sense Publishers, 2011, p. ix.

47 Although there are many of books and journals that explore their linkages to varying degrees, they often tend to be either generally descriptive, non-critical of the law or library science-oriented.

regimes are reaching desirable outcomes or, in other words, if the public is being benefited in the most optimal way.

Universities and copyright are imperfect systems that constantly encounter changing cultural and technological realities, but as long as they continue to benefit the public, they can be perpetuated between many generations. The benefits of these systems include reduced transaction costs, increased civic-mindedness, and an investment into public goods and infrastructure through a "spirit of public consciousness and willingness to abstain from free-riding behavior...."[48] Especially in complex societies, systems that reduce transaction costs facilitate most other necessary social interactions.[49] The public trust, along with various privileges, is given to the institutions with the hope that they achieve their goals, thereby benefiting society. Their goals are formulated externally by laws and government support and, on the other hand, internally through centuries of practice and adaptations to technology, among other factors.[50]

B. General Structure

This work consists of two main parts, first focusing on private, nonprofit universities (Part I) and, second, on copyright law (Part II). Each part begins with a detailed description of the system's historical and legal background along with the expectations set by their interested parties; this is designed to demonstrate the systems' purposes and goals (*telos*). More specifically, Part I establishes the goals and purposes of universities

---

48 Mokyr, *Culture of Growth*, *supra* note 13, at 12–13.

49 Salamon, Lester M., and Stefan Toepler. "The Impact of Law on Nonprofit Development: A Framework for Analysis." In *Met Recht Betrokken: Opstellen Aangeboden Aan Prof. Mr. T.J. Van Der Ploeg*. Edited by C. H. C. Overes and T. J. van der Ploeg, Kluwer, 2012, p. 277.

50 Both of these systems at least indirectly lead to increased economic productivity, but that is not my purpose for choosing them. Rather, I chose to analyze these systems for knowledge creation and dissemination specifically with regard to their role in the knowledge process, which, in many instances, does not have a positive, direct economic effect. Quite the contrary, knowledge systems that undertake basic research tend to consume a substantial amount of resources that may not be recouped, not to mention some of the problems associated with economic free-riding. The greatest economic impact from these knowledge systems will be measured indirectly; better-educated individuals with improved access to academic works will then go on to participate in society, develop businesses, create processes and patent inventions.

by looking at their historical development, the privileges that they are afforded, their curricula, the expectations of their students, their financial structures as well as their legal, nonprofit structures. The goals and purposes of copyright law are detailed in the first sections of Part II, covering its historical and legal development, its constitutional basis, an overview of how it functions, its major exceptions, the effect of international law and the alternative regimes that currently co-exist alongside copyright law. Once the systems' purposes and goals are ascertained, they are used as elements for analyzing the Questions Presented (*see* Questions Presented below). Throughout the analyses in both Part I and Part II, special attention is paid to the interrelationship between the two systems. The two systems will be synthesized together to identify the linkages between them and how each system affects the other. After the questions are analyzed in Parts I and II, Part III will provide a summary and conclusion.

C. *Questions Presented*

1. *Are the knowledge proliferating systems of private, nonprofit universities and copyright law benefiting the public?*
2. *If so, are they benefiting the public in accordance with how both systems are legally structured? What linkages are there between the two systems?*
3. *How can university and copyright regimes be improved through the law?*

D. *Methods*

In order to effectively understand and analyze nonprofit universities and copyright as legal sub-systems within the general legal system, this dissertation will adopt the methods of *General Systems Theory* (hereinafter, GST). "Systems," for the purposes of a GST analysis, can be defined as collections "... of interdependent flows and activities linking shifting coalitions of participants embedded in wider material-resource and institutional environments."[51] GST is an extension of classical *systems theory*, which sought to analyze individual systems for the purpose of finding solutions to prob-

51 Scott, W. Richard. *Organizations: Rational, Natural and Open Systems*. 5th ed., Prentice Hall, 2003, pp. 25–29 (including numerous definitions for rational, natural and open systems; the definition cited in this text is referring to open systems).

lems, optimizing efficiency, developing analytical procedures and creating scientific order.[52] One of the major shortcomings of the classical systems theory was that, following its extensive interpretation and theorizing, it often led to unsuccessful attempts to develop mathematical theories that could be applicable to other systems or sub-systems. This difficulty is further exacerbated by the fact that there are differing system types, including natural and social systems, which may be either "open" or "closed" to inputs from their environments.[53]

GST operates on the premise that an analysis focusing on one system alone is inadequate when it is an "open system," i.e. when the system has a flow of inputs and outputs from other systems.[54] The inputs and outputs can consist of "materials, energy and information."[55] Open systems, best represented by living organisms and social institutions, have inputs and outputs that contribute to a steady state in which it can continue to function.[56] In addition to promoting stability, a system's inputs can even improve order and organization within the system.[57] A system's inputs are also highly determinative for the effectiveness of a system's functioning; one author fittingly reminds that "great universities do not arise in deserts or other sparsely inhabited areas."[58] Regardless of the system type, one presumption of GST is that all systems begin in a complex, dynamic arrangement, and, while they can become more organized and efficient, they eventually break down in their ability to function and are diminished.[59]

GST requires observing every system as part of a hierarchy of interactions with larger overarching systems and smaller sub-systems. When the smaller subsets are capable of functioning autonomously, the entire hierarchy benefits.[60] Due to the many possible "linkages" across systems and sub-systems, drawing boundaries can be quite complicated.[61] "Open"

---

52 Bertalanffy, Ludwig von. *General System Theory: Foundations, Development, Applications*. Penguin, 1969, pp. 4, 8.

53 *Ibid.* at 9, 14, 34 (explaining that formal organizations include armies, bureaucracies and business, for example, whereas informal organizations are observable in social structures and interactions. Further, natural systems also lack teleology and other indispensable factors present in non-natural systems).

54 *Ibid.* at 39.

55 Scott, *supra* note 51, at 83.

56 Bertalanffy, *supra* note 52, at 39.

57 *Ibid.* at 41.

58 Scott, *supra* note 51, at 91.

59 Bertalanffy, *supra* note 52, at 44.

60 Scott, *supra* note 51, at 92.

61 *Ibid.* at 90.

systems, such as private nonprofit universities and copyright, still maintain boundaries although the boundaries may not be clearly defined and may require an investment of resources for their maintenance.[62] The hierarchy of higher education could be observed through the interactions of the types of universities—public nonprofits, private nonprofits and private for-profits—with an infinite amount of overarching and parallel social and natural systems. Similarly, copyright, being a sub-system of IP and the entire legal system as a whole, can be observed through its linkages with an expansive web of systems for promoting knowledge. Extending the scope of observation to view systems at every level, GST is meant to develop better methods for approaching systems, even at their highest, most general levels. Because of this, GST requires no mathematical formulation, seeking, instead, only a "guiding idea."[63] GST may contribute more concise theories, it may develop unifying principles and, finally, it may contribute to the communication and education within and among all of the disciplines.

The goal of GST is to "find constructs and possibly laws within the individual levels," and the only necessary unifying principle is "that we find organization at *all* levels."[64] Once a system is reduced to its working pieces and its organization is identified, GST requires an "interdisciplinary synthesis."[65] An interdisciplinary synthesis should go beyond isolating system parts in the search for causation; in its holistic, gestalt-based search for linkages between systems, GST aims to incorporate teleology, direction, adaptation along with other major driving factors.[66] Intensive focus on these linkages is meant to elucidate an understanding of the systems, something from which we can learn and adapt, not a means of "predict[ing] the future."[67] GST provides a basis for today's organizational theorists, although they are still forced to humbly admit that our systems for analyzing are substantially less complex than those being studied.[68]

Perhaps a GST analysis of a living organism is illustrative of how one can approach social systems. An animal could be dissected down to its lowest level by its organs, tissues and cells, but it can also be observed through the lens of its overarching taxonomy. Observing its taxonomy

62 *Ibid.* at 89.
63 Bertalanffy, *supra* note 52, at 9, 16, 24.
64 *Ibid.* at 49.
65 *Ibid.* at 51.
66 *Ibid.* at 45.
67 Junker, Kirk W. *Legal Culture in the United States: an Introduction*. Routledge, 2016, p. 77.
68 *See e.g.*, Scott, *supra* note 51, at 82, 84.

steps away from the one specific animal and, instead, looks upward toward its entire species, genus, family, order and so on. While considering the animal's biology, a more holistic GST approach must also include the animal's interaction with its own species, diseases, its natural environment, competing species, predators, prey and "the relations or forces between them."[69] There is a good argument that Charles Darwin in his famous work, *On the Origin of Species by Means of Natural Selection,* applied a GST analysis of his own. Darwin observed animals with regard to their individual biology, reproductive systems, genealogy, adaptation and "web of complex relations" in order to develop a theory related to the animals' complex systems and hierarchies in relation to the outside world.[70] With more modest goals in mind, this dissertation similarly seeks to develop an intricate understanding of the university and copyright systems, and then to describe the linkages in and among them. GST is useful in analyzing complex legal structures that need to be broken down into their many levels, understood as individual components and put back together as "a coherent whole."[71]

In writing about the law, lawyers tend to downplay the political, economic, financial, sociological, psychological and other external factors, while reducing their writing to what they believe is a pure legal analysis. Such an approach is unwarranted and this work will show that the legal system is very much an "open system," to borrow GST terminology. US jurisprudence is riddled with interdisciplinary approaches; one need look no further than a Supreme Court opinion written by an "originalist" to get a history lesson or to punishments written into the criminal law, creating, at least theoretically, economic incentives to abstain from antisocial behavior. Looking at other fields aids us in forming our "understanding of what law is" and that "law is a social institution that shapes society, while also being shaped by it."[72] This dissertation, in attempting to create a more intricate understanding of what nonprofit universities and copyright law are and how they function, is made possible by the invaluable prior

69 Bertalanffy, *supra* note 52, at 32.

70 Winther, Rasmus Grønfeldt. "Systemic Darwinism." *PNAS*, vol. 105, no. 33, 2018, pp. 11833–37.

71 Nimmer, David and Melville Nimmer. *Nimmer on Copyright.* Matthew Bender Elite Products, 2019, vol. 5, § 19E.02 (suggesting that a thorough analysis of legal systems is dependent on studying their underlying theories, which goes beyond textual analysis to assure "better analytic consistency and coherence" as well as to "[reflect] the nature of human rights as principles of morality.").

72 Junker, *supra* note 67, at 100–101.

contributions of historians, economists, sociologists and, not to mention, jurists. The aforementioned disciplines are drawn upon extensively in this work in order to conduct an interdisciplinary, primarily qualitative review, incorporating various primary and secondary sources.

E. Literature Review

At the forefront of research on higher education, are authors such as Cole, Kerr, Shapiro, Karabel, Vedder, Brint, Roche and Armstrong. They provide extensive sociological, economic and administrative insight into many aspects of higher education. University history is also a well-researched area; the publications from Rüegg, De Ridder-Symoens and Drake provide a thorough foundation for subsequent researchers. The study of nonprofit law is similarly well developed but has not been written on with the same frequency as higher education, for example. Hansmann remains the standard-bearer in the area of nonprofit law, especially with his inquiry into the non-distribution constraint, while Cafardi and Cherry provide a broader picture of how nonprofit law is structured. When universities' legal structures are addressed in other academic literature, either public or for-profit university forms tend to be the focal points; private, nonprofit universities are greatly understudied. The analyses by Weisbrod, Salaman, Frumpkin, Keating, Galle, Walker, Fuchs and Sandoval also add many valuable contributions to the study of nonprofit law.

Authorship in the area of copyright law is extensive, while still dominated by a few decided leaders: Melville and David Nimmer, Netanel and Lessig. These standard-bearers for copyright are not only influential through their publications, but some have also actively formed copyright law by arguing cases in front of the Supreme Court. Others such as Crews, Darnton and Baldwin have also made significant contributions to the field. One note on these authors, which is especially relevant for this dissertation; the Nimmer treatises are of top-quality and highly authoritative but can only be accessed with access to expensive databases, whereas Lessig has made all of his books openly accessible with user-friendly licensing terms. This is just one of the many examples addressed in this dissertation of how legal and technical controls on works affect subsequent academic research.

Most authors that are drawn upon for this dissertation tend to focus intensively on the specific areas of their expertise, leaving a wealth of authoritative sources to build upon, but stopping short of exploring the boundaries between theirs and other systems. Bertalanffy provides a method for analyzing across systems that is adopted here as a methodic structure. Beyond this work, Bertalanffy's contributions have also laid the groundwork for most of today's organizational theorists. Mokyr's writing on economic history is both an intrepid and brilliant attempt to cross boundaries between systems. Finally, Rooksby's writing, bridging higher education to trademark law, not only added insight to many of the substantive areas of study in this dissertation, but was also exemplary for its analysis across systems.

F. *Contributions of this Research*

Universities and copyright law are both highly researched areas, so this work explores the most neglected areas of study within these systems. Topics concerning higher education are discussed by a broad-spectrum of experts in many fields but are neglected when it comes to the study of universities' legal structures, especially in relation to their nonprofit characteristics. Copyright law too suffers no lack of research, but most of the research and case law tends to take a narrow, microscopic focus on issues under the broad category of copyright law, paying little attention to the overarching purposes of the system. Thus, this dissertation addresses these respective shortcomings in order to provide a more comprehensive understanding of universities as legal systems and how their interactions with copyright law spur knowledge creation and dissemination. In order to do so, this work makes an essential distinction between academic works and works made for entertainment while introducing new terms, which distinguish "first-" from "second-class works." This GST approach draws out linkages between the two systems throughout the entire work and is summarized in Part III. Although, in order to make such observations, this dissertation first undertakes an analysis of each of the systems and their inner workings.

Part I delves into university goals and their outcomes in relation to their legal structure. More specifically, this research lays a groundwork for universities' purposes (*telos*). While many researchers tend to focus on the various roles of universities, they rarely present them in the relevant context of how universities are legally structured. When so, the nonprofit form is generally neglected. Universities' purposes are defined here through a thorough look into their historical development, privileges, curricula, student expectations, funding structures and nonprofit legal requirements. Following this study of universities' purposes, Part I conducts a detailed analysis of the overall access to higher education and universities' roles as institutions for education, research, certification and social mobility. In addition to avoiding the legal structuring issues, most other research also tends to avoid using such a holistic approach to define the actual roles that universities have come to play. Finally, universities' legal structures are considered in terms of their commercial activities, administrative compensation and capital accumulation, all of which are shown to exceed the parameters of universities' nonprofit legal structuring and have been both understudied and underenforced. This dissertation addresses the likelihood that some structural safeguards have been neutralized.

Part II similarly lays out a groundwork for copyright law's purposes (*telos*). In assessing access to knowledge through copyrighted works, this dissertation lays out a new conceptualization of the many rings of regulation to which copyrighted knowledge is subjected. This dissertation also details how accessing knowledge is different in the various private, public and nonprofit sectors, a vital distinction that has previously not received enough attention. Finally, copyright's production, structural and expressive functions are thoroughly analyzed in order to view them in the context of their relationship to academic works; this analysis makes a key distinction between academic works and works made for entertainment, which is elsewhere most often avoided or ignored.

In the attempt to cover a vast swath of information regarding universities and copyright, some general assumptions are made in this work. First, it is assumed that access to higher education and knowledge are both essential for an innovative, functioning society. Structural impediments, hindering access to higher education and knowledge, arise over time for various reasons and can be identified and changed. Higher education should be available to those who desire it and who are academically qualified, including those of historically disadvantaged groups. Policies encouraging institutional longevity, the inter-generational flourishing of an institution, are in the best interests of society, the universities themselves as well as their graduates. Adherence to nonprofit standards and principles can add to private universities' longevity. At the same time, outside interference, such as intensive government involvement or adoption of for-profit models, can detract from private, nonprofit universities' ability to flourish over long periods. The three major sectors—private, public and nonprofit—all perform different functions, and their individual functions must be understood. This process can aid policymakers who are able to adapt the systems in line with the systems' underlying purposes. Similarly, US copyright law has a set of foundational goals that must guide the system to function and serve the public.

Part I: Universities

This work focuses on private, nonprofit universities, but public nonprofit and private for-profit universities are also brought up for points of comparison as well as to discuss the linkages between these institutions. One overarching theme is that, because the state and federal governments have failed to distinguish between the university types and their legal structures, their boundaries have become excessively blurred. Those closest to university administration are seeing growing "cracks" throughout the whole of higher education due to, among other things, universities' financing models and rising costs.[73] These cracks are not the result of a lack of resources. Private universities have enjoyed such extensive support from all levels of government that students at private, nonprofit universities enjoy significantly more state-support than students elsewhere. Thus, in terms of finance, many private universities are becoming indistinguishable from the other forms, despite their substantially different underlying structures.[74] For reasons that will be addressed in Part I, public universities are also attempting to adopt private financing models, while both public and private types have been affected by the growth of for-profit institutions. Notwithstanding the blurred boundaries between systems in terms of finance, significant differences remain.

Because of the major legal and social differences between the types of universities, Part I first starts out by establishing the unique historical development, privileges, curricula, student expectations, funding structures and nonprofit legal requirements of private, nonprofit universities. One initial distinction is that private, nonprofit universities are neither obliged to guarantee the protection of students' constitutional rights nor do they enjoy the state-immunity that exists for public universities. Moreover, private universities have traditionally used *selectivity* as a measurement of success, whereas public universities have traditionally encouraged *access* as a rubric; this Part will demonstrate how the adoption of standards across

73 Johnson, Daniel M. *The Uncertain Future of American Public Higher Education: Student-Centered Strategies for Sustainability*. Palgrave Macmillan, 2019, p. 8.

74 Vedder, Richard. "There Are Really Almost No Truly Private Universities." *Forbes*, 8 Apr. 2018, https://www.forbes.com/sites/richardvedder/2018/04/08/there-are-really-almost-no-truly-private-universities/#a61d0c757bc5.

systems has resulted in changing approaches to education. Whether a university focuses on "elite" or "open" education is likely determinative as to what is at the core of their curriculum.[75] Open-universities do not focus primarily on character or leadership skill development and opt, instead, to focus on streamlined programs tailored to train more students in more professional fields. Over time, the tendency has been for the curricula of the most open access schools to creep upward through the educational spectrum, as opposed to the liberal arts of the most elite schools filtering downward. Part I will show how this has affected the university system, leading to more professional training overall, and why that is relevant for this knowledge system.[76] The general goals of universities go beyond providing access to *education* to also include *research*, *certification* and *social mobility*.[77]

These five elements—access, education, research, certification and social mobility—will be analyzed to determine whether private, nonprofit universities benefit the public. Whether these goals are realized, and to what extent, is highly dependent on the type of institution, the expectations of all interested parties and the institution's adherence to its legal and educational standards. The interested parties of a nonprofit organization, to name a few, could be the beneficiaries of nonprofit goods or services—students in the case of nonprofit universities—donors, faculty, administrators, members of the community and the local, state and federal authorities. Where the success of a for-profit company could be measured by profits, dividends and overall shareholder satisfaction, properly functioning nonprofit organizations have an entirely different set of economic incentives, different legal obligations and no *shareholders* to whom profits are distributed. Determining if universities are benefiting the public entails an in-depth look at the expectations set by their interested parties in terms of education, research, certification and social mobility, and establishing

---

75 Brint, Steven. *Two Cheers for Higher Education: Why American Universities Are Stronger than Ever, and How to Meet the Challenges They Face*. Princeton University Press, 2018, pp. 29–30.

76 *Ibid*. at 32.

77 Graduates, as private beneficiaries, stand to earn higher wages and will have better employment opportunities, while society stands to indirectly benefit from higher productivity, better public health, more stable families, lower crime, etc; *See generally Ibid*. at 76 (discussing university involvement in various goals such as being cultural organizations, vehicles for upward mobility and economic drivers through local community connections).

whether their activities in these areas meet the obligations set by nonprofit law.

A. Background and Development of the American University

American universities have their roots in several European systems, especially those of the British and Germans. Some of the most notable advances were made by the eighteenth century Scottish and English universities, promoting philosophy and the sciences, and, eventually, German universities and their reforms during the Enlightenment.[78] While progress in the development of new sciences and analytical approaches was sparse and unpredictable, it occurred and was likely fostered by the sheer quantity of European institutions.[79] American universities have similarly come to make an impact through meaningful areas of study and the sheer volume of institutions. The advances made by early universities were complimented by the numerous independent academies and societies; all of these institutions, formal and informal, laid the groundwork for the American system.[80] Thus, by describing the roots of the American university system, this section also begins to define their role in society and the public's expectations of these institutions.

I. Early European Societies and Universities

The Republic of Letters was a decentralized intellectual community of international scholars, sharing their ideas in the time leading up to the Enlightenment.[81] Because of the distance and informality between contributors, such associations have since been dubbed "invisible colleges."[82] Enabling communication between scholars throughout the West, the Republic reduced the obstacle of political fragmentation and opened the discussion up to thousands of other individuals who would have otherwise been

78 Roche, *supra* note 40, at 21–24.
79 Mokyr, *Culture of Growth*, *supra* note 13, at 173.
80 Roche, *supra* note 40, at 43–45.
81 Mokyr, *Culture of Growth*, *supra* note 13, at 179.
82 Crow & Dabars, *supra* note 12, at 190.

left out of the discussion.[83] In other words, this system reduced "access costs" by making science more open.[84] The Republic was ideally meant to be egalitarian, opening the door to all based on "merit, originality, achievement and erudition," and to provide the opportunity to stake one's claim on these factors.[85] This noble attempt at knowledge proliferation did not effectively include the poorest classes, but, nonetheless, it served to drive the useful sciences until other institutions would become more relevant.[86]

At the beginning of the nineteenth century, France initiated a few reforms that were notable for the university system's development. This "French model" relied on special colleges, state centralization and the isolation of faculties to offer tightly regimented curricula in accordance with the desires of its "enlightened despotism."[87] The French model emphasized strict discipline, even with regard to personal habits, and the adherence of personal views to official doctrines while tightly controlling the issuance of degrees. After this model was passed on through a few successive regimes, it was eventually substituted, in most part, for the "German model" in the late 1800's.[88] The French model, while it was still prevalent, had its greatest influence in the French colonies in North Africa, French West Africa, Syria and Indo-China.[89]

The German Model for university research and education is primarily attributed to the efforts of Wilhelm von Humboldt, who persuaded the King of Prussia, despite the King's preference for the French Model, to found a university in Berlin in 1810.[90] His namesake institution, Humboldt

83 Edelstein, Dan, et al. "Historical Research in a Digital Age: Reflections from the Mapping the Republic of Letters Project." *The American Historical Review*, vol. 122, no. 2, 2017, pp. 412–417.

84 Mokyr, *Culture of Growth*, *supra* note 13, at 183.

85 *Ibid.* at 200.

86 Mokyr, *Gifts of Athena*, *supra* note 12, at 291.

87 Rüegg, Walter. "Themes." In *A History of the University in Europe: Volume III, Universities in The Nineteenth and Early Twentieth Centuries*, edited by Walter Rüegg, Cambridge University Press, 2004, pp. 3–5 (noting that there were hints of these characteristics already during the early modern period, but the French Model acted to formalize them under Napoleon).

88 *Ibid.*

89 Shils, Edward, and John Roberts. "The Diffusion of European Models Outside Europe." In *A History of the University in Europe: Volume III, Universities in The Nineteenth and Early Twentieth Centuries*, edited by Walter Rüegg, Cambridge University Press, 2004, p. 163.

90 Crow & Dabars, *supra* note 12, at 79–80.

University, was founded on the principle of studying how knowledge is acquired in order to stimulate students' minds, while encouraging them to think scientifically in all fields.[91] This comes in contrast to previous systems, which acted merely to pass on "settled" knowledge.[92] The German Model was characterized by "freedom;" the manner of study, curricula and relationships with governmental authorities were all liberalized.[93] Humboldt proposed a multi-faceted, educational system for the good of the whole public. It would aid peoples' moral development, general education, skills necessary for occupations, training for leadership roles as well as to cultivate research and scholarship.[94] Humboldt's aspiration to promote the development of multidimensional individuals is evident in his writing:

> [t]here are undeniably certain kinds of knowledge that must be of a general nature and, more importantly, a certain cultivation of the mind and character that nobody can afford to be without. People obviously cannot be good craft workers, merchants, soldiers or businessmen unless, regardless of their occupation, they are good, upstanding and—according to their condition—well-informed human beings and citizens. If this basis is laid through schooling, vocational skills are easily acquired later on, and a person is always free to move from one occupation to another, as so often happens in life.[95]

Humboldt believed that there should only be state involvement in two respects; first, the state should guarantee and protect academic freedom and, second, that it would appoint professors.[96] This ideal relationship with the state suffered some drawbacks in its implementation due to governmental restrictions on speech and censorship that were not removed until after 1848.[97] Access to seminars and laboratories gradually gave students a start in their scientific research; eventually this system became prominent, attracting researchers to Berlin and replacing Paris as the

---

91 *Ibid.*

92 Rüegg, *Themes*, *in* Volume III, Universities in the Nineteenth and Early Twentieth Centuries, *supra* note 87.

93 *Ibid.*

94 Günther, Karl-Heinz. "Profiles of Educators: Wilhelm Von Humboldt (1767–1835)." *Prospects-Quarterly Rev. of Edu.*, Translated by Karl-Heinz Günther, vol. 18, no. 65, 1988, pp. 127, 132.

95 *Ibid.*

96 Rüegg, *Themes*, *in* Volume III, Universities in the Nineteenth and Early Twentieth Centuries, *supra* note 87.

97 *Ibid.*

"Mecca for scholars and scientists from all over the world."[98] As the nineteenth century progressed, and as more German universities followed Humboldt's model, more Europeans and Americans began streaming into the German research universities.[99] By the end of the nineteenth century, the German Model was accepted as the modern university model throughout Europe as well as in the United States.[100] The German Model owes its success, in large part, to both secularization and bureaucratization of the respective states in which it flourished.[101] While this coincided with the transformation of public universities into lay institutions, it did also subject universities everywhere to increased state bureaucracy.[102]

Indeed, the German model was implanted in the US out of the desire to provide students higher education, which would otherwise not be possible through apprenticeships or other experience-based training and to form universities into "the symbolic apparatus of progressive civilization."[103] Taking the legal training in the US as an example, the apprenticeship model was gradually phased out in favor of the professionalized university education. The influence of the German model resulted in full-time university professors using case law to scientifically analyze legal reasoning and theories.[104] Any American universities that experienced this transition experienced it gradually. American universities throughout the nineteenth century still had small faculties, inadequate research equipment and libraries, many students were not trained to research and there were very few doctoral candidates; of the few, they were primarily doctors of divinity.[105]

The distinctive goals of the liberal British model such as enforcing discipline, strengthening character and promoting good leadership continued to live on despite the gaining influence of the German model. Retaining

---

98 *Ibid.* at 3, 6.

99 Crow & Dabars, *supra* note 12, at 82–83.

100 Roche, *supra* note 40, at 23–24, 27 (noting that, along with the Humboldt University in Berlin, German universities in Göttingen, Halle and Jena were significant in the early days of the German model).

101 Crow & Dabars, *supra* note 12, at 80–81.

102 Rüegg, *Themes*, *in* VOLUME III, UNIVERSITIES IN THE NINETEENTH AND EARLY TWENTIETH CENTURIES, *supra* note 87, at 3, 6 (noting that a number of ecclesiastical institutions reintroduced in France and Spain at this time were not capable of surviving; elsewhere, the study of theology was moved into the seminaries).

103 Shils & Roberts, *Diffusion of European Models*, *supra* note 89, at 163–64.

104 Angulo, A.J. *Diploma Mills: How For-Profit Colleges Stiff Students, Taxpayers, and the American Dream*. Johns Hopkins University Press, 2016, p. 31.

105 Shils & Roberts, *Diffusion of European Models*, *supra* note 89, at 163, 166.

its influence today, the British model is still to be found in American legal training as well as in the undergraduate sphere, especially at private liberal arts colleges.[106] Undergraduate studies have therefore remained the sphere in which students are instructed and trained to be better market and political leaders. Although, universities, in addition to the liberal arts programs, became more active in creating specialized and professionalized students; there was a tendency to make a science out of traditional trades, reestablishing universities as the gatekeepers to numerous professions in a new way.[107] In doing so, professors who taught were increasingly becoming involved in research, providing new knowledge for new professions and new fields of study. Such advancements were based on having a corps of committed professors who were "true experts, qualified to train others and evaluate the importance of developments within specialized monopolies of competence."[108] Signs of influence from the German model were noticeable in the US beginning in the 1850's.[109]

II. The Emergence of the American System

American universities today are the worldwide standard bearers for higher education. Their rise to prominence was not only a result of decreased competition internationally following the Second World War, but also because of their ability to drive innovation.[110] While the substantial German influence on American universities is undeniable, it should also be noted that the German structural model was adopted, Americanized and became a unique American system of its own. Of the many public and private American universities that adopted the German model, it is clear that this German influence is most recognizable in their development of

106 Kerr, Clark. *The Uses of the University*. Harvard University Press, 2001, p. 144.

107 McSherry, *supra* note 15, at 58–59 (noting that university engineering degrees eventually became an indication of professional quality and pressed many people, who would have otherwise undergone apprenticeships, into specialized programs. Despite resistance from the trades, the 226 engineering degrees awarded in 1880 rose to around 11,000 by 1930).

108 *Ibid*. at 115, 123.

109 Shils & Roberts, *Diffusion of European Models*, *supra* note 89, at 163, 167.

110 Roche, *supra* note 40, at 35.

graduate schools.[111] Prior to the expansion of postgraduate programs in the US, many American graduates had been traveling to Germany for further research experience.[112] Separate graduate schools, those offering master's and doctoral degrees, were an American concept, essentially a compromise allowing for a liberal undergraduate education, based on the British model, as well as higher, research-based, study. The Germans never traditionally had a need for graduate schools because these research aims were already integrated within one's general university studies.

American universities adopted various features of foreign systems while simultaneously allowing for uniquely American features to develop; this came to form the modern university landscape. For example, the principle of *Lehr- und Lernfreiheit*, academic freedom increased the regard for and dignity of the academic profession, thus creating an environment in which academics were free to express opinions and pursue non-orthodox studies.[113] With varying degrees of acceptance around the US, the principle of *Einheit von Forschung und Lehre*, the unity of research and teaching, was also adopted.[114] Some universities began elevating research to the level of importance of teaching, providing scientific equipment for the natural sciences and founding libraries for the study of the humanities and social sciences.[115] Another feature adopted from the German model was the *Seminar*, a small gathering where students could present research and have critical discussions with a professor and their fellow students.[116] "Tenure" became the American approach for protecting professors and

---

111 *Ibid.* at 52–53. While the German university structure was highly influential in the US, both systems still maintained their own standards and levels of academic rigor.

112 Shils & Roberts, *Diffusion of European Models*, *supra* note 89, at 163, 167–69 (noting that between 9,000 and 10,000 American students attended German universities, of these were Daniel Cold Gilman, the first president of Johns Hopkins University, Granville Stanley Hall, the first president of Clarke University, William Rainey Harper, the first president of the University of Chicago, and Charles William Eliot, president of Harvard who had studied chemistry in Germany).

113 Lerg, Charlotte A. "Academic Freedom in America: Gilded Age Beginnings and World War I Legacies." *The Journal of the Gilded Age and Progressive Era*, vol. 17, no. 4, 2018, pp. 693–94.

114 *Ibid.*

115 Shils & Roberts, *Diffusion of European Models*, *supra* note 89, at 163, 170 (noting that the University of Chicago, Johns Hopkins University and Clark University were some of the first to seriously undertake research).

116 Roche, *supra* note 40, at 26. *Journal of the Gilded Age and Progressive Era*, vol. 17, no. 4, 2018, pp. 693–94; Lerg, *supra* note 113.

their academic freedom by guaranteeing lifetime employment, by faculty having a say in the hiring of other faculty and by allowing professors to determine their own curricula.[117] While constitutional rights to academic freedom of individual professors exist on First Amendment free expression grounds, the most contentious academic freedom issues on tenure usually come down to contractual issues between faculty and their universities.[118]

The omissions of some aspects of the German model proved to be substantial in the formation of a uniquely American research model. Perhaps most notable was the inclusion of technical disciplines in the American universities, whereas, in Germany, such disciplines would typically be found in separate technical schools.[119] Although it could be argued that such professional training programs in American universities are more education- than research-based, their related masters and doctoral programs do allow for research within the various fields. Also, the German academic *Institut* was generally not adopted in the United States.[120] These German *Institute* tend to isolate top professors according to discipline, giving them "exclusive domain" to manage their departments. Universities in the US, rather, favored grouping professors together in departments, which came with the benefit of better access to funding for labs and libraries and well as more interdisciplinary and interdepartmental work.[121] Finally, the concept of the German *Habilitation*, a specialized monograph and defense thereof, beyond the doctoral dissertation, also was not adopted in the US.[122] This may have been primarily due to financial constraints. The German *Privatdozent* traditionally needed to be independently wealthy to support his teaching and research, whereas, in the US, academics were already in short supply and tended to come from the lower middle class.[123]

By the outset of the First World War, in 1914, the flow of Americans studying in Germany had already subsided.[124] American universities had

---

117 McSherry, *supra* note 15, at 59–60; Brint, *Two Cheers for Higher Education*, *supra* note 75, at 44.

118 Post, Robert. "Academic Freedom and the Constitution" In *Who's Afraid of Academic Freedom?* Columbia University Press, 2015, pp.132–33.

119 Hammerstein, Notker. "Universities and War in the Twentieth Century." In *A History of the University in Europe: Volume III, Universities in The Nineteenth and Early Twentieth Centuries*, edited by Walter Rüegg, Cambridge University Press, 2004, pp. 637, 67.

120 Shils & Roberts, *Diffusion of European Models*, *supra* note 89, at 163, 172.

121 Gumport, *supra* note 19, at 7.

122 Roche, *supra* note 40, at 25.

123 Shils & Roberts, *Diffusion of European Models*, *supra* note 89, at 163, 173.

124 Lerg, *supra* note 113, at 694.

grown enough in prestige and research output to the extent that it was no longer perceived as necessary to travel to Europe.[125] The German model was still held in high regard. Many academics were able to read the German language and many physicists continued traveling to Germany throughout the 1920's and 1930's to research alongside some of the world's leading physicists.[126] There was also a growing trend in the US for universities to focus more on applied sciences, as opposed to the German tendency to conduct basic scientific research.[127] Following the Russian Bolshevik Revolution and the rise of fascism in Europe, the flow of intellectuals was reversed, now in the direction of the US. Many refugee scholars found a new home in the American universities.[128]

As the Second World War broke out, American universities were regarded as on par or even, perhaps, more advanced than their European counterparts.[129] Their focus on applied research and practical applications was aided by their structural organization; broad departments, as opposed to individual institutes, facilitated internal cooperation for tasks regarding war research, namely atomic research.[130] University departments added a diversity of approaches because each discipline has its own "boundaries, priorities, [systems for] knowledge, and preferred concepts, methods and principles of inquiry."[131] Numerous federal government bodies, such as the National Defense Research Committee, were established to streamline research for the war effort now among universities, industry and the army.[132] Aside from the controversial and ethical aspects associated with weapons research, the atom bomb's development was a remarkable feat. German atomic research for military applications was abandoned in 1942 and the US had its first functional test by July 1945.[133] For better or for

125 Shils & Roberts, *Diffusion of European Models*, *supra* note 89, at 163, 174.

126 *Ibid.*

127 *Ibid.* at 163, 174–45.

128 Siegmund-Schultze, Reinhard. *Mathematicians Fleeing from Nazi Germany Individual Fates and Global Impact*. Princeton University Press, 2009, pp. 267-98.

129 Hammerstein, *Universities and War in the Twentieth Century*, *supra* note 119.

130 *Ibid.*

131 Gumport, *supra* note 19, at 7.

132 Hammerstein, *Universities and War in the Twentieth Century*, *supra* note 119, at 637, 67–68 (mentioning the role of other bodies such as the Office of Scientific Research and Development, the Medical Research Committee and the Joint Committee on New Weapons and Equipment).

133 Sullivan, Neil J. *The Prometheus Bomb the Manhattan Project and Government in the Dark*. Potomac Books, an Imprint of the University of Nebraska Press, 2016, p. 134.

worse, the Manhattan Project, the army and industrial collaboration with the University of Chicago and the University of California at Berkley, proved to be highly effective.[134] Along with the progress made in this era in the natural sciences, such as physics, mathematics and statistics, American universities also took a worldwide leadership role in the social sciences and humanities (*see* the discussion on curriculum below).[135]

American universities became preeminent following the Second World War. Ever since that point, the American model has been exported around the world.[136] A primary characteristic of the American model is its "entrepreneurial organization," in which a director answers to a board of trustees, but is otherwise unrestrained to manage as he or she sees best fit.[137] Private, nonprofit universities' ability to amass great amounts of private funding also allow for a large degree of autonomy.[138] Although autonomous, universities still often willingly subject themselves to monitoring by regional accreditation organizations.[139] Perhaps one of the greatest privileges that American universities enjoy is academic freedom in education and research.[140] The modern American university, sometimes referred to as the "multiversity," is an entanglement of interests, between private donors, tuition fee-paying students and state funding bodies, and the cooperation between the universities and local, regional and even international outside partners.[141] Ironically, though, many nations are now emulating the American model, despite American universities' current efforts to move away from this resource-intensive, twentieth century structure.[142]

---

134 Hammerstein, *Universities and War in the Twentieth Century*, *supra* note 119, at 637, 68.

135 *Ibid.*

136 Rüegg, Walter. "Themes." In *A History of the University in Europe: Volume IV, Universities Since 1945*, edited by Walter Rüegg, Cambridge University Press, 2011, pp. 3, 27.

137 *Ibid.* at 3, 28.

138 *Ibid.*

139 Mohrman, Kathryn. "Excellence and Mass Higher Education in China and the United States." In *Questioning Excellence in Higher Education: Policies, Experiences and Challenges in National and Comparative Perspective*. Sense Publishers, 2011, p. 99.

140 Cole, Jonathan R. *Who's Afraid of Academic Freedom?* Columbia University Press, 2015, p. 41; *see also* Mohrman, *supra* note 139, at 102 (describing how higher education in China is centrally, state controlled).

141 Kerr, *supra* note 106, at 31.

142 Cole, Jonathan R. *Toward a More Perfect University*. PublicAffairs, 2016, p. 190.

B. Society's Expectations and University Privileges

The supreme special treatment afforded to today's universities also has its roots in Europe. While the concept of the university as we know it first came about in the high Middle Ages (ca. 1000 – 1250 A.D.), it was not until the early modern period (ca. 1450-1800) that there was a surge in European universities being founded.[143] These early institutions started exhibiting features that would be familiar to today's universities such centralized locations, a corpus of proficient instructors, students, curricula, academic standards and administrations.[144] Between 1500 and 1800, there were roughly 190 universities in Europe.[145] The majority of universities were founded either at the behest of the pope or the emperor of the Holy Roman Empire, although a few were founded by the prerogative of regions, communities or private individuals.[146] Following Luther's 1520 denunciation of the Catholic Church, the pope lost the authority to legitimize universities in Protestant lands. The Emperor of the Holy Roman Empire assumed this authority, but, eventually, the Empire's boundaries were reduced and the power to legitimatize fell to local rulers or other sovereign municipal republics.[147] Because of the many potential benefits arising out of universities, they have always enjoyed a privileged position in society, with many tangible advantages to show for it. Therefore, considering these privileges, this section demonstrates the social balancing of interests where resources are invested into universities with the expectation that they serve a particular purpose.

---

143 *See generally* Frijhoff, *Patterns*, *in* Volume II, Universities of Early Modern Europe, *supra* note 21, at 43.

144 Kerr, *supra* note 106, at 8.

145 Frijhoff, *Patterns*, *in* Volume II, Universities of Early Modern Europe, *supra* note 21, at 43, 47, 79 (listing the alternative institutions that arose alongside the universities: "schools of practitioners (the Inns of Court in London), semi-university colleges (as in Milan), illustrious schools with professorial chairs (as in Amsterdam), and occupational schools (such as the school of the Barcelona Chamber of Commerce), or research academies and learned societies").

146 *Ibid.* at 43, 49.

147 *Ibid.* at 43, 51.

I. University Privileges

The term "privilege" is used throughout this dissertation to refer to some type of law or favor that is given to an individual or organization, derived from a sovereign authority and that serves as an exception to a standard rule.[148] Universities have further sought "legitimation" from sovereign or religious authorities through legal founding charters. Once a charter was granted, European universities often received privileges with corresponding sovereign involvement in their affairs.[149] The universities of the Middle Ages generally enjoyed their privileges well into the early modern times. The privileges included:

> ... special jurisdiction, the right of self-management (drafting of statutes, co-optation of members, governmental and academic liberty), exemptions (from various kinds of taxation or military service or quartering) and special protective measures (control on prices in the town; priority in case of food scarcity). In addition to this, the members of the universities, as recognized state bodies, had certain social and political rights and advantages (delegations to diets and councils, reserved clerical prebends, seats on the councils). From the sixteenth century certain new privileges were acquired—a monopoly on printing, forms of legal deposit, milder forms of censorship....[150]

Some universities were founded without a religious or sovereign legitimizing authority, which meant that they did not have the valuable privilege to confer degrees.[151] Their ability to confer degrees acted as both a control mechanism and a mark of quality in the only four faculties that existed at the time: law, medicine, theology and philosophy.[152] As it would later develop in Germany, academic freedom was also a privilege of sorts; this

---

148 Looking at a legal dictionary, one finds nearly four pages full of the various legal privileges within our modern legal system, all offering substantially different meanings. The definition provided above in this text is most closely related to the concept of "*privilegium*," derived from the Roman law. *See* "Privilegium." *Black's Law Dictionary*, Edited by Bryan Garner, 9th ed., West Group, 2009, p. 1320.

149 De Ridder-Symoens, Hilde. "Management and Resources." In *A History of the University in Europe: Volume II, Universities in Early Modern Europe*, edited by Walter Rüegg, Cambridge University Press, 1996, pp. 155, 164.

150 *Ibid.* at 155, 164–65.

151 Frijhoff, *Patterns*, *in* Volume II, Universities of Early Modern Europe, *supra* note 21, at 43, 49–50.

152 McSherry, *supra* note 15, at 51.

was meant to allow free inquiry without fear of government interference. Academic freedom has come to incorporate faculty's ability to choose what they research, what they teach and to express themselves through publication without concern of legal or internal discipline procedures.[153] Independence in the "search for truth" originally served to attract some of the most brilliant researchers to the German universities.[154]

The individual expectations of the founding authorities, local communities and students are telling as to what exactly the early universities of the Middle Ages purposes and goals were. From the perspective of monarchs and popes, their involvement in granting privileges was worthwhile in order to deter involvement by other religious orders and local bishops. Papal interest in higher education was also incentivized by the desire to enhance doctrinal scholarship.[155] Monarchs all over Europe saw universities as institutions capable of training professionals in governmental and administrative capacities; the growth of a strong bureaucracy acted as a defensive mechanism towards the power grabs of competing aristocrats.[156] Additionally, some rulers wished to create institutions on par with the oldest, well-reputed universities as well as to spare their subjects the burdens of traveling abroad to study.[157] By contrast, local communities and their municipal authorities were mostly not interested to exempt scholars from tolls and taxes, nor did they wish to grant other privileges; there was very little local demand for higher education.[158]

If the earliest European universities received any privileges from municipal authorities during the twelfth-century, it would have been on an *ad hoc* basis.[159] When some of the benefits of specialization made themselves clear in the thirteenth century, municipalities began playing a more active

---

153 AAUP, "1940 Statement of Principles on Academic Freedom and Tenure with 1970 Interpretive Comments," in *Policy Documents and Reports* (Washington, D.C.: AAUP, 2006).

154 Stone, Geoffrey R. "A Brief History of Academic Freedom." In *Who's Afraid of Academic Freedom?* Columbia University Press, 2015, p. 4.

155 Rüegg, Walter. "Themes." In *A History of the University in Europe: Volume I, Universities in The Middle Ages*, edited by Hilde De Ridder-Symoens, Cambridge University Press, 1992, pp. 3, 17–18.

156 *Ibid.* at 3, 18.

157 Nardi, Paolo. "Relations with Authority." In *A History of the University in Europe: Volume I, Universities in The Middle Ages*, edited by Hilde De Ridder-Symoens, Cambridge University Press, 1992, pp. 77, 97.

158 Rüegg, *Themes*, *in* Volume I, Universities in the Middle Ages, *supra* note 155, at 3, 18.

159 *Ibid.* at 3, 19.

role, supporting universities with paid professorships and other privileges, while exercising numerous controls over the institutions.[160] Local municipalities first fully came around to universities in the early modern period when the flourishing book-publishing industry showed great promise of economic benefits for their cities.[161] University students enjoyed collective representation, protecting them from bothersome public officials and the resulting legal difficulties.[162] Above all, students were most often attracted to the universities for the prestige associated with academic degrees.[163] While university degrees were not necessary for most types of employment during the Middle Ages, they became more important during the fifteenth-century, demonstrating candidates' high qualifications for both religious and secular posts.[164]

II. Privileges in the US

Early American universities, like their European counterparts, received privileges that supported independence, political representation and financing. Being founded as corporations or trusts, their founders would first receive state charters, and then be free to operate autonomously, but within the boundaries of their by-laws.[165] Out of a desire to integrate their new institutions into their communities, they still ceded control to external "magistrates and ministers," in the case of Harvard University (Massachusetts), as Yale University (Connecticut) turned its governance over to an independent board.[166] The College of William and Mary's charter

---

160 *See* Burrell, Thomas H. "A Story of Privileges and Immunities: From Medieval Concept to the Colonies and United States Constitution." *Campbell Law Review*, vol. 34, no. 1, 2011, pp. 24–30; Rüegg, *Themes*, *in* VOLUME I, UNIVERSITIES IN THE MIDDLE AGES, *supra* note 155, at 3, 19.

161 *Ibid.* at 3, 20.

162 *Ibid.*

163 Cobban, Alan B. "Medieval Student Power." *Past & Present*, no. 53, 1971, p. 33.

164 *Ibid.* at 49.

165 Shils & Roberts, *Diffusion of European Models*, *supra* note 89, at 163, 165; Roberts, John, et. al. "Exporting Models." In *A History of the University in Europe: Volume II, Universities in Early Modern Europe*, edited by Walter Rüegg, Cambridge University Press, 1996, pp. 256, 272.

166 Morison, Samuel Eliot. *Three Centuries of Harvard, 1636-1936*. Harvard University Press, 1986, p. 12.

even granted professors representation in Virginia's colonial legislature.[167] Around the time of the American Revolutionary War, changes came in the founding of American universities, especially with regard to how they were financed. Institutions such as Dartmouth College (New Hampshire), Williams College (Massachusetts), and Dickinson College (Pennsylvania) were privately founded on individual and group philanthropy.[168] This trend toward funding through private charity stepped away from the direct state endowments, which initially funded universities through legislative grants of taxpayer revenue.[169] Untaxed private charitable giving, which is a privilege, and tuition fees became regular sources of revenue for American universities in the late eighteenth century.[170]

Although taking many forms and no longer going by the name "privileges," the privilege system remains in the US, stronger than ever.[171] The federal government provides "tens of billions of dollars annually" in grants to universities, not to mention nearly $200 billion in financial aid to students.[172] Billions in state grants further supplement this, albeit to a much-lesser extent at nonprofit universities. Tax-deductible private gifts, going toward university endowments, usually amount to between $20 and $25 billion annually.[173] Other notable privileges include federal,

---

167 Wenger, Mark R. "Thomas Jefferson, the College of William and Mary, and the University of Virginia." *The Virginia Magazine of History and Biography*, vol. 103, no. 3, July 1995, pp. 365, 373–74.

168 Roberts et. al, *Exporting Models*, *in* VOLUME II, UNIVERSITIES IN EARLY MODERN EUROPE, *supra* note 165, at 256, 274.

169 *Ibid.* at 256, 276.

170 *Ibid.*

171 In distinguishing between privileges and ordinary government services, whether a good or service is a *private* or *public* good in the economic sense may be illustrative, although not determinative. For example, government spending toward national defense and the building of highways are classic examples of public goods. For this dissertation, citizens being safe from international threats and having facilitated interstate travel would not be considered recipients of a privilege. As will be discussed below in further detail, higher education is likely not a public good. Thus, individuals and institutions within the higher education system are privileged to receive substantial state funding, among other privileges. It may also be helpful to juxtapose privileges with rights, which are "due to a person by just claim, legal guarantee, or moral principle." "Right." *Black's Law Dictionary*, Edited by Bryan Garner, 9th ed., West Group, 2009.

172 Vedder, Richard K. *Restoring the Promise: Higher Education in America*. Independent Institute, 2019, p. 19.

173 *Ibid.*

state and local university tax-exemptions on excess revenues, the ability to accept gifts tax-free, tax-free municipal bonds for cheap borrowing, tax-free endowment investing, tax-free property transactions and exemptions from certain state and local sales taxes.[174] By one estimate, these tax-exemptions alone cost federal taxpayers nearly $20 billion yearly.[175]

C. *University Objectives as Seen in the Curriculum*

The transformation of European universities' structures and priorities over the early modern period is especially relevant to the structures and priorities of the modern American university. The universities of the late Middle Ages could be characterized as institutions focused on the *studium generale* or *universitas*, meaning that they were involved with regulating students' lifestyles and instructed to "cover the entire extent of knowledge."[176] This curriculum went unchallenged up until around the eighteenth century.[177] The late-fifteenth century gave rise to the study of classical thought in order to understand scientific truths; based on this, the "exact sciences" developed and mathematics were the foundation for studies in the seventeenth century.[178] The eighteenth century was heavily influenced by the development of the "experimental method."[179] It was the experimental scientific method that served as a foundation for applied sciences and the

---

174 Hansmann, Henry B. "Why Are Colleges and Universities Exempt From Taxes?" *25th Annual Conference, Colleges and Universities: Legal Issues in the Halls of Ivy*, 2013, p. 3.

175 Saul, Stephanie. "Endowments Boom as Colleges Bury Earnings Overseas." *The New York Times*, The New York Times, 8 Nov. 2017, https://www.nytimes.com/2017/11/08/world/universities-offshore-investments.html.

176 *See* Verger, Jacques. "Patterns." *A History of the University in Europe: Volume I, Universities in The Middle Ages*, edited by Hilde De Ridder-Symoens, Cambridge University Press, Cambridge University Press, 1992, pp. 35, 37 (noting that the term *universitas* refers to the "totality" or the "whole" of a particular body, community or corporation. The terms *universitas scholarium* and *universitas magistrorum et scholarium*, for example, refer to "the university of students" or "the university of masters and students.").

177 Stone, *supra* note 154, at 2.

178 Frijhoff, *Patterns*, *in* Volume II, Universities of Early Modern Europe, *supra* note 21, at 43–44.

179 Fulton, JF. "The Rise of the Experimental Method: Bacon and the Royal Society of London." *The Yale Journal of Biology and Medicine*, vol. 3, no. 4, 1931, pp. 301–08.

many accompanying specialized institutions and disciplines.[180] This transition from the general university education to instruction in specialized areas, incorporating both basic and applied sciences, "foreshadowed the modern western university system."[181] Thus, understanding the curriculum is essential for defining the purposes and goals of universities.

I. The Early Curriculum in Europe

The courses of study requiring a formal degree or professional certification provided the universities their greatest monopoly; students who wished to become medical doctors, lawyers and later, scientists, teachers and "academics in every discipline" first needed to attend university for their training.[182] Throughout the seventeenth and eighteenth centuries, the universities, as a response to unemployment amongst their graduates and the resulting social problems, geared themselves for professional training.[183] Furthermore, professionalization was, in particular areas, an attempt to "separate the quacks and charlatans from the experts and authorities."[184] Concerned that apprenticeships could lead to inconsistent training outcomes, universities, as well as many outside societies, organizations and publications, pushed for standardized training and specialization.[185] Reforms throughout this era resulted in a reduction of students attending universities as well as an increase in more practical, professionalized higher education.[186] These reforms, spanning the late-fifteenth century through the nineteenth century, coupled with the general availability of printed materials, led to a general rise in the level of education of the European

180 *Ibid.*

181 Frijhoff, *Patterns*, *in* VOLUME II, UNIVERSITIES OF EARLY MODERN EUROPE, *supra* note 21, at 43, 46, 54 (noting that institutions, which failed to adapt to new specializations generally failed to keep their student enrollments up; some of the specialties included the natural sciences, teaching, clerical training, medical and legal studies as well as training for civil service).

182 *Ibid.* at 43, 61–62 (suggesting that university curricula were flexible to students' demand for diplomas that were connected to their future employment); Angulo, *supra* note 104, at 21.

183 Frijhoff, *Patterns*, *in* VOLUME II, UNIVERSITIES OF EARLY MODERN EUROPE, *supra* note 21, at 43, 56.

184 Angulo, *supra* note 104, at 21.

185 *Ibid.*

186 Frijhoff, *Patterns*, *in* VOLUME II, UNIVERSITIES OF EARLY MODERN EUROPE, *supra* note 21, at 43, 56.

populations as well as more specialized religious and political elites.[187] Although, any university that replaced its traditional *studium* with professional training programs, only acting to serve its "material interests... would have shared the fate of other medieval institutions; it would have long since disappeared."[188]

II. The Developing Curriculum in the Americas

While European universities were beginning to flourish in the early modern period, such knowledge-based institutions were only emerging in the New World. At first, the colonial powers, Spain, France and England, had the largest impact on the founding, governance and teaching at universities in the Americas.[189] Spanish colonists imposed their influence in Central and South America, whereas French influence took over in what is modern day Canada. It was the British, though, who had the single greatest influence over the colonies that would later form the United States.[190] Many former students, especially those coming from Cambridge, carried over the traditions and curricula of English universities with them to New England.[191] Early modern universities were hardly interested in academic research. University research would only become significant, following the above-mentioned reforms in Germany; until then, the greatest innovators of the era were found predominately outside of the universities.[192]

The first universities in British colonial America were primary focused on training clergy. Propagating knowledge, and especially religious knowledge, was viewed as the means of passing civilization down to subsequent generations.[193] These institutions had the primary focus of teaching and, similar to European universities of the time, did not show a great inter-

187 *Ibid.* at 43, 62.

188 Rüegg, *Themes*, *in* Volume I, Universities in the Middle Ages, *supra* note 155, at 3, 17.

189 *See generally* Feldmann, Horst. "The Long Shadows of Spanish and French Colonial Education." *Kyklos*, vol. 69, no. 1, 2016, pp. 32–64.

190 Roberts et. al, *Exporting Models*, *in* Volume II, Universities in Early Modern Europe, *supra* note 165, at 256, 272–73.

191 *Ibid.* at 256, 273.

192 Porter, Roy. "The Scientific Revolution and Universities." *A History of the University in Europe: Volume II, Universities in Early Modern Europe*, edited by Walter Rüegg, Cambridge University Press, 1996, pp. 531, 547–49.

193 These first institutions of higher education were actually founded as colleges, with many of them subsequently transforming into universities. Roberts et. al,

est in original scholarship.[194] While many European universities had already taken root throughout the sixteenth century, the settlers in the Massachusetts Bay Colony established the US' first institution of higher learning, Harvard, in 1636. Its mission, although significantly different to that of most modern universities, was typical for the seventeenth century:

> [a]fter God had carried us safe to New England and we had builded [sic.] our houses, provided necessaries for our livelihood, reared convenient places for God's worship, and settled the civil government: One of the next things we longed for and looked after was to advance learning and perpetuate it to posterity; dreading to leave an illiterate ministry to the churches, when our present ministers shall lie in the dust.[195]

Other universities founded in the seventeenth century shared the same central tenant, that religion should be the core of the curriculum and college mission.[196] The American curricula underwent significant changes in the late eighteenth century.[197] The curriculum of small colonial institutions focused on classical studies; the students would typically learn Latin, Greek, Hebrew, logic, rhetoric and Aristotelian physics.[198] This changed in the second half of the eighteenth century when the curricula were adapted to the modern educational demands. Many universities then offered applied studies in "surveying, measuring, navigation, commerce, husbandry, law and government" to name a few.[199] Note, though, that despite the multiplying areas of study, many universities retained the British model

---

Exporting Models, *in* Volume II, Universities in Early Modern Europe, *supra* note 165, at 256, 269.

194 Shils & Roberts, *Diffusion of European Models*, *supra* note 89, at 163–64.

195 "History and Mission." *Harvard Divinity School*, https://hds.harvard.edu/about/history-and-mission.

196 Roberts et. al, *Exporting Models*, *in* Volume II, Universities in Early Modern Europe, *supra* note 165, at 256, 273.

197 The European university structure for faculties of law, medicine, theology and philosophy was not carried over to the New World. The small institutions founded in the Americas hardly even discerned between disciplines. Rather, the professors or ministers who were educating did so as "generalists" across all areas of the curriculum. Specialization only began to take root in the US with the creation of departments in the first half of the nineteenth century. *See* Gumport, *supra* note 19, at 5–9.

198 *Ibid.* at 5.

199 Roberts et. al, *Exporting Models*, *in* Volume II, Universities in Early Modern Europe, *supra* note 165, at 256, 275.

in their approach toward education; students had little choice as to which courses they would take, they had to attend all of their classes and had to abide by strict moral codes.[200]

The first American medical and law schools were founded in 1765 and 1784, respectively. Before then, students seeking specialized studies had to travel to Europe.[201] The changing educational focus led to an overall decline in the number of graduating ministers and increase in graduating physicians and lawyers, reflecting demand for these positions in society.[202] Moreover, moving into the nineteenth and twentieth centuries, universities, their departments, their professors and curricula became continuously more specialized and professionalized.[203] "A more complex and richer society was reflected" through this specialized professional training in American colleges and universities.[204]

The Founding Fathers of the US were the politicians, philosophers and soldiers who led the American colonies to revolt against Great Britain, and, once independent, their enlightened philosophy laid the groundwork for the new nation.[205] Many had views on formalized education systems, which they envisioned being implemented within their own states.[206] Their greatest contributions are reflected in American culture, especially in the aspiration that one can succeed through merit. Jefferson believed that higher education was the means of promoting the most "talented and virtuous" citizens, not the "wellborn," to positions of leadership; this ideal, for example, was present in Jefferson's founding of the University of Virginia.[207] Furthermore, he believed that higher education existed to form experts to further a "sound spirit of legislation" both domestically and internationally, to promote agriculture and manufacturing, to teach

---

200 Shils & Roberts, *Diffusion of European Models*, *supra* note 89, at 163, 165.

201 Roberts et. al, *Exporting Models*, *in* VOLUME II, UNIVERSITIES IN EARLY MODERN EUROPE, *supra* note 165, at 256, 279.

202 *Ibid.*

203 Gumport, *supra* note 19, at 6.

204 Roberts et. al, *Exporting Models*, *in* VOLUME II, UNIVERSITIES IN EARLY MODERN EUROPE, *supra* note 165, at 256, 279.

205 Crow & Dabars, *supra* note 12, at 27–28.

206 *See generally* Holowchak, Mark. *Thomas Jeffersons Philosophy of Education: a Utopian Dream*. Routledge, 2014.

207 *Ibid.* at 35; Wenger, *supra* note 167 (founding the University of Virginia initially as "Central College," Jefferson wished to abolish old "pedagogical habits, social rituals" and even architecture. Some of the most influential aspects regarded less formal relationships between students and professors as well as the secularization of the institution).

mathematics and natural sciences, and, finally, to develop "reasoning faculties of our youth, enlarge their minds, cultivate their morals, and instill into them the precepts of virtue and order."[208] Therefore, through higher education, Jefferson believed that the *artificial aristoi*, positioned only by wealth and birth, would be overcome by a *natural aristoi* of the virtuous and talented.[209] Jefferson's philosophy and implementation of it served to nudge the new nation in the direction of more social equality, while rejecting the inflexible and insurmountable social structures of Great Britain.

D. The Various Types of Students and Their Expectations

American students' perceptions of what universities are, and their expectations of higher education are highly influential as to what the university system has become and how it may transform. Because of financial factors, which will be described in the section below, relentless competition among universities and students' diverse backgrounds, interests and goals, American universities have been forced to continuously adapt. It is helpful to distinguish the following student pathways that have been integrated into university curricula and infrastructure to approximate an understanding of the diverse student interests: the *professional pathway*, *mobility pathway* and *social pathway*.[210] Students on the professional pathway are characterized by their high ambition, focus on academic achievement and intensive preparation at the secondary level, often with large amounts of support from their families.[211] Of all of the students on campus, the overwhelming majority are on the mobility pathway; students on the professional pathway are a minority on most US university campuses.[212] The mobility pathway is descriptive of students wishing to improve their economic, and perhaps social, status. Finally, the social pathway consists of students, usually from affluent families, seeking socialization and university certification without being subjected to a rigorous curriculum.[213] All

208 Holowchak, *supra* note 206, at 35–36.

209 *Ibid.* at 31–32 (noting that the word "*aristoi*" is Greek for "best men").

210 Armstrong, Elizabeth A., and Laura T. Hamilton. *Paying for the Party How College Maintains Inequality*. Harvard University Press, 2013, p. 15 (noting these three categories, but instead of calling it the *social pathway*, these authors referred to the third group as the *party pathway*).

211 *Ibid.*

212 Brint, *Two Cheers for Higher Education*, *supra* note 75, at 151–52.

213 Armstrong & Hamilton, *supra* note 210.

three pathways are present at most institutions to varying degrees, and, accordingly, the universities must direct funding for infrastructure necessary to facilitate them.[214] Thus, most universities must make compromises when admitting students. Balancing the pathways inevitably leads to the admission of less-than-desirable students who can pay full tuition fees, although the more-qualified students who are not admitted ultimately pay the price for such tradeoffs.[215] Keeping this in mind, this section describes students as interested parties and how their expectations shape higher education.

---

214 Because most students are enrolled in bachelors' programs and the majority of bachelors' programs are not humanities-based, the above-mentioned pathways are dominated by other non-humanities programs. Nonetheless, students studying in the humanities, including increasing amounts of students from historically disadvantaged groups, can be found within each of the pathways but overwhelmingly at private and public universities. The absolute number of bachelors' degrees issued for the humanities has stagnated over the last few decades, but, as a percentage of all degrees issued, the humanities has been in a steady decline. As of 2015, about thirteen percent of degrees issued at private, nonprofit universities were in the humanities, with a slightly lower rate at public institutions. The percentage of for-profit bachelors' degrees issued in the humanities never surpassed three percent of all degrees. However, doctoral degrees in the humanities were better represented in the most-recent data from 2013, comprising about sixty-two percent of all doctoral degrees at public institutions and around thirty-eight percent at private nonprofits. For-profit universities issued no doctoral degrees in the humanities. "Humanities Bachelor's Degrees as a Percentage of All Bachelor's Degrees Awarded by Public versus Private Institutions, 1987–2015." *Humanities Indicators*, American Academy of Arts & Sciences, 2017, https://www.humanitiesindicators.org/content/indicatordoc.aspx?i=201; "Percentage of All U.S. Doctorates in the Humanities Awarded by Public versus Private Institutions, 1987–2013." *Humanities Indicators*, American Academy of the Arts & Sciences, 2015, https://www.humanitiesindicators.org/content/indicatordoc.aspx?i=10846; "Percentage of Bachelor's Degrees Awarded to Members of Traditionally Underrepresented Racial/Ethnic Groups, Selected Academic Fields, 1995–2015." *Humanities Indicators*, American Academy of Arts & Sciences, 2017, https://www.humanitiesindicators.org/content/indicatordoc.aspx?i=38.

215 Armstrong & Hamilton, *supra* note 210, at 21 (highlighting that even public universities have become involved in these balancing-acts, often to the detriment of qualified, low-income students).

I. The Professional Pathway

The professional pathway is highly competitive in terms of "financial awards, entry to top programs, internships and attention from professors;" the competition begins long before students are enrolled in higher education.[216] To be admitted to a desirable program, students are subjected to a competitive sorting process and undertake intensive standardized test preparation, highly competitive high school programs, community service and anything else to improve their chances of being admitted to top programs.[217] These students, although invariably hard working and intelligent, are likely to have received significant support from their families in order to be competitive in the admissions process and, subsequently, during their studies. Because these students are high achieving and able to pay full tuition fees, they are the ideal complement to the most elite universities. The professional pathway and mobility pathways both have driven, serious students, but the mobility pathway is more pragmatic and open to students with less financial and familial support.[218]

II. The Mobility Pathway

Students entering higher education on the mobility pathway will have to invest a great amount of resources and work into their studies, while the universities seek to promote their access to higher education and better upward mobility. Historically, and still to a certain extent, this group was most heavily represented by the "children of immigrants, sons and daughters of rural farmers, blacks, Jews and women of all classes."[219] It is likely that the majority of all students fall into this category; roughly sixty percent by one estimate.[220] For this reason, universities provide financial aid, which is usually need-based, and students are further supported by government grants and loans. Once admitted, the curriculum for students on the mobility pathway is rather practical, substantive and vocation-ori-

---

216 *Ibid.* at 18.

217 *See e.g.*, "The Ultimate Admissions Guide: 75 Steps for Getting into Your Dream College." *YesCollege*, yescollege.com/guides/get-into-your-dream-school/.

218 Armstrong & Hamilton, *supra* note 210, at 18–20 (suggesting that most public universities have difficulty attracting such students from elite private schools).

219 *Ibid.* at 12.

220 Vedder, *Restoring the Promise*, *supra* note 172, at 17.

ented.[221] As a result, students on the mobility pathway are trained for jobs such as nursing, engineering and accounting and their future employment will be primarily connected to the substance of their studies and less dependent on their social networks.

III. The Social Pathway

The social pathway has been made possible by an "implicit agreement between the university and students to demand little of each other."[222] Because this demographic is characterized by its mediocre academic achievement at the secondary level, the universities admitting them compromise high academic standards, receiving in return affluent students whose families can pay full tuition and "legacy" preferred students sometimes with accompanying donations.[223] Campus amenities are necessary to attract such students. Modern student dormitories, fitness facilities and sports programs are just a few of the many showcases. Once admitted, students on the social pathway will be held to relatively low academic standards, accommodating their activities without serious concern of failing out. For this reason, universities have developed "easy majors," allowing students to enroll in professional training programs such as "business, public administration, communications, tourism, recreational studies, education, human development, fitness and fashion" among others.[224] This pathway also offers numerous electives, giving students alternatives to the more challenging math, sciences and language requirements. Campus life for these students could include extensive partying and experimentation with sex and drugs.[225] Students on the social pathway are highly dependent on universities to be certifying institutions.[226]

As mentioned, these pathways are found at all universities to varying degrees. The Ivy League universities, all private and nonprofit, enroll relatively few students, but continue to set themselves apart from all other institu-

221 Armstrong & Hamilton, *supra* note 210, at 17.

222 *Ibid.* at 15.

223 Meer, Jonathan, and Harvey S. Rosen. "Altruism and the Child Cycle of Alumni Donations." *American Economic Journal, Economic Policy*, vol. 1, 2009, p. 258.

224 Armstrong & Hamilton, *supra* note 210, at 15–16 (contrasting the easy majors with more challenging majors, which are nestled under science and arts departments).

225 Vedder, *Restoring the Promise*, *supra* note 172, at 17.

226 Brint, *Two Cheers for Higher Education*, *supra* note 75, at 303.

tions; the gap is wide and continues to widen.[227] Ivy League selectivity is likely due to its inputs; most of their students are high achieving and from affluent families. Average students from the same affluent background are mostly attracted to large public universities.[228] Higher-achieving students from less affluent families are more likely to end up in middle-tier private or large public universities because, despite exhibiting top ability, they tend not to apply to top-institutions and are usually "undermatched" to less-prestigious universities.[229] Finally, average students from low-income families tend to attend community colleges and for-profit universities.[230] The proportions of students on each of the pathways are noticeably different within all of the various university-types.

E. How Form Affects Substance: University Finance

As of 1869, when reliable statistics for higher education in the US were first recorded, only one percent of eighteen to twenty-four year old Amer-

---

227 "Ivy League Schools." *U.S. News*, 23 Sept. 2019, https://www.usnews.com/education/best-colleges/ivy-league-schools (listing the following Ivy League schools: Princeton University, Harvard University, Columbia University, Yale University, Pennsylvania University, Dartmouth College, Brown University and Cornell University).

228 Armstrong & Hamilton, *supra* note 210, at 5, 21.

229 Even when advertised student costs are shockingly high, it could be more affordable for a low-income student to attend a prestigious private university than a community college. Vance, a graduate of Yale Law School, noted the following in his autobiography that traced his family's escape from Appalachian poverty to his graduation from Yale Law School:

I was sufficiently committed to going to Yale Law that I was willing to accept the two hundred thousand dollars or so in debt that I knew I'd accrue. Yet the financial aid package Yale offered exceeded my wildest dreams. In my first year, it was nearly a full ride. That wasn't because of anything I'd done or earned—it was because I was one of the poorest kids in school. Yale offered tens of thousands in need-based aid. It was the first time being so broke paid so well. Yale wasn't just my dream school, it was also the cheapest option on the table.

Vance, J. D. *Hillbilly Elegy*. Harper Collins Books, 2016, p. 198; Ovink, Sarah, et al. "College Match and Undermatch: Assessing Student Preferences, College Proximity, and Inequality in Post-College Outcomes." *Research in Higher Education*, vol. 59, no. 5, 10 Nov. 2017, p. 574 (indicating that "lower levels of parent income and education, lower student academic achievement, lack of proximity to a match school and preferences for a low-cost institution close to home consistently predict undermatching.").

230 Armstrong & Hamilton, *supra* note 210, at 5.

icans were enrolled in higher education; by 2018, this number reached nearly forty percent, equaling roughly twenty million students.[231] This surge in the number of institutions and student enrollment is the outcome of decades of federal government involvement in the area of higher education. The uptick in institutions and students also corresponds with the growing debt burden on Americans. $1 billion in student debt was accumulated by 1971, it exceeded $1 trillion by 2012 and is currently well over $1.5 trillion.[232] This section will show how government support for higher education spiraled out of control and, specifically, how it has influenced private, nonprofit universities and their goals. This is particularly important to understand before looking into the nature of nonprofit organizations below.

I. The Funding Schemes

The first major involvement by the federal government in higher education came in the aftermath of the Second World War. By means of the *Servicemen's Readjustment Act of 1944*, better known as the *GI Bill*, the returning servicemen had access to grants covering university fees, books, room and board, along with an additional cash allowance.[233] This program is generally regarded as a success, having provided benefits to about two-thirds of returning servicemen to attend universities or other vocational schools.[234] Another impetus to enroll more students was the arms race with the Soviet Union, where science, research and innovation became synonymous with national security. As a result, the *National Defense Education Act of 1958* (hereinafter, NDEA) was enacted, granting federal student loans to bolster education for teachers, scientists, mathematicians, engineers and translators.[235] Eventually the scope of the program broadened to allow other areas of study, more students began enrolling and the amounts being borrowed increased. By 1962, the federal government was allocating around $100 million per year for NDEA loans.[236] These programs were effective in their goals, but small in scale relative to later programs.

231 Haidt, *supra* note 20, at 197.
232 Best & Best, *supra* note 23, at 157.
233 *See* 58 Stat. 268 (1944); (codified as amended at 38 U.S.C. § 34, 37 (2011)).
234 Best & Best, *supra* note 23, at 24.
235 *See* 2 U.S.C. § 17 (1958).
236 Best & Best, *supra* note 23, at 27–30.

Another effort to promote funding for higher education followed the civil rights movement of the 1960's where the unequal access to higher education for low-income families and racial minorities was highlighted. The *Higher Education Act of 1965* (hereinafter, HEA) set aside little grant and scholarship funding for low-income students and, instead, established guaranteed student loans for anybody qualified to enroll in higher education.[237] In this attempt to promote private lending, the federal government allowed students to seek out private lenders, whereby the government would subsidize the interest during the period of study and guarantee the loan if the students were to default in their repayment.[238] The HEA suffered from the inability to calculate how much interest the government would eventually have to pay, the volume of students taking loans as well as the amounts being borrowed, but it unquestionably led to higher enrollment rates.[239] HEA lending, and subsequent programs based on the HEA, shaped the modern university landscape.

As the lending programs expanded, private lenders were still hesitant to get involved with student loans because market interest rates exceeded the six percent interest guaranteed by the government and the transaction costs of administering relatively small student loans were high. Therefore, private lenders were more likely to lend their money elsewhere.[240] The government, wishing to incentivize lending, created a secondary market to increase lenders' liquidity. To promote the secondary market for student loans, the federal government created the *Student Loan Marketing Association* (hereinafter, Sallie Mae) in 1972.[241] The concept was that banks would lend directly to students, then sell the loans to Sallie Mae. This created liquidity for the banks to do more lending, without having to wait for the student-borrowers to repay.[242] Sallie Mae would, in turn, bundle the student debt and resell it into secondary, capital markets where it could be bought and sold as long-term investments.[243] While this program achieved its goal to provide access to education for as many students as possible, there were some serious, unintended consequences.

---

237 *See* 20 U.S.C. ch. 28 § 1001 et seq. (1965) (amended through P.L. 116-91 (December 19, 2019)).

238 *Ibid.*

239 Best & Best, *supra* note 23, at 33.

240 *Ibid.*

241 *See* P. L. 92–318, title I, § 133(a), 86 Stat. 265 (1972); (codified as amended at 20 U.S.C. § 1087 (2006)).

242 *Ibid.*

243 *Ibid.*

From the inception of all these lending programs, there was a constant and exponential growth in student lending, the founding of institutions and, until recently, student enrollment. All of these factors corresponded with massive increases in tuition fees and associated costs from the late 1980's onward.[244] The Federal Reserve observed that there is a strong relationship between student loans and tuition fee increases; for every dollar increase in subsidized student loans, tuition fees increase by sixty cents.[245] At the same time, the frequency of borrowing for higher education became normalized and many students with access to large loans became desensitized to the rising costs, leading to a self-perpetuating cycle of rising costs and more student debt.[246] When adjusting for inflation, tuition and other costs, the advertised tuition fees for both private and public institutions were stable throughout the early 1980's, but they began growing thereafter, far outpacing the cost of living. Not only was student borrowing normalized, but in many cases it became necessary where it had not been before. Most students would have preferred to finance their education by working part-time jobs, summer jobs, or out of personal or family savings when possible, leaving long-term debt as a last option. Although, with the rising costs, taking out student loans became the only option for many.[247]

On a related matter, federal Pell Grants, grants for low-income students that do not need to be repaid, were and continue to be substantial. Unfortunately, lending programs have essentially flooded the grants out and raised college prices to the extent that students dependent on Pell Grants often do not bother applying to institutions beyond the most affordable community colleges.[248] This is a result of the dwindling ability of grants to cover costs and prospective students' fear of being buried in student debt. Federal grant support today is only a fraction of students' overall financial

---

244 Baum, Sandy, et al., editors. *The Effectiveness of Student Aid Policies: What the Research Tells Us*. The College Board, 2008, p. 40.

245 Lucca, David O., et al. *Credit Supply and the Rise in College Tuition: Evidence from the Expansion in Federal Student Aid Programs*. Vol. G28, I22, Federal Reserve Bank of New York Staff Reports, 2017, pp. 30–31.

246 Baum, *supra* note 244, at 40–44.

247 Best & Best, *supra* note 23, at 47, 70, 82 (explaining that, despite the intention to provide access to education to low-income individuals, the lending programs raised costs so much that many people in the middle-class were forced to borrow. Furthermore, the wealthy were also able to use this as an opportunity to take out college loans, "subsidized as low rates by taxpayers" and either keep or reinvest their money elsewhere).

248 Brint, *Two Cheers for Higher Education*, *supra* note 75, at 212.

aid, despite having accounted for around fifty percent of aid in 1971.[249] This has not only led to a vast underrepresentation of low-income students at elite universities, but many flagship state universities also experienced major drops in Pell-eligible student enrollments as lending became more available.[250]

II. Negative Outcomes of Federal Funding

Guaranteed loans, granting access to higher education to potential students across the country, also opened the door to financially "high-risk" students.[251] A student might be considered high-risk for a number of reasons, whether it be poor previous academic achievement, lack of ability to pay back loans or a course of study that is not likely to lead to employment.[252] Under other circumstances, if a high-risk individual sought a loan for a house or a car, the lending institutions would either deny their request, or use the house or car as a security against the loan. In the case of student loans, lenders had every incentive to offer the greatest amount possible while facing no risk. The possibility of borrowers defaulting on their payments was of no concern to the private lenders because the federal government, i.e. the taxpayers, assumed that liability. This no-risk lending also created competition on the lending side; most lending institutions made generous campaign contributions and spent extensive sums on political lobbying. Corruption, such as lending institutions giving kickbacks to universities, also occurred.[253] Since virtually all universities base their

---

249 Vest, *supra* note 45, at 61–62.

250 Brint, *Two Cheers for Higher Education*, *supra* note 75, at 213.

251 Best & Best, *supra* note 23, at 62.

252 The HEA was signed into law by President Johnson to increase funding that would enable individual students to choose which institutions they would like to attend, regardless of price. It is my contention that this goal was well intentioned and that the resulting skyrocketing tuition fees and declining study in the humanities were the product of economic realities being disregarded by the politicians enacting these laws. In other words, students' aversion to the humanities, i.e. courses of study that are perceived to lead to less lucrative careers, was an unintended consequence of student loans being injected into the higher education system.

253 Dickinson, Tim. "Obama's Real Reform." *Rolling Stone*, 6 Aug. 2009, pp. 41–43 (stating that:

... the incentives have ranged from $100,000 in stock options (Columbia University) to lucrative consulting fees (Johns Hopkins University). In one egregious

income on money derived from student loans, it is clear that institutions of all types have formed a dependence on this type of funding, thereby, becoming, in some regards, indistinguishable from one-another, generally less independent and, in terms of nonprofits, less private.

Federally guaranteed student loans also led to stratification and, thereby, intense competition within higher education. For many Americans, especially those on the mobility pathway, the attitude towards higher education is pragmatic; potential students and their families weigh the benefits of a college education, higher future income, against the price to determine if it is a worthwhile *investment*. Several university ranking guidebooks, namely that of the *U.S. News & World Report*, began ranking colleges and universities in the 1980's.[254] This information was and continues to be used by students to decide which university to attend. They might choose to attend a more expensive university if they perceive it as a superior institution. Area of study is also important for future earnings prospects. Although the humanities provide a degree of flexibility, professional training programs such as accounting, engineering or nursing are generally seen as a better *investment* by prospective students who wish to earn more.[255] Such rankings are demonstrative of the shift toward universities acting like "business," trying to attract "customers" with superior

---

attempt to persuade the University of Maryland to list it as a "preferred lender," loan giant Nelnet gave the school a $50,000 "donation." Several lenders also created "revenue sharing" that kicked back a portion of the profits on student loans to schools, meaning that universities like Duquesne were directly profiting from helping drive their students into debt.).

254 Morse, Robert. "U.S. News Best Colleges Rankings Turn 30 Years Old." *U.S. News & World Report*, 27 Nov. 2013, www.usnews.com/education/blogs/college-rankings-blog/2013/11/27/us-news-best-colleges-rankings-turn-30-years-old.

255 Best & Best, *supra* note 23, at 73, 133; *but see* Adams, William D. "Not by Earnings Alone: A New Report on Humanities Graduates in the Workforce and Beyond." *American Academy of Arts & Sciences*, 29 Jan. 2018, www.amacad.org/news/not-earnings-alone-new-report-humanities-graduates-workforce-and-beyond (decribing the tendency in recording statistics on the humanities to rely overwhelmingly on the quantitative indicators that are most important to vocational areas of study such as business or engineering. Calling also for more research regarding how graduates of the humanities are faring in the workplace as well as how their overall thinking and communication abilities develop); *see also* "World Happiness Report 2019." Edited by John F. Helliwell et al., *World Happiness Report*, United Nations, 2019, s3.amazonaws.com/happiness-report/2019/WHR19.pdf (analyzing "happiness" along with factors including community participation, voting, digital media and addiction, but not along the lines of graduates' life-satisfaction following studies in various fields).

goods and services.[256] Rankings have raised the stakes and heightened competition between American universities, pushing them to extremes to improve their standing.[257]

Universities bitterly competing for national prominence seek to attract prospective students with a broad array of amenities such as high-end residences, classrooms, fitness facilities, manicured landscapes, expensive sports programs and stadiums. The magnitude, breadth and frequency of university spending on campus amenities is shocking.[258] Because these amenities were effective at attracting students, who were increasingly becoming less price sensitive, most universities became caught up in the whirlwind of competition.[259] The rush to attract desirable students is a means of "positional warfare," to protect or improve a university's rankings; sometimes this even manifests itself in the form of scholarships for top athletes or stellar graduate students.[260] Failing to compete effectively with other universities leads to a reinforcing circle of lower-rankings, admitting fewer top students and faculty, fewer donations, fewer research grants as well as fewer commercial partnerships.[261] These amenities were made possible in large part through significant increases in tuition fees as increased tuition fees were aided by the availability of massive student loans and "the normalization of student debt culture."[262]

---

256 Karabel, Jerome. *The Chosen: the Hidden History of Admission and Exclusion at Harvard, Yale, and Princeton*. Houghton Mifflin Company, 2014, p. 514.

257 Westerheijden, Don, et.al. "Ranking Goes International." In *Questioning Excellence in Higher Education: Policies, Experiences and Challenges in National and Comparative Perspective*. Sense Publishers, 2011, p. 180.

258 Vedder, *Restoring the Promise*, *supra* note 172, at 212 (describing administrators' push to build recreational centers, climbing walls, lazy rivers, eccentric entranceways, indoor sports fields, the most expensive lab equipment and student apartments with granite countertops worth well into the hundreds of thousands of dollars per student bed).

259 Best & Best, *supra* note 23, at 73.

260 Kirp, David L. *Shakespeare, Einstein and the Bottom Line: the Marketing of Higher Education*. Harvard University Press, 2004, p. 2.

261 *Ibid.* at 4.

262 Brint, *Two Cheers for Higher Education*, *supra* note 75, at 211 (explaining that the expansion of for-profit universities and increased graduate school enrollments were also major contributors to heightened college costs).

III. How Finance Affected the Various Types of Universities

Public institutions, such as state universities, have always provided a less-expensive alternative to private universities. In addition to providing quality education for the sake of education, states subsidize education for in-state residents with the expectation that the students will go on to be productive taxpayers.[263] The lion's share of student-aid at state universities used to come directly from state budgets, but, as costs rose throughout higher education, the states were strained to keep their contributions up. Tuition fees at public state universities were low in the 1970's but have ballooned since. Public universities' costs, similar to private and for-profit universities, went up drastically because of the race to accentuate their campuses, even requiring them to take on substantial amounts of debt in the form bond issuances, adding new debt-servicing expenses.[264] Despite charging less than private institutions in absolute terms, this rising tide of tuition fees actually led to a more rapid increase at public universities; between 1976 and 2010, adjusting for inflation, tuition fees rose more than three hundred percent at public universities as opposed to around 275 percent at private, nonprofit universities.[265]

As tuition fees increased, state contributions remained stable until the 1990's and the remainder of the costs were pushed on to the students who had access to federally subsidized loans.[266] Because of these two factors, i.e. skyrocketing tuition costs and student loans, there was at least a twenty-five percent drop off in state support, per student, between 1990 and 2010.[267] This financing model has negatively affected the goal of public universities to provide increased access to higher education to broader swaths of the population. In fact, public universities, to improve their bottom lines, have rushed to enroll international students who can pay—sometimes more than—full tuition fees.[268] Public universities also cannot offset their growing expenses and debt with endowments; if they have endowments, they are likely to be small.[269] Because of dwindling

263 Schrum, Ethan D. *The Instrumental University: Education in Service of the National Agenda after World War II.* Cornell University Press, 2019, pp. 46–50.

264 Best & Best, *supra* note 23, at 149.

265 *Ibid.* at 71.

266 Snyder, *Digest of Education Statistics*, *supra* note 43, at Table 331.20.

267 Best & Best, *supra* note 23, at 81.

268 *Ibid.* at 148 (noting the negative effect that this may have on potential in-state students).

269 Kirp, *supra* note 260, at 24.

state resources, public universities have sought out more private alumni donations, thereby diminishing a major distinction between public and private universities and making both their revenue and expenditures much more similar than ever before.[270]

The growth of for-profit universities since 2000 and ensuing competition to attract students has affected all universities. To put their growth in perspective, public and private, nonprofit universities increased their enrollment by twenty-two percent between 2000 and 2010, whereas for-profits increased by four-hundred percent.[271] For-profit enrollment peaked in 2010 at 1.3 million students, while dropping to 700,000 students by 2016.[272] These institutions put large financial burdens on both their students and society. For-profit universities can be characterized by their incredibly high dropout rates, where only twenty-two percent of students are likely to graduate; this is, in no small part, attributable to their very low admission standards. Their students, similarly, can be characterized as high-risk prospects, unlikely to graduate once they are enrolled, unlikely to be able to transfer credits to other universities and, once they dropout, will be much more likely to have large debt burdens without the degree or credentials necessary to find jobs.[273] Public and private, nonprofit universities have followed suit, adapting their advertising tactics and distance learning programs, similar to those of for-profits, to attract students back to their institutions. Additionally, public and private, nonprofit universities have come to resemble for-profits in terms of higher tuition fees, centralized administration as well as their declining support for the tenure system.[274]

Unfortunately, for-profit dropout and unemployment rates are the tip of the iceberg. Using a very conservative estimate of student loan default rates, excluding students who have "deferred" payment, over fifteen percent of students from for-profit universities will default on their payments

---

270 Vest, *supra* note 45, at 51.

271 Gelbgiser, Dafna. "College for All, Degrees for Few: For-Profit Colleges and Socioeconomic Differences in Degree Attainment." *Social Forces*, vol. 96, no. 4, 2018, p. 1785.

272 Snyder, *Digest of Education Statistics*, *supra* note 43, at Table 303.70.

273 Best & Best, *supra* note 23, at 107–10, 116 (noting that the graduation rate for public universities is fifty-five percent and sixty-five percent for private universities and that students who attended for-profit universities have a higher unemployment rate, around twenty-three percent, and will earn less than students from nonprofit universities).

274 Hansmann, *Evolving Economic Structure*, *supra* note 44, at 159, 181; Best & Best, *supra* note 23, at 127.

within three years of it becoming due.[275] More than ten percent of graduates from public universities and seven percent from private, nonprofit universities will also default.[276] As a comparison, the default rate on subprime mortgages, leading to the Great Recession in 2008, was around nine percent.[277] Since debt from student loans cannot be discharged through bankruptcy, delinquency in repayment can later lead to wage garnishment and, in many cases, capitalizing interest leading to students owing substantially more than they originally borrowed.[278] Meanwhile, the federal government continues to finance for-profit schools with well over $30 billion per year, subsidizing about ninety percent of their income through grants, student loans and work-study programs.[279]

Nonprofit universities maintain a level of prestige and independence through their selectivity, endowments and involvement in research. Endowments are particularly useful in guaranteeing future financial stability in times of market-downturns. Both public and private universities face the same potential market downturns, but, due to having smaller endowments, public universities have greater volatility in their budgets.[280] The resulting financial freedom also contributes to the quality of course offerings and the maintenance of traditional classroom education; financially pressed universities may resort to increased class sizes or alternative, online course offerings. Cost-cutting measures can result in a deluge of other negative outcomes such as the hiring of fewer professors (with PhDs), smaller graduate programs, fewer majors, fewer sub-specialties as well as the neglect of entire bodies of knowledge.[281] The sources from which rev-

---

275 "National Federal Student Loan Cohort Default Rate Continues to Decline." *National Federal Student Loan Cohort Default Rate Continues to Decline | U.S. Department of Education*, U.S. Department of Education, 25 Sept. 2019, www.ed.gov/news/press-releases/national-federal-student-loan-cohort-default-rate-continues-decline.

276 *Ibid.*

277 Best & Best, *supra* note 23, at 138 (noting that these student loan statistics are very optimistic and that the number of lenders in risk of defaulting can be up to thirty-five percent).

278 *Ibid.* at 140.

279 Snyder, *Digest of Education Statistics*, *supra* note 43, at 333.55; Kelchen, Robert. "How Much Do for-Profit Colleges Rely on Federal Funds?" *Brookings*, 10 Jan. 2017, www.brookings.edu/blog/brown-center-chalkboard/2017/01/11/how-much-do-for-profit-colleges-rely-on-federal-funds/.

280 Vest, *supra* note 45, at 11–12 (mentioning the push by public universities to attract more private giving).

281 Brint, *Two Cheers for Higher Education*, *supra* note 75, at 288, 355.

enue is derived, whether it be from states, the federal government, tuition fees or donors, is directly related to the degree of university autonomy. Endowments allow for a high level of autonomy, whereas dependence on tuition fee revenue puts universities in a position of treating students as customers.[282]

Private giving to private, nonprofit universities is significant; in 2015, around $22.8 billion was donated, accounting for 12.5 percent of nonprofit university revenues.[283] Although, most nonprofit universities with smaller endowments are like for-profit universities in that they are dependent on student loans. The most elite universities do not have this kind of dependence.[284] Their high-costs and the drop of student enrollment since 2010 exemplify the struggles of non-elite, private nonprofit universities.[285] Of their students who pay tuition fees, 87.1 percent are receiving government grants and 65.9 percent obtain loans from the Department of Education.[286] Nevertheless, private, nonprofit universities, just the same as the other types, are "hooked on student loans," in the race to accentuate campuses and attract more students.[287] Beyond the massive costs associated with this growth-based model, the shrinking pool of high school graduates looking to enroll in higher education is already proving that this model is neither sustainable nor wise.

As is the case with any for-profit undertaking, for-profit universities regularly go in- and out of business. There have been a shocking number of cases in which, without warning and in the middle of the semester, schools would dismiss their faculties and literally leave their students locked out.[288] Some of the institutions have become metaphorically *too big to fail* and, because they enroll tens of thousands of students each with hundreds of thousands of dollars in student debt, the Department of Education often becomes directly involved in their restructuring, resale and reorganization schemes once they have neared the brink of bankruptcy.[289]

282 *Ibid.* at 382.

283 Snyder, *Digest of Education Statistics*, *supra* note 43, at 389.

284 Best & Best, *supra* note 23, at 165.

285 Snyder, *Digest of Education Statistics*, *supra* note 43, at Table 331.70.

286 *Ibid.* at Table 331.10.

287 Best & Best, *supra* note 23, at 152.

288 Cowley, Stacy, and Erica L. Green. "A College Chain Crumbles, and Millions in Student Loan Cash Disappears." *The New York Times*, The New York Times, 8 Mar. 2019, www.nytimes.com/2019/03/07/business/argosy-college-art-insititutes-south-university.html.

289 *Ibid.*

Sometimes the universities survive their financial problems, but, all too often, they go bankrupt, leaving their students with massive debt burdens and non-transferable credits. Ultimately, the federal government, at the taxpayers' expense, forgives these debts.[290]

The Obama administration, in 2010, eliminated federally guaranteed loans and nationalized the lending program.[291] As a result, most loans made today are directly from the Department of Education. Furthermore, the reforms created a "Pay-As-You-Earn" option, allowing all indebted graduates with federally guaranteed loans to make payments of up to ten percent of their income for a period of twenty or twenty-five years before the debt would be forgiven.[292] As a conservative estimate, there is about $36 billion of debt in the Pay-As-You-Earn program, $1.3 trillion overall in outstanding loans, whereas the federal government continues issuing around $30 billion in grants to students, not to mention the $200 billion issued in student loans every year.[293] These reforms were also preceded by the spin-off of Sallie Mae, into a publicly traded corporation. Now that it is a private lender without guaranteed loans, it has demonstrated a tendency to lend to low-risk students from wealthier families, or to high-risk students with less-favorable terms of repayment and higher interest rates.[294]

As a response to the crippling student debt burdens, a growing number of private, nonprofit universities have taken the initiative to weed out and eliminate student loans in higher education. In this recent drive to

---

290 *Ibid.*

291 Brooks, John R. "Don't Let the G.O.P. Dismantle Obama's Student Loan Reforms." *The New York Times*, 9 Apr. 2018, www.nytimes.com/2018/04/09/opinion/student-loan-reform-prosper-act.html.

292 Despite the student loans being forgiven after this period, the remainder is to be treated as taxable income, requiring the students to pay tax on the forgiven amount. This program acted retrospectively back to loans issued in 2007, so, barring any radical changes to the program, the first wave of loan-forgiveness will occur in 2027 for those with bachelor's degrees and 2032 for those who have studied at the graduate and postgraduate levels. This sudden tax debt that will come due has colloquially come to be known at the student-loan "tax bomb."

293 Brooks, *supra* note 291.

294 Best & Best, *supra* note 23, at 155; Friedman, Zack. "Trump's New Plan to Make Student Loans Great Again." *Forbes*, Forbes Magazine, 21 Dec. 2019, www.forbes.com/sites/zackfriedman/2019/12/21/trump-plan-student-loans-great-again/#5763208b4c0c (indicating that the Trump administration has not yet taken any legal action on student loan debt, but that many different approaches are being considered).

disentangle themselves from the student debt mess, at least seventy-five institutions now have "No Student Loan" programs, financed by grants, scholarships and affordable tuition fees.[295] The financial aid packages vary from institution to institution, but the majority calculate tuition fees based on the financial need of students and their families, granting much more financial aid to low-income students.[296] Based on these calculations, students from the poorest families can attend at virtually no cost. Some public universities have moved in this direction, but the list of institutions with no student loan rules is dominated by private, nonprofits, including many of the most prestigious universities in the US.

F. The US' Third Sector: Nonprofits

Nonprofit organizations are deeply rooted in the US' legal and cultural tradition, complementing both the governmental and private, for-profit sectors. Because they play such a large role, nonprofits are often referred to as the US' "third sector." Although all three sectors are all distinguishable and based on different economic premises, there are many linkages between them. The designation "nonprofit" was originally coined to distinguish between for-profit organizations and those with purposes other than serving shareholders.[297] This "nonprofit" distinction, as will be shown below, has come to be clearly defined in the law. Some of today's most recognizable nonprofits were founded very long before the US itself.[298] These

---

295 Friedman, Zack. "75 Colleges with Free or Reduced Tuition." *Forbes*, 27 Nov. 2018, www.forbes.com/sites/zackfriedman/2018/11/27/colleges-no-student-loans/#37e51ece6156.

296 *Ibid.*

297 *See generally* Hansmann, Henry B. "The Role of the Nonprofit Enterprise." *Yale Law Journal*, vol. 89, no. 5, 1980, ft.nt. 32 (indicating that chartered nonprofits long preceded their for-profit counterparts; American universities have their roots in the twelfth century English and European universities, while many ecclesiastical corporations and monasteries date back even further).

298 Kerr, *supra* note 106, at 115 (stating that:
... it might be said that "everything else changes, but the university mostly endures"—particularly in the United States. About eighty-five institutions in the Western world established by 1520 still exist in recognizable forms, with similar functions and with unbroken histories, including the Catholic Church, the Parliaments of the Isle of Man, of Iceland, and of Great Britain, several Swiss cantons, and seventy universities. Kings that rule, feudal lords with vassals, and guilds with monopolies are all gone. These seventy universities, however, are

older, but still-living organizations demonstrate that charities, volunteer groups, religious organizations and the many other types of nonprofits have an independent growth, separate from government and they have a tendency towards longevity. Governments and for-profits have not traditionally enjoyed such lengthy tenures.[299]

A number of similarities endure between the earliest nonprofits and today's: first, self-government allows for governing boards to make essential decisions, second, they are not subject to taxation due to their designation as privileged organizations and third, they are able to receive donations for the purpose of furthering charitable purposes.[300] Today's massive nonprofit sector has humble roots, going back to America's colonial era, when small associations would provide goods and services, socialize, evangelize and undertake many other activities. Perhaps the best example of this is Harvard University, which was founded through the permission of a Great and General Court of Massachusetts decree and endowed with an initial £400 from the Massachusetts Colony.[301] This public endowment was greatly surpassed, though, by private donations from donors such as John Harvard.[302] Harvard University would go on to set the standard for American higher education with its usage of professional governing boards, adaptations to the curriculum as well as its culture of alumni support.[303] Political writer Alexis de Tocqueville noted the unique nature of such private associations following his visit to the US in the 1830's, stating "[w]herever at the head of some new undertaking you see the government

---

still in the same locations with some of the same buildings, with professors and students doing much of the same things, and with governance carried on in much the same ways...).

299 *See* Madison, James. "Memorial and Remonstrance against Religious Assessments." *National Archives and Records Administration*, 20 June 1785, founders.archives.gov/documents/Madison/01-08-02-0163 (stating that "for it is know that this religion both existed and flourished, not only without the support of human laws, but in spite of every opposition from them.").

300 Hall, Peter Dobkin. *The Jossey-Bass Handbook of Nonprofit Leadership and Management*. Edited by Robert D. Herman and David O. Renz, Jossey-Bass, 2010, p. 6.

301 Morison, *supra* note 166, at 12.

302 *Ibid.* (noting that, in addition to the initial £400 colonial endowment, private donors such as John Harvard (£1000 contribution), Lady Anne Radcliffe-Mowlson (£100), and individual planters ranging from a few shillings up to £40 made an immense difference in financing Harvard College's early activities).

303 Veblen, Thorstein. *Higher Learning in America: a Memorandum on the Conduct of Universities by Business Men*. Nabu Press, 2010, p. 8.

in France, or a man of rank in England, in the United States you will be sure to find an association."[304]

Today's formalized American nonprofit organizations are conceptually similar to those created under England's Charitable Uses Act of 1601, which enumerated various charitable purposes and allowed the formation of charities aimed to serve the public benefit.[305] If a charity fit within one of the Act's listed purposes, it could be chartered. This support for charities was necessary because of legislative attempts in England to interfere with private groups, namely religions that tended to accumulate wealth indefinitely, without it ever escheating to the lords or to the crown.[306] The British carried over these laws permitting limited charitable uses to the American colonies. Following the American Revolution, the states initially shifted to discourage charitable giving.[307] Most attempts to discourage charity came in the form of states seizing assets,[308] setting narrow limitations on who the beneficiaries could be (*cestui que*),[309] applying the rule against perpetuities,[310] implementing taxes on charities or creating

---

304 Tocqueville, A. de. *Democracy in America,* vol. 2 (Henry Reeve, *trans.*). New York: Random House, 1945. (Originally published in 1840), p. 106.

305 Statute of Charitable Uses 1601, 43 Eliz. I, c. 4 (Eng.).

306 Nuzhat, Malik. "Charity and Charitable Purposes in the United Kingdom." *The International Journal of Not-for-Profit Law*, vol. 11, no. 1, Nov. 2008.

307 Hall, *supra* note 300, at 7 (describing how Virginia restricted charitable uses and confiscated the Anglican Church's endowments. Further, indicating that the trend towards making charity a matter for public funding was a stronger trend in the southern and newer western states).

308 Trustees of Dartmouth College v. Woodward, 17 U.S. (4 Wheat.) 518 (1819) (ruling that the Constitution's Contracts Clause protected the college as founded under its corporate charter from New Hampshire's legislative attempts at delegating trustee appointments to the state's governor. This case serves as a landmark, protecting private charters from governmental subsumption).

309 Vidal v. Executors of Girad, 43 U.S. (2 How.) 127 (1844) (The court ruled that the extensive estate of Stephen Girard may be distributed as per his testament and not subject to the restrictive limitations of the no longer effective Statute of Charitable Uses. The bequeath to a large class of people was shown to have been supported in the English system, prior to its adoption of the Statute of Charitable Uses, through its allocation in the Courts of Chancery. Courts of Chancery had permitted charitable trusts created for indefinite charities along with more specified charitable recipients. Chancery had even gone as far as permitting charitable trusts which failed to name a competent trustee or any trustee at all).

310 The arcane rule prohibits the creation of future interests or estates which may not become vested within the life or lives in being at the time of the effective date of the instrument creating the future interest and 21 years thereafter.

true mortmain statutes that set limits on the assets that could be held by charities.[311] Over time, these restrictions were loosened and, either by means of legislative enactment or judicial decision, charitable trusts and corporations are recognized in every US state today.[312]

From the beginning of the twentieth century up through the 1930's, there was a boom in the founding of nonprofits. This boom also coincided with increased formalization and professionalization within the organizations.[313] Following exponential growth in the governmental and for-profit sectors, from 1930 to 1980, the nonprofit sector became increasingly more linked with the other two sectors. The federal government initiated a wave of subsidies for nonprofits, creating tax deductions, charitable tax-exemptions, voucher programs and large funding grants.[314] Because of increasing federal taxes and the corresponding deductions that were available for charitable giving, Americans poured funding into these private, nonprofit organizations.[315] As these nonprofit organizations became more expansive, professionalized and reliant on federal funding, general public participation was significantly reduced.[316]

G. *Nonprofit and University Governance*

I. The Third Sector

In the "third sector," *nonprofit organizations*, *tax-exempt organizations*, *charitable organizations* and *foundations* make up the corps of organizations receiving special treatment from the government for the delivery of goods and services that are otherwise not delivered by the governmental or

311 Being derived from the Latin *morta manus*, mortmain literally translates into "dead hand." Knaplund, Kristine S. "Charity for the Death Tax: The Impact of Legislation on Charitable Bequests." *Gonzaga Law Review*, vol. 45, 2010, p. 714.

312 Fremont-Smith, Marion R., Governing Nonprofit Organizations: Federal and State Law and Regulation, Harvard University Press, 2009, p. 47.

313 *See generally* Hwang, Hokyu, and Walter W. Powell. "The Rationalization of Charity: The Influences of Professionalism in the Nonprofit Sector." *Administrative Science Quarterly*, vol. 54, no. 2, 2009, p. 268.

314 Hall, *supra* note 300, at 16.

315 *Ibid.* at 17 (noting that, while these incentives were effective for the wealthy, the average Americans did not even earn enough money to have to pay an income tax).

316 Putnam, R.D. *Bowling Alone: The Collapse and Renewal of American Community.* New York: Simon & Schuster, 2000.

private, for-profit sectors. Upon careful observation, one would see that *nonprofits* are the most general category under the tax code; as an organization goes on to become tax-exempt, charitable or a foundation, the regulations become increasingly more restrictive. *Tax-exempt* organizations are those that are exempt from the federal income tax, because of their involvement in particular activities, as defined by the Internal Revenue Code (hereinafter, IRC).[317] *Charitable organizations*, a yet more narrow group, are defined by 501 (c)(3) of the IRC; they are tax-exempt and their donors may receive tax deductions for any gifts given to the charity.[318] Both tax-exemptions and deductions for gifts to charitable organizations are recognized as being government subsidies to promote particular activities.[319] Although charities are greatly advantaged by the rules that promote private giving, the advantages are counterbalanced by restrictions on lobbying, political campaigning and, of course, the distribution of excess profits to various parties. Private universities are one of the many different types of nonprofits, and, due to their educational role, they are usually designated as *nonprofit*, *tax-exempt* and *charitable*.[320]

---

317 26 U.S.C. § 501 (2006).

318 26 U.S.C. §§ 170, 501 (c)(3) (2006) (Granting tax-exemptions to:
[c]orporations, and any community chest, fund, or foundation, organized and operated exclusively for religious, charitable, scientific, testing for public safety, literary, or educational purposes, or to foster national or international amateur sports competition (but only if no part of its activities involve the provision of athletic facilities or equipment), or for the prevention of cruelty to children or animals, no part of the net earnings of which inures to the benefit of any private shareholder or individual, no substantial part of the activities of which is carrying on propaganda, or otherwise attempting, to influence legislation (except as otherwise provided in subsection (h)), and which does not participate in, or intervene in (including the publishing or distributing of statements), any political campaign on behalf of (or in opposition to) any candidate for public office.).

319 Rubin, Eric. "Knowing an 'Educational Institution' When You See One: Applying the Commerciality Approach to Tax Exemptions for Universities Under § 501 (c)(3)." *Washington Law Review*, vol. 92, 2015, p. 1055.

320 *See e.g.*, Letter from Internal Revenue Service to President and Fellows of Harvard College (Dec. 28, 2011), http://internal.procurement.harvard.edu/files/procurement/files/certificate_501.pdf.

1. Overcoming Contract Failure through the Nonprofit Form

Nonprofits are distinguishable from for-profit enterprises and government entities through their unique legal structuring, which provides a means of overcoming *contract failure*. Contract failure, arising primarily in the provision of public goods or in cases of price discrimination, occurs when not enough information is available to evaluate the quality of a good or a service being provided. This could lead to higher prices for sub-optimal goods and services.[321] Such breakdowns in market efficiency have been dubbed "contract failure," because of the inability of consumers to police producers through arm's length contracts. Contract failure is the distinguishing factor of what makes an undertaking more suitable for a nonprofit, as opposed to a for-profit entity. Nonprofits are thought to be better in the provision of goods or services that are subject to contract failure as opposed to normal commodities whose values and prices are more apparent.[322] If consumers are well-informed and well-situated to bargain for abundant goods and services, their demand and the competition among suppliers should lead to the highest quality goods and services available at the lowest possible prices.[323] In the case of activities normally undertaken by nonprofits, normal market competition could be inadequate to incentivize profit-seeking producers to charge reasonable prices; rather, it is likely that they will charge excessive prices for inferior goods and services.[324] In determining if contract failure applies to higher education,

321 Hansmann, *Role of the Nonprofit Enterprise*, *supra* note 297, at 846.

322 Notice that consumer electronics, for example, are constantly improving in quality while their prices continuously drop. If somebody buys a smart phone or television this year, they are likely to see an improved version released in the next year for a similar or, perhaps, lower price. This availability of high-quality goods at reasonable prices is a result of widespread market information, consumers' ability to evaluate their purchases, outside competition providing comparable alternatives and internal controls to ensure shareholders' profits. In the case of higher education, universities need only compete to attract students to enroll, so that they can collect massive tuition fees that will be subsidized by the federal government without regard to the students' abilities or the quality of the education provided by the university. As will be discussed further, private nonprofit universities still provide access to quality higher education, but some of the mechanisms for economic restraint have been removed.

323 Smith, Adam. *An Inquiry into the Nature and Causes of the Wealth of Nations*, edited by S.M. Soares. MetaLibri Digital Library 2007, original published in 1776, p. 48; Salamon & Toepler, *supra* note 49 (referring to situations where parties are not well informed as "information asymmetries").

324 Hansmann, *Role of the Nonprofit Enterprise*, *supra* note 297, at 843–44.

which has major implications for pricing, one must first ask if it is a *public good or service*.[325]

Higher education is most likely not a *public good or service* in the economic sense, i.e. a good or service that is *non-rivalrous* and *non-excludable*.[326] Education is *excludable* in that all universities have admissions criteria that exclude some segment of the population. Even open-enrollment universities require that applicants have a high school (or equivalent) degree; this excludes applicants who have never met that prerequisite. Likewise, education is *rivalrous* in that, as class sizes increase, the learning atmosphere simultaneously becomes less intimate, and traditional classroom capacities will eventually be met. Universities' financial resources also serve as a limitation. Even though higher education is best considered a private good due to the individual benefits enjoyed by students, it does create down-stream public goods such as increased tax revenues, better-funded state programs, lower crime rates, more active public participation and lower health care costs. Despite not being a public good or service, higher education is prone to contract failure.

Contract failure applies to higher education because students cannot know the content and quality of their education in advance and certainly are in no position to weigh the long-term outcomes when first deliberating whether to make such an investment. The fact that parents or the government often pay students' tuition fees, with very little feedback regarding the programs' quality and nearly no recourse in cases of unsatisfactory service, breaks down the student's ability to be fully informed. The outcomes may only materialize years later. As a further means of determining if contract failure applies to higher education, the fact that universities charge essentially all their students different prices, based on scholastic

325 It is essential to begin by determining if any particular good or service is a *public* good or service in the economic sense. The contract failure theory applies to private goods, because these are the types of transactions that could theoretically be policed by arm's length contracts. On the other hand, public goods, such as knowledge, are better analyzed by the market failure theory, which will be described in Part II. *Ibid.* at 838; *but see* Weisbrod, Burton Allen. *The Nonprofit Economy*. Harvard University Press, 1988 (explaining that nonprofits derive their role in cases of "government failure analogous to private market failure" to provide public goods or services).

326 Examples of non-excludable goods include fresh air, sidewalks, sunshine or national defense, which are accessible regardless of whether a beneficiary has paid for them. The risk of economic free-riding makes the provision of public goods in private markets inefficient and often undersupplied. Hansmann, *Role of the Nonprofit Enterprise*, *supra* note 297, at 860.

ability, family income and financial need, indicates that they partake in price discrimination. This extensive price discrimination is made possible by universities' access to information. Virtually all students complete the Free Application for Federal Student Aid (FAFSA) application, providing universities unrestricted access to their students' financial information.[327] Nonprofits exist to counteract contract failure, and their special structure is meant to facilitate this. Of the numerous features unique to nonprofits, the cornerstone is the *non-distribution constraint.*

2. The Non-Distribution Constraint

The foremost theorist on the role of nonprofits, Henry B. Hansmann, was the first to identify the non-distribution constraint, which inherently existed within the nonprofit form.[328] The non-distribution constraint is the legal requirement that nonprofit organizations neither distribute excess profits to shareholders, which they do not have, nor may they inure a private benefit to specified individuals, such as officers, directors, trustees or their close relatives. Rather than distributing to shareholders, nonprofits are required to retain excess revenues and put them toward future nonprofit, charitable activities. The non-distribution constraint is, at least theoretically, meant to restrain the individual profit motive within nonprofits, what economists would call "rent-seeking," by ensuring donors that their gifts are ultimately put toward the specific purposes or beneficiaries, or both, that they intended to help.[329] Recall that this mechanism is necessary due to contract failure, especially because the donors are not among the recipients of the goods and services provided by the nonprofits and cannot make accurate assessments of their quality.[330] Theoretically, nonprofits, due to the non-distribution constraint, should be committed to using excess revenues for their exempt purposes and should lack the incentive to raise prices and cut quality, thereby additionally alleviating the need for marginally informed students to search for better options.[331]

---

327 Note that this access to information is unparalleled; no service provider in any other context has such an extensive knowledge of their "customers" financial situations.

328 Hansmann, *Role of the Nonprofit Enterprise*, *supra* note 297, at 835.

329 *Ibid.* at 862.

330 *Ibid.*

331 Frumkin, Peter. *On Being Nonprofit: A Conceptual and Policy Primer.* Harvard University Press, 2009, pp. 70–71.

Incidentally, nonprofit activities also tend to correspond better with the provision of services, rather than with the production of goods. Services are not quite as standardized as goods and not as objectively comparable. Thus, the protection afforded by nonprofits should aid in providing quality services at reasonable prices.[332]

As a major caveat, all the above discussion of the non-distribution constraint as a means for overcoming contract failure is made primarily in the context of a relationship among donors, service providers and beneficiaries. The assumption is that the donor gives financial support to the service provider for the beneficiary. In the context of universities, this is usually implemented by alumni gifts to universities that are intended to benefit the students. Hansmann makes a vital distinction between *donative* and *commercial* nonprofits wherein *donative* nonprofits are those that "receive most or all of their income in the form of grants or donations" and *commercial* nonprofits are those that "receive the bulk of their income from prices charged for their services...."[333] Churches, museums and performing arts groups are some examples of donative nonprofits whereas modern nonprofit hospitals depict how commercial nonprofits might work. These distinctions are made as rough approximations that are unlikely to be fully descriptive of any single organization.

Private, nonprofit universities have both *donative* and *commercial* characteristics. They are donative in the sense that the majority have endowments, which are means of "transfer[ing] private dollars to public purposes" with certain assurances, adding a great deal of financial stability.[334] Although, the endowments are quite stratified among the universities; a small majority of, predominately private, universities have the largest endowments and the rest have somewhere below ten million dollars.[335] Beyond endowments, these private nonprofit universities are also, to varying degrees, the recipients of government grants from both state and federal governments. Despite their strong donative features, the fact that most universities charge tuition fees demonstrates commercial characteristics. Furthermore, another quality of commercial nonprofits—that they are better suited for providing complex and non-standardized services—

332 Hansmann, *Role of the Nonprofit Enterprise*, *supra* note 297, at 872.

333 *Ibid.* at 840.

334 "Understanding College and University Endowments." *American Council on Education*, 2014, www.acenet.edu/Documents/Understanding-Endowments-White-Paper.pdf.

335 *Ibid.* (noting that most public universities "have no substantial endowments").

comports with the services provided by many universities.[336] Because both elements, *donative* and *commercial*, are present, such university attributes should be thought of as being on a spectrum in-between the two, while occasionally moving toward one extreme or the other. First writing on the non-distribution constraint in 1980, Hansmann classified universities as donative because of universities' extensive alumni support that was used to supplement the payment of manageable tuition fees.[337] Nobody in 1980 could have contemplated how big a role student lending and thereby, tuition fee-based revenues would come to play; these two factors suggest that universities today are more commercial.[338]

It is also necessary to understand the role of "demand-side subsidies," which, in the context of university finance, are the massive subsidies given to students in the form of student loans.[339] For-profits have consumer dissatisfaction as an inherent control mechanism to protect against abuses when demand-side subsidies are employed. On the other hand, nonprofits are dependent on the non-distribution constraint. This suggests that non-profits are theoretically better suited for situations involving demand-side subsidies, although the commercial provision of services can put them in competition with for-profit enterprises.[340] One benefit of demand-side subsidies is that they "reinforce market selection," empowering students to choose among *all* institutions, which still requires students to be well

336 Hansmann, *Role of the Nonprofit Enterprise*, *supra* note 297, at 862.

337 *Ibid.* at 861.

338 *See* Frumkin, *supra* note 331, at 77, 89 (describing the phenomenon of public subsidies "crowding out" private charitable giving).

339 Hansmann, *Role of the Nonprofit Enterprise*, *supra* note 297, at 848 (giving "re-deemable coupons, such as food stamps or housing vouchers" as examples of demand-side subsidies).

340 Hansmann, *Evolving Economic Structure*, *supra* note 44, at 159, 161–64 (describing the effect of supply-side private donations and supply-side governmental subsidies as well. The supply-side private donations, primarily from alumni, can be conceptualized as *ex post facto* repayments for subsidized education, a significant source of revenue guaranteeing stability as well as being an effective means of financial "risk sharing" between institutions and their students; although, private giving is inadequate to fully support an institution and not all institutions have access to these subsidies. Supply-side governmental subsidies operate differently; these incentivize state and local governments to operate their own institutions and are unlikely to promote any major nonprofit expansion. Non-profits, "regardless of the kind or quantity of subsidies offered," tend to grow rather slowly in light of their aims to be relatively more selective. Nonprofits do expand but primarily in response to increased demand).

informed.[341] If the non-distribution constraint fails to restrain rent-seeking, the result could be twofold: there could be both contract failure and massive amounts of demand-side subsidies being disbursed without any control mechanism. Other outcomes of massive government subsidies being pumped into universities include the loss of independence, the distortion of university goals in the competition to attract more subsidies as well as the growth of expansive administrative infrastructures.[342]

Nonprofits are most advantaged in the delivery of services that are desired only by a small percentage of the population because they are more responsive to individual needs, have smaller internal bureaucracies and have better market discipline than governments.[343] Especially with commercial nonprofits potentially being involved in areas also occupied by for-profit enterprises, there is a great amount of public trust and discretion endowed upon these nonprofits, with the expectation that the non-distribution constraint will prevent abuses.[344] Despite the large and important interests protected by the non-distribution constraint, it is still a "blunt instrument" and a "rather crude consumer protection device."[345]

The non-distribution constraint is written into all the states' statutes regarding nonprofit organizations. The Model Nonprofit Corporation Act (MNCA) mirrors this, stating: "... a nonprofit corporation shall not pay dividends or make distributions of any part of its assets, income, or profits to its members, directors, members of a designated body, or officers."[346] Naturally, nonprofit officers should be compensated, but as a limitation, they may only receive "*reasonable* compensation" or be reimbursed for "*reasonable* expenses" for their services rendered."[347] While it has never been observed, Hansmann suggests that any salaries paid within the non-distribution constraint be fixed. That is, any yearly variation in the salaries, especially when they correspond to annual surpluses, should be viewed by

---

341 Hansmann, *Why Are Colleges and Universities Exempt*, *supra* note 174, at 11.

342 Salamon, Lester M. *Partners in Public Service Government-Nonprofit Relations in the Modern Welfare State*. The Johns Hopkins University Press, 1996, p. 109.

343 Hansmann, *Role of the Nonprofit Enterprise*, *supra* note 297, at 895.

344 *Ibid.* at 863.

345 *Ibid.* at 871.

346 This model legislation was first drafted 1964 by the Business Law Section of the American Bar Association to propose nonprofit standards for the states. With minor variation between state statutes, all incorporate the non-distribution constraint; ABA Model Nonprofit Corporation Act, Third Edition § 6.40. (2008).

347 ABA Model Nonprofit Corporation Act, Third Edition § 6.41. (2008).

state authorities or the Internal Revenue Service (hereinafter, IRS) as being a distribution of profits.[348]

In contrast to nonprofits, government entities are best suited to deliver public goods and services because of their dependable access to capital, accountability mechanisms and taxing power that eliminates the risk of free-riding.[349] For-profit service providers, furthermore, are most efficient in the provision of goods that can be standardized and objectively observed for their quality. Their provision of services, though, are highly dependent on the level of communication between provider and recipient, universities and students in this context.[350] This high level of information and communication is simply not present in higher education. Because of this contract failure, nonprofits have traditionally played a leading role in American higher education but, for reasons that will be discussed below, many students are now receiving (possibly inferior) educations at exorbitant prices, calling the functioning of the nonprofit structure into question.

II. The Nonprofit Tests

All nonprofits must satisfy several requirements through both formal filings and actual practices to attain and retain their charitable, tax-exempt statuses. First, they have to uphold the *commerciality doctrine*, which is derived from the common law.[351] The IRC does not expressly prohibit nonprofits from partaking in commercial activity—other than requiring that they operate solely for their filed exempt purposes—so courts have created a patchwork requirement, questioning nonprofits' tax-exemptions when they actively compete with for-profit companies or provide similar products or services.[352] The most essential element for the commerciality doctrine to be considered is whether there is substantial commercial activ-

348 Hansmann, *Role of the Nonprofit Enterprise*, *supra* note 297, at 900.

349 *Ibid.* at 894.

350 *Ibid.* at 843.

351 *See* Trinidad v. Sagrada, 163 U.S. 578 (1924); Better Business Bureau of Washington D.C. v. U.S. 326 U.S. 279 (1945); Scripture Press v. U.S. 285 F.2d 800 (Ct. Cl. 1961).

352 Cafardi, Nicholas P., and Jaclyn Fabean Cherry. *Understanding Nonprofit and Tax Exempt Organizations*. Carolina Academic Press, 2012, p. 95.

ity.[353] The remedy for substantial commercial activity is revocation of a tax-exempt status. Although, this common law doctrine is seen as being somewhat draconian, and, as is discussed below, a few other remedies are available. Beyond the *commerciality doctrine*, courts and the IRS[354] apply four tests to determine whether nonprofits comply with the IRC: the *organizational test*, *operational test*, *private inurement test*, and *political activities test*.[355]

1. The Organizational Test

The *organizational test* requires that an organization's founding document, i.e. articles of incorporation or charitable trust indenture, establish the organization for a charitable purpose. The document must expressly specify the exempt purpose, as defined by § 501 (c)(3), state that the organization will only undertake that exempt activity and that it will abstain from substantial non-exempt activity.[356] Put another way, the organizational test requires that all of the proper "magic words" are included in an organization's founding document.[357] Once the IRS determines that an organization has properly filed, they may receive a tax-exempt status and the other three tests then become important for nonprofit activities.

353 *Ibid.* at 97–98 (describing that some courts have taken a quantitative approach, finding twenty percent commercial revenues to be "substantial non-exempt activity," whereas another jurisdiction found ten percent to be "not substantial." Despite their attempts to draw a bright line, the Tax Court rejected the notion that having below ten percent commercial revenues would serve as a safe-harbor. More qualitative approaches have also been developed in other courts, focusing on whether a nonprofit has competed with for-profit entities, provided below-cost service, had an excessive amount of profits or engaged in commercial advertising).

354 The IRS is the federal government agency responsible for tax collection, enforcement of the IRC and clarification of issues regarding the IRC.

355 The IRS's involvement is primarily in the initial filing phase, determining whether an entity is qualified to receive tax-exemption. Once a tax-exemption is received and, if it were to be challenged by the IRS, then the courts become involved in applying the IRC-derived tests. 26 U.S.C. § 501 (c)(3).

356 A number of other clauses, including a renunciation of lobbying and political campaigning and a plan for dissolution or termination, must be included as well.

357 Cafardi & Cherry, *supra* note 352, at 65.

2. The Operational Test

The *operational test* requires courts to examine a tax-exempt organization's activities. As required by the IRC, charities must operate *exclusively* for a tax-exempt purpose, although the IRS later interpreted this to mean *primarily*.[358] If any of a tax-exempt organization's primary activities are in furtherance of a non-exempt purpose, it does not meet the operational test. However, it still may meet the operational test if its non-exempt activities are found to be insubstantial.[359] If a court were to examine a non-exempt activity and find it to be substantial, it would revoke the organization's tax-exemption.[360] The commerciality doctrine is very-much related to the operational test; courts often consider whether a tax-exempt organization's activities have a certain "commercial hue" or profit making motive and use this as a consideration as to whether it is undertaking non-exempt, for-profit activities. Similarly, courts have inquired as to whether tax-exempt organizations have acted "commensurate" with their resources in an exempt manner.[361] Finally, the operational test requires that a tax-exempt organization shall not privately benefit anyone. They exist for the good of the public, and a private benefit to a small or limited group ought not to occur because of the non-distribution constraint.

3. The Private Inurement Test

The third IRC test for tax-exemption is called the *private inurement test*. This test prohibits inurement of the organization's assets to private interested parties or individuals. These are an organization's "insiders," those who may be officers, managers, members of the board of directors or otherwise operating in a control capacity.[362] A violation of this test is

---

358 *See e.g.*, Rameses School of San Antonio, Texas v. Commissioner, T.C. Memo 2007-85 WL 1061871 (T.C. 2007).

359 *Ibid.*

360 Redlands Surgical v. Commissioner, 113 T.C. 47, 71–72, 1999 WL 513862 (T.C. 1999), *affd.*, 242 F.3 d 904 (9th Cir. 2001) (noting that, regardless of the inclusion of truly exempt purposes, the presence of a single nonexempt purposes that is substantial in nature will bring an organization's tax-exempt status into question).

361 Cafardi & Cherry, *supra* note 352, at 68.

362 Family Trust of Massachusetts, Inc. v. U.S., 892 F. Supp. 2d 149, 155 (D.D.C. 2012).

proven by a showing that there is an overlap of control and benefit within the exempt organization. Private inurement most typically occurs through organizational business deals with officers, members, directors or their family members. If these individuals were to be excessively overpaid for goods or services, the organization could lose its exemption. However, this does not prohibit insiders dealing with the organization; it just requires that their exchanges be conducted in a reasonable and fair, "arm's-length" manner.[363]

Nonprofits universities are, at least in theory, regulated and overseen by various government agencies at both the state and federal levels. At the state level, attorneys general usually play the largest role in oversight, but their secretaries of state, corporation commissions, departments of tax and revenue as well as consumer protection agencies may aid them.[364] The IRS plays the most substantial role at the federal level.[365] In most instances, due to lack of standing, private parties cannot bring an action to enforce legal rules against nonprofits. Private parties are essentially limited to the role of reporting violations to governmental bodies or generating media attention to increase public awareness.

III. Enforcement Remedies

Prior to 1996, the only remedy for private inurement or excess benefit was for the IRS to *revoke an organization's tax-exemption*.[366] Excess benefit is defined in the IRC as "any transaction in which an economic benefit is provided by an applicable tax-exempt organization directly or indirectly to or for the use of any disqualified person if the value of the economic benefit provided exceeds the value of the consideration (including the

---

363 *Ibid.*

364 Fremont-Smith, Marion R. *The Nonprofit Sector: a Research Handbook*. Edited by Walter W. Powell and Richard Steinberg, Yale University Press, 2006, pp. 301, 364–65, 368–70, 372–73.

365 Mayer, Lloyd Hitoshi. "Fragmented Oversight of Nonprofits in the United States: Does It Work – Can It Work." *Chicago-Kent Law Review*, vol. 91, 2016, p. 938.

366 Note that private benefit, private inurement and excess benefit transactions are three distinct categories. Although they are all relevant to a certain extent, this dissertation focuses mostly on private inurement, which is the impermissible benefit to nonprofit insiders. Private benefit, on the other hand, is an impermissible benefit to individuals outside of the nonprofit. *See* Orange County Agr. Soc. v. C.I.R. 893 F.2 d 529 (2 d Cir. 1990).

performance of services) received for providing such benefit."[367] This was perceived as being too draconian; therefore IRC § 4958 was drafted to implement *intermediate sanctions*, allowing the IRS to punish groups without eliminating their exemption.[368] Intermediate sanctions target organizations that improperly benefit "disqualified persons." A disqualified person is somebody who exercised substantial control over an organization within the last five years (or one of his or her family members). The intermediate sanctions also provide a safe-harbor provision for organizations and their officers.

1. Safe-Harbor

While compensation may be facially exorbitant, the IRC safe-harbor permits it if it was previously laid out as a fixed contract, if an internal controlling panel preapproved it, due diligence was conducted and if the panel's reasoning is documented.[369] When these requirements are satisfied, payments made to disqualified persons under the compensation arrangement are presumed to be reasonable.[370] Nonprofits should seek to compensate their executives comparably to other nonprofit executives working within the same geographic area, within the same sector, and who manage similar sized operations. The failure of an organization to satisfy the safe-harbor requirements will result in the IRS conducting a review.[371] These intermediate sanctions and their related safe-harbor will be particularly relevant in the analysis section below regarding university administrator compensation.

This presumption in favor of a safe-harbor may be rebutted if the IRS provides sufficient evidence to rebut the probative value of the in-

---

367 26 U.S.C. § 4958 (c)(1)(A) (2012).

368 Fishman, James J. "Improving Charitable Accountability." *Maryland Law Review*, vol. 62, 2003, pp. 253–54.

369 "Rebuttable Presumption – Intermediate Sanctions." *IRS*, 8 Jan. 2020, https://www.irs.gov/charities-non-profits/charitable-organizations/rebuttable-presumption-intermediate-sanctions (requiring advance approval by a body within the nonprofit consisting of individuals who do not have a conflict of interest, prior due diligence on comparative pay at other similar nonprofits by this authorized body and that the body documented its basis for the compensation during the decision-making process).

370 *Ibid.*

371 *Ibid.*

ternal panel's comparability data.[372] The IRS makes its determination as to whether a nonprofit's compensation is reasonable by comparing it to what other, similar, nonprofits would pay for such services under similar circumstances. This comparison and enforcement is made possible by the requirement that all nonprofits annually report, "all compensation paid to [their] directors, officers, trustees, key employees, five highest compensated employees, and five highest compensated independent contractors receiving more than $100,000.[373] When the subject does not fall under a safe-harbor, the disqualified person must pay a tax on twenty-five percent of the excess benefit received. This is essentially a "warning shot" for them to remedy the excess benefit within the tax period. If they fail to do so, they shall then be taxed an additional two hundred percent rate on the excess benefit. The organization's manager may also be subject to a ten percent tax on the excess benefit, unless his conduct was not willful and has a reasonable justification.[374]

2. UBIT Taxes

Finally, the IRC created a separate tax for instances of nonprofits undertaking commercial, for-profit activity. The Unrelated Business Income Tax (hereinafter, UBIT) applies to "any trade or business the conduct of which is not substantially related to the exercise or performance by such organization of its charitable, educational, or other purpose or function constituting the basis for its exemption under section 501."[375] This is a remedy for infractions that are considered to be substantial business activities, but not frivolous enough to warrant revocation of the organization's tax-exemption. Instead of taxing all income, the unrelated activities may be *fragmented* away from the remainder of the income and only the fragmented portion is subject to the UBIT tax. There is still a lack of clarity, though, as to exactly what activities are "related" and "unrelated." The university

---

372 *Ibid.*

373 "About Form 990, Return of Organization Exempt from Income Tax." *IRS*, 5 Nov. 2019, https://www.irs.gov/forms-pubs/about-form-990 (including the following as forms of compensation: all forms of cash and non-cash compensation, including salary, fees, bonuses, deferred compensation and severance payments, the payment of some insurance premiums, fringe benefits, such as medical, dental, life and disability insurance, and foregone interest on loans).

374 26 U.S.C. § 4960 (2017).

375 26 U.S.C § 513 (a) (2017).

provision of dormitories and dining halls is an example of activities falling into a grey area.[376]

The UBIT is a result of Congress' concerns, in the early 1950's, that nonprofits were involved in for-profit, commercial activities, and, due to their nonprofit status, payed no federal taxes. More specifically, the Mueller Macaroni Company was donated to the New York University Law School in 1948 and its profits went untaxed due to NYU's nonprofit status.[377] Because of nonprofit involvement in commercial activity, Congress created the UBIT to make only activities "related" to a nonprofit core purpose tax-exempt.[378] Although, despite the tax on "unrelated" activity, very little money has been paid in taxes, and is, instead, reinvested into a broadly defined "related" activities such as real estate investment and contracting to perform research and publishing.[379] Advocates for for-profit enterprises argue that nonprofits entering into competition with for-profits is unfair because, first, the nonprofits might be able to undercut for-profit firms with lower prices and second, nonprofits can accumulate capital faster than for-profits, which have to pay taxes.[380] Especially due to their ability to accumulate wealth, nonprofits capable of obtaining capital are in a favored position over for-profits operating in similar areas.[381]

IV. State Regulation

State governments regulate and oversee nonprofits in four primary ways. First, the legal means of formation and related fiduciary duties are created and supervised by the states. Second, attorneys general are responsible for the oversight of nonprofit charitable assets. Third, charitable solicitations are covered by state consumer protection laws. Fourth, states often grant

---

376 Hansmann, *Why Are Colleges and Universities Exempt*, *supra* note 174, at 19.

377 C.F. Mueller Co., v. Commissioner of Internal Revenue, 190 F.2d 120 (3d Cir. 1951); *see also* Rose-Ackerman, Susan. "Unfair Competition and Corporate Income Taxation." *Stanford Law Review*, vol. 34, May 1982, pp. 1017–39 (noting that beyond NYU's macaroni, leather, piston ring, and chinaware operations, many other universities had ownership stakes in auto part manufacturing, cotton gins, food production, airport operations, public transportation, electricity plants, radio stations, etc.).

378 26 U.S.C. § 502–514 (2006).

379 Rose-Ackerman, *supra* note 377, at 1018.

380 *Ibid.* at 1023.

381 *Ibid.* at 1035.

their own exemptions from income, property, sales, or other taxes, thus, necessitating a certain level of oversight.[382] Furthermore, municipalities may also challenge tax-exemption if they have grounds to believe that a charitable organization is not operating in line with state exemption laws.[383]

Regarding the first point's means of formation, it should be recognized that state secretaries of state have essentially a ministerial role in entity formation; they merely ensure that entities can pass the *organizational test*.[384] The organizational test requires that all tax-exempt nonprofit organizations have a clearly defined exempt purpose stated in their founding document. Furthermore, they must expressly state that they will only engage in permissible tax-exempt activities and will not engage non-exempt activities, unless they are insubstantial. Although this dissertation is primarily concerned with federal nonprofit law, it is important to note that state law controls the nonprofit formation process. Just as with for-profit organizations, nonprofits may choose where to incorporate, thus choosing the state laws to which they will be subject. A prospective nonprofit founder would find a degree of variation in the level, nature, and details of nonprofit state regulation between all of the state jurisdictions.[385] The largest variations in state laws arise in terms of "accountability standards, the number of directors required, donor standing with respect to lawsuits, liability standards, layers of supplemental regulation by specialized state agencies, the nature of approvals for fundamental transactions, and the intensity of enforcement by state charity officials."[386] While there are differences between the jurisdictions, they are not as pronounced as they are in the for-profit field. Thus, nonprofit jurisdiction shopping happens relatively infrequently.[387]

---

382 Mayer, *supra* note 365, at 939.

383 *See generally* City of Washington v. Washington & Jefferson College, 550 Pa. 175 (1997).

384 Sidel, Mark. "The Nonprofit Sector and the New State Activism." *Michigan Law Review*, vol. 100, no. 6, 2002, p. 1317 (noting that new nonprofit approval is a "virtual entitlement").

385 Jenkins, Garry. "Incorporation Choice, Uniformity, and the Reform of Nonprofit State Law." *Georgia Law Review*, vol. 41, 2007, p. 1125.

386 *Ibid.* at 1126–27.

387 *Ibid.* at 1126.

At the state level, nonprofit enforcement is primarily in the hands of the attorneys general.[388] More specifically, state laws cover the fiduciary duties owed by nonprofit board members as well as the creation of standing for donors to enforce their rights.[389] The duties owed are similar to those owed in for-profit enterprises; boards owe the duty of care,[390] the duty of loyalty[391] and the duty of obedience.[392] Note that the internal governance of nonprofits is different from that of for-profits; for-profit board members and officers are accountable to shareholders.[393] Due to the non-distribution constraint and the lack of shareholders and owners, nonprofits are, conceptually, to be held accountable by the public.[394] As for the oversight of charitable assets, almost all of the states have created the duty, through either statute or case law, for attorneys general to ensure that assets are used for charitable purposes.[395] There are very few cases holding directors liable for breaches of fiduciary duties, but when there is an enforcement, prosecutors tend to enforce the duty of loyalty.[396]

---

388 Sidel, *supra* note 384, at 1317 (emphasizing the inconsistency of nonprofit governance enforcement within and among the states).

389 Jenkins, *supra* note 385, at 1126.

390 The duty of *care* requires that a nonprofit board member actively participates in the governance and oversight of an organization's activities.

391 The duty of *loyalty* requires that nonprofit board members act in the best interest of the organization at all times.

392 The duty of *obedience* requires that board members work to ensure compliance with applicable laws and regulations, that the organization acts in accordance with its own policies, and that it carries out its mission. Mayer, *supra* note 365, at 939.

393 *See generally* Bovens, Mark, et al. "Accountability and the Nonprofit Sector." *The Oxford Handbook of Public Accountability*, Aug. 2014.

394 *Ibid.*

395 Fremont-Smith, Marion R. *Governing Nonprofit Organizations: Federal and State Law and Regulation*. Belknap, 2008, pp. 301, 306 (distinguishing the attorneys general "enforcement power" from the "regulatory power" of the courts; in terms of nonprofit asset management, the courts also enjoy broad equitable powers).

396 Sugin, Linda. "Strengthening Charity Law: Replacing Media Oversight with Advance Rulings for Nonprofit Fiduciaries." *Tulane Law Review*, vol. 89, 2015, p. 877–78 (indicating that prosecutions for breach of care alone are very rare, but if there is a co-existing breach of loyalty, the chances of prosecution are increased. For example, if an administrator were to be embezzling funds from an organization, he would likely be prosecuted based on his duty of loyalty, and, only then, would the board likely be prosecuted based on its duty of care, *i.e.* their failure to properly monitor the administrator's activities).

In the rare event that an organization and its officers are prosecuted for a breach of their duty of loyalty, the states may invoke harsh equitable measures along with numerous legal remedies.[397] For example, in 2013, a New York court implemented a number of equitable and legal remedies against a sham charity.[398] The state attorney general proved that the charity's directors owned a number of for-profit fund raising services, which were exclusively used for the charity's fund raising efforts.[399] Of the ten million dollars that was raised by the private consultant, only about four percent of the funds were used for their advertised charitable purposes of providing public awareness for breast cancer and providing aid to breast cancer caregiver organizations.[400] Thus, the defendants were ordered to pay around $1.5 million in restitution, the charity was dissolved, the defendants were enjoined from soliciting future charitable contributions in the State of New York and they had to provide an accounting of the charity's assets.[401] Cases such as these, though rare, show the strength of the remedies available to enforce nonprofit duties.

A survey of forty-nine states and the District of Columbia uncovered some startling realities of state-level nonprofit enforcement. Seventy-four percent of the responding jurisdictions admitted to having "one or fewer full-time equivalent attorneys working on nonprofit oversight, with seventeen states reporting no such lawyers at all."[402] Even with the ever-increasing number of nonprofits, the resources devoted to nonprofit oversight have remained stagnant at their original, low levels. This could be attributable to other concerns receiving higher prioritization as well as common budget constraints.[403] Not only has this lack of resources contributed to significantly less oversight of nonprofits, but it also leads to a marked void of bureaucratic expertise upon which legislatures can rely when deliberating policy changes.[404]

---

397 *Ibid.*

398 State of New York v. Coalition Against Breast Cancer, Inc., 2013 WL 4283360 (May 2, 2013); *affirmed*, People v. Coalition Against Breast Cancer, Inc., 134 A.D.3 d 1081 (N.Y. App. Div. 2015).

399 State of New York v. Coalition Against Breast Cancer, Inc., 2013 WL 4283360 (May 2, 2013).

400 *Ibid.*

401 *Ibid.*

402 Jenkins, *supra* note 385, at 1128.

403 *Ibid.* at 1130.

404 *Ibid.* at 1129–30.

V. Federal Regulation

Due to the historically larger role played by the states in the realm of nonprofits, the federal government initially had very little to do with nonprofit oversight. The most substantial shift toward federal regulatory involvement came with the Sixteenth Amendment in 1913, establishing the federal income tax and creating the need for related statutory nonprofit exemptions and charitable deductions.[405] These exemptions and deductions create two different regulatory roles for the IRS; it must first determine if a nonprofit is qualified for tax benefits and, second, it must oversee the subsequent nonprofit activities.[406]

Ever since the ratification of the Sixteenth Amendment of the US Constitution, the federal regulatory and oversight role has continuously expanded. This expansion is also due in part to the constraints on states' resources.[407] As previously mentioned, the IRS is involved in the oversight of private inurement activities, the imposition of intermediate sanctions, when appropriate, and the annual collection of information from nonprofits with significant assets.[408] With the larger role of the federal government, the state regulatory agencies have shown increasing amounts of deference to nonprofits that have satisfied the requirements for federal tax-exemption and deductions. Several states automatically provide state tax-exemptions based on nonprofits' federal exemption approvals.[409]

Although the state and federal governments have distinct roles in the oversight and regulation of nonprofits, there still are a few notable divisions and overlaps in their competencies. The federal intermediate sanctions, for example, impose essentially the same duties as most states' laws.[410] The states remain the primary regulators of the fiduciary duties, but federal regulations and remedies, such as sanctions and revocation of exemption, still exist parallel to the state regimes. In order to relieve the regulatory burdens at all levels, the IRS created a set of normative best practices for fiduciary duties, which act to advise nonprofits on the premise that "a well [self-] governed charity is more likely to obey the tax

---

405 Fremont-Smith, *Governing Nonprofit Organizations*, *supra* note 395, at 56; U.S. CONST. amend. XVI.

406 These duties arise in the above-mentioned organizational, operational, private inurement, and political activities tests.

407 Jenkins, *supra* note 385, at 1130.

408 Mayer, *supra* note 365, at 942.

409 Fremont-Smith, *Governing Nonprofit Organizations*, *supra* note 395, at 368.

410 Mayer, *supra* note 365, at 941.

laws."[411] In other words, there is a presumption by government regulators that nonprofit boards will seek to fulfill their legal duties.

The intensity of oversight seems to correspond with organizational size. Boards of nonprofits that are small and all-volunteer, for example, tend not to receive very much regulatory attention due to their small budgets and relatively insubstantial responsibilities.[412] The level of scrutiny will be elevated when boards of directors are charged with the governance of organizations that run multiple programs, receive large government contracts or have for-profit subsidiaries. This larger role in society therefore attracts more oversight of the boards of director's fiduciary duties.[413] To their credit, nonprofit universities generally satisfy the various requirements to zealously defend their tax-exemptions and to avoid penalties, but the law that they are conforming to no longer strictly implements the non-distribution constraint. Because of the weakened non-distribution constraint and skyrocketing costs for higher education, the public is now paying a much higher cost than ever before to attend American universities.

H. Assessment of Universities

As mentioned previously, *access* is a precondition to all the other factors that will be analyzed in this dissertation, so this assessment begins by analyzing the nature of access to higher education. Beyond *access* to higher education, the previous sections depicted the many expectations of universities, the sources from which they arise as well as the legal standards to which nonprofits are held. Thus, this assessment will examine some of the most central goals of the universities and ask specifically, within the context of each goal—*to educate, research, certify and promote social mobility*—if universities can be considered successful. Considering university goals and the many privileges given to them, I will return to the question of whether are benefiting the public. This analysis also inquires into the relationship between university activities and the law of nonprofits, asking: are universities in the US complying nonprofit law? Finally, this part identifies features within the university system that need improvement and suggest potential improvements that can be made within its legal framework. Such

411 "Governance of Charitable Organizations and Related Topics." *IRS*, 4 Feb. 2008, www.irs.gov/pub/irs-tege/governance_practices.pdf.

412 Bovens, *supra* note 393.

413 *Ibid.*

an assessment is needed in order to understand university functions, outcomes and relationships with the culture and the law. A mere superficial glimpse depicts an innovative American university system constantly occupying the top world-rankings, also with the greatest numbers of affiliated Nobel Prize recipients.[414] A deeper look paradoxically presents a system burying millions of individuals and the federal government in debt and bloated university expenses, draining public resources. The public benefit lies somewhere between these two realities.

I. Access

American universities are stratified, and they are stratified primarily by their degree of selectivity. The most prestigious universities with the most selective standards, which are often nonprofits, outperform lower-ranked universities by every metric relating to education, social mobility and certification and are quite strong in the research area as well. Their outcomes for student achievement, graduate employment and student debt are also significantly better. The concept of inclusion comes into direct contravention with top universities' means of generating perceived prestige. That is, the top-ranked universities are the most selective, usually to the detriment of prospective minority and low-income applicants.[415] With near-ubiquitous access to higher education, via federal funding programs, the question often asked by employers "did you go to college?" now looks more like "where did you go to college?" As demonstrated in this and the following sections, the answer to this second question plays a major role. Universities are now so accessible that seventy percent of on-time high school graduates will go on to enroll at a university, including essentially every ethnic group.[416] Although, in addition to disparities in admissions between highly selective and open access universities, certain minority students tend to graduate at significantly lower rates.[417] Access to higher education has been greatly increased since the early 1970's, but, now, there is a new stratification among universities and students' outcomes.

---

414 "50 Universities with the Most Nobel Prize Winners." *BestMastersPrograms.org*, 5 Oct. 2018, www.bestmastersprograms.org/50-universities-with-the-most-nobel-prize-winners/.

415 Brint, *Two Cheers for Higher Education*, *supra* note 75, at 39.

416 Snyder, *Digest of Education Statistics*, *supra* note 43, at Table 302.20.

417 *Ibid.* at Table 326.10.

1. Access Statistics

The US federal government's student financing programs were implemented with the specific goal of expanding overall access to every type of college and university for the most disenfranchised members of society. With more students enrolled today than ever, it is worthwhile exploring who has benefited most from this wave of government support for higher education. Of the ca. twenty million students currently enrolled in the American universities, about a quarter are attending private nonprofit universities.[418] It should also be recognized that, although private nonprofit universities enroll only around a quarter of all students in higher education, they are actually the most common type of institution: of 4,298 US institutions, 1,687 are private nonprofits, 1,626 are public and 985 are private, for-profit.[419] The sheer volume of institutions has improved access to higher education. This immense enrollment number is generally viewed as a success, but it has come at the expense of monstrous public and private debt burdens. Furthermore, the social stratification that many of these programs were meant to eliminate still exists, but just in a new configuration; this time social stratification is observable within the hierarchy of university rankings, prestige and graduates' outcomes long after graduation. Prior to the Second World War, around five percent of Americans had college degrees; this has since increased to nearly thirty percent.[420]

2. Campus Diversity

The growth in number of institutions and students contributed to a greater degree of diversity on campuses through new educational opportunities for women and racial minorities. Enrollment rates for African-Americans in higher education improved: around two percent of African-Americans were enrolled in 1940 and, today, nearly twenty percent are.[421] Women made the most progress in enrollment numbers, now outnumbering

418 *Ibid.* at Table 317.40.

419 *Ibid.* at Table 317.40.

420 Vedder, *Restoring the Promise*, *supra* note 172, at 96–97 (factoring in those with two-year degrees and others who have dropped out, around fifty percent of all Americans have spent at least some time in higher education).

421 Snyder, *Digest of Education Statistics*, *supra* note 43, at Table 306.30; Best & Best, *supra* note 23, at 18.

their male peers.[422] Although, the most disadvantaged poor and minority students are most likely to be drawn into for-profit universities; these are essentially open access and require students to take on substantial debt.[423] Students from higher-income families still accumulate student debt, but the majority falls on low-income and, disproportionately, African-American students.[424] The distribution of debt is not the only disparity; minority enrollment rates at the highest- and lowest-ranked institutions have come to resemble the previous racial disparities between those admitted to and left out of college.

College-ranking lists base their classifications on all types of available data such as graduates' debt, their employment outcomes and university endowments.[425] Looking at *Forbes*' 2018 rankings of the top 650 undergraduate programs in the US—based on alumni salary, student debt, retention rates, alumni achievement, fellowships, Ph.Ds. and graduation rates—some interesting observations can be made.[426] First, the absolute top of the list is weighed heavily in favor of private nonprofit universities, and, second, of the 650 universities, 399 are private nonprofits.[427] These rankings are essential in understanding the new stratification that is occurring within the university system: eighty percent of prospective white students will go to the most selective colleges on lists such as these, whereas seventy percent of African American and Hispanic applicants will end up at one of the ca. 3,500 other universities.[428] Less apparent, but even stronger indicators of disparate student enrollment are wealth and family income:

> [h]igh-income students were forty-five percentage points overrepresented compared to population share in the most selective colleges while white students were "only" fifteen points overrepresented. African-American and Hispanic students were underrepresented in the most selective colleges, relative to population share by nine percentage

422 Snyder, *Digest of Education Statistics*, *supra* note 43, at Table 306.10.

423 Angulo, *supra* note 104, at xiv.

424 Best & Best, *supra* note 23, at 86.

425 *See* Coudriet, Carter. "Top Colleges 2018: The Methodology." *Forbes*, 23 Aug. 2018, www.forbes.com/sites/cartercoudriet/2018/08/20/top-colleges-2018-the-methodology/#40b889ee3098.

426 *Ibid.*

427 Conklin, Justin, et al. "America's Top Colleges 2019." *Forbes*, 15 Aug. 2019, www.forbes.com/top-colleges/list/#tab:rank.

428 Carnevale, Anthony P., and Jeff Strohl. "Separate & Unequal How Higher Education Reinforces the Intergenerational Reproduction of White Racial Privilege." *Georgetown University Center on Education and the Workforce*, 2013, p. 8.

points; low-income students were underrepresented by twenty percentage points.[429]

Although wealth and family income seem to be the strongest indicators of where students are enrolled, racial disparities are very-much correlated.[430] In light of the extensive minority enrollment over the last decades, it is clear that these students have overwhelmingly gravitated toward less-selective institutions.[431] Even once admitted, a majority of African-American and other minorities, such as Native Americans, are likely to not complete their studies.[432] Similarly, those in the bottom quartile of family income are less likely to graduate, while their graduation rates have recently begun to slowly decline. Since the early 1970's, following the creation of the federal government's finance programs, students from the least wealthy quartile graduated slightly more frequently, but these programs' ballooning of university costs are now acting to dissuade these same students from ever attending.[433] Because access is the precondition to receiving the direct benefits of higher education, the access disparity is by default also present in universities' efforts to promote education, research, certification and social mobility.

3. Access and University Type

For how troubled the university system is, the greatest concerns of dropping enrollment, unstable finances and questionable academics do not appear to be present at the top-ranked, elite private universities. These institutions are as selective as they have ever been, even while their posted tuition fee rates continue to rise. Private, nonprofit universities have always been a more expensive option relative to the public and, even, for-profit alternatives.[434] Students attending private universities tend to be

---

429 *Ibid.* at 12.

430 Brint, *Two Cheers for Higher Education*, *supra* note 75, at 176–77 (listing other potential factors such as father's education, father's occupation, social background, academic achievement, verbal test scores and high school grades).

431 Carnevale & Strohl, *supra* note 428, at 17.

432 Vedder, *Restoring the Promise*, *supra* note 172, at 275–76.

433 *Ibid.* at 153.

434 *Ibid.* at 34–35 (describing the skyrocketing tuition fees, in relation to median family income, created by federal funding programs from his time as a student at Northwestern in 1958 until 2017. The tuition fee at Northwestern University, a private nonprofit, was $795 a year in 1958, accounting for 15.6 percent of that

less affected by tuition fee increases, whereas low-income students, often enrolled in public universities, may choose not to attend. As a result, many public universities without reliable endowments tend to increase class sizes and reduce tenured faculty.[435] As a side-note, some of the top public universities have also pursued the prestige-through-selectivity approach, resulting in higher costs for students and, subsequently, reduced admission rates for potential low-income students.[436]

As discussed above, for-profit universities are relatively expensive, have either low or no standards for admission and are highly unsuccessful in terms of student retention and many other similar metrics. While they generally fail to serve the low-income and otherwise disadvantaged in terms of professional outcomes and student debt, they nonetheless continue to attract a disproportionally large amount of low-income and disadvantaged students.[437] Despite the government's student loan programs being clearly well intentioned, they led to significant post-graduation debt burdens on the students who were originally in the greatest need of financial aid. Some effects of student debt are that graduates may be passing up on preferable jobs for higher-paying ones, moving back in with their parents, buying fewer houses, fewer cars, putting off marriage, having fewer children, postponing graduate studies, not to mention the high school graduates that may never go to college because they do not want to take on debt.[438]

---

year's median family income. As of 2003, Northwestern's tuition fee reached 53.3 percent of a median family income and, in 2017, the percentage shot up to 69.4 percent of the median family income).

435 The historical bulwark of tenure, meant to protect academic freedom, is weakening at the moment; the push to create more economical, professional training programs has led to a surge of hiring adjunct and part-time professors who are retained by limited contracts. Snyder, *Digest of Education Statistics*, *supra* note 43, at 382; Brint, *Two Cheers for Higher Education*, *supra* note 75, at 238.

436 *Ibid*. at 237.

437 Angulo, *supra* note 104, at 143.

438 A 2017 study by the Pew Research Center showed the "education gap" between married people with bachelor's degrees or more, at sixty-five percent, and married people with high school degrees or less, at fifty percent. Although marriage rates have fallen across the board since 1990, university graduates' numbers have not changed substantially, whereas the drop-off for people with less education was precipitous. Especially because the search for potential partners takes resources into consideration, men who are former students with significant student debt may be viewed as potential financial liabilities. This is particularly true for male students taking on massive debt at mid- to low-ranked universities, who may have never even graduated. Many women may have to wait to meet

4. The Outcome of the HEA's Student Lending

The federal government's reason for providing financing was to assist low-income and minority students, but higher-income and middle-income students took greatest advantage of these programs, enrolling at much higher rates. Rather than helping low-income students, the biggest beneficiaries of federal financing, by far, were university presidents, football and basketball coaches and other senior administrators such as university investment managers. Federal finance programs, such as the HEA, have inflated the overall costs of attending college, regardless of which type of institution students wish to attend. In terms of increasing low-income and minority student participation, the programs have "failed [miserably]."[439] This leads to the conclusion that, although higher education is now generally more accessible than ever, the programs designed to promote higher attendance and graduation rates for low-income and minority students has, at best, shown lackluster results, and, at worst, burdened these same students with astronomical debt while, in many cases, leaving them with nearly-worthless degrees.

Some suggest, as a counterpoint, that the affordability crisis of higher education is exaggerated.[440] This basic argument is that college is generally a good investment, due to both graduates earning substantially more over the course of their careers and the better employment prospects. Whether this argument is valid is subject to what the observer's definition of a "good investment" is; different definitions could lead to different results. A second point would be that graduates with the average student-debt burden generally find repayment to be manageable; the exceptions being underemployed people with graduates' degrees, those who studied at for-profit universities and those who never completed their studies. Although this second point is in and of itself true, it disregards the fact that the lending programs were initially created to aid low-income and

their matches, at least until there is some guarantee of earnings potential from their prospective partners. Thus, because of the narrowing pool of potential, suitable partners, "the marital benefits of college do not extend to the least advantaged of college-goers." Parker, Kim, and Renee Stepler. "As U.S. Marriage Rate Hovers at 50%, Education Gap in Marital Status Widens." *Pew Research Center*, 14 Sept. 2017, www.pewresearch.org/fact-tank/2017/09/14/as-u-s-marriage-rate-hovers-at-50-education-gap-in-marital-status-widens/; Best & Best, *supra* note 23, at 84–85; Armstrong & Hamilton, *supra* note 210, at 12–13.

439 Vedder, *Restoring the Promise*, *supra* note 172, at 153, 185.

440 *See* Brint, *Two Cheers for Higher Education*, *supra* note 75, at 329.

minority students. These are the very students who are attending for-profit universities and dropping-out at the highest rates. Student lending, once viewed as a solution to the problem of access to higher education, is now, paradoxically, the problem itself; the lowest-income students will have the least-favorable financial prospects, while their higher-income peers are still, unnecessarily, pressed to take on student-debt that they would otherwise not require. Student loans have transformed access issues into issues of *affordability* and all prospective university students should be aware of this in their search for well-matched institutions of higher education.

II. Education

Being one of the core university goals, the education of students will be assessed in this section to determine if private, nonprofit universities are succeeding in their educational goals and whether the public is benefiting from these institutions. As this section will demonstrate, there are numerous ways to determine if universities are successful in their efforts to educate and it will begin with a quantitative overview of the resources devoted to this goal. Other elements that will be considered in this section are universities' focus on education in the humanities or professional training, their protection of free debate and inquiry on campus as well as how the various university types have influenced each other in the realm of higher education.

1. Education Statistics

All the university types derive revenue from various sources and to varying degrees. Therefore, to draw an initial comparison between the different types of universities, I will show how the different types of universities vary with regard to their annual expenditures for instruction[441] per full-time

441 Snyder, *Digest of Education Statistics*, *supra* note 43, at 842 (defining "instruction" as:

> [t]hat functional category including expenditures of the colleges, schools, departments, and other instructional divisions of higher education institutions and expenditures for departmental research and public service that are not separately budgeted; includes expenditures for both credit and noncredit activities. Excludes expenditures for academic administration where the primary function is administration (e.g. academic deans).).

student, in relation to the amount that they derive from annual tuition fee revenues per student, using constant 2016-17 dollars.[442] Observing higher education from the standpoint of expenditures toward instruction, public universities offer a high-value outcome in terms of their yearly revenue derived from *tuition fees* per student, $7,400, versus their per student expenditures for *instruction*, $10,400.[443] Nonprofit universities also invest extensive amounts of their revenues into instruction, but while charging significantly more in tuition fees; for the average $21,400 per student derived from *tuition fees*, $17,850 is spent on *instruction*.[444] Finally, as a stark contrast, one can see the low-value relationship between tuition fees and instruction at for-profit universities. For-profits charge an average $15,800 per student in *tuition fees* and devote only $4,400 to *instruction*.[445] Using only expenditures as a metric, these statistics demonstrate that instruction is still at the core of the public and private nonprofit university missions whereas other core interests likely guide for-profits. Statistics regarding other types of expenditures also shed light on the further spending priorities within public and private nonprofit universities, along with where for-profits are directing most of their funding.

Student tuition fees have expanded rapidly because of both the availability of federally backed student loans as well as rising costs within universities for budget items such as "academic support,"[446] "student ser-

442 In light of the many possible ways of observing the extensive data created by the National Center for Education Statistics, the most consistent with this dissertation's definition of "university" is to use the data from "all levels," and not to restrict it to the data of two or four year universities alone. Using revenues derived from tuition fees as a point of comparison is ideal because tuition fees are the one universal and relatively comparable revenue source across all university types. Other revenue derived from grants or contracts from federal, state and local governments are tied heavily to particular types of universities and do not offer a meaningful comparison as other university types are not reliant on them. The same is true for sources of revenue from auxiliary services, i.e. residence halls and food services, and university hospitals. *Ibid.*

443 *Ibid.* at Tables 333.10, 334.10.

444 *Ibid.* at Tables 333.30, 334.20.

445 *Ibid.* at Tables 333.55, 334.50.

446 *Ibid.* at 831 (defining "academic support" as:

... expenditures for support services that are an integral part of the institution's primary missions of instruction, research, or public service. It also includes expenditures for libraries, galleries, audio/visual services, academic computing support, ancillary support, academic administration, personnel development, and course and curriculum development.).

vices"[447] and "institutional support."[448] Institutional support happens to be the largest category of spending on university administrators such as registrars, presidents, provosts, campus police and athletic coaches.[449] Public universities annually spend $2,850 per student on academic support, $1,950 on student services and $3,300 on institutional support.[450] These total up to 23.7 percent of overall spending, whereas 30.5 percent is devoted to instruction.[451] Using the same metrics, private nonprofit universities spend around $4,750 on academic support, $4,760 on student services and $7,360 on institutional support.[452] These total up to 30.2 percent of overall spending, while 31.9 percent is directed toward instruction.[453] For-profit universities are an outlier. For the $10,400 per student devoted to these three categories of spending, i.e. 63.1 percent of all expenditures, only 26.6 percent of expenditures go to instruction.[454] These non-instructional costs, mostly to compensate administrators, are passed on to the students that will inevitably be forced to rely on student loans, thus, enabling universities to spend even more on non-instructional budget items. While costs are rising within all university types, for-profit universities have by far the highest non-instructional costs.

2. The Focus of University Instruction

Universities are involved in a wide range of tasks, so the degree to which they focus on instruction is certain to be different from institution to insti-

---

447 *Ibid.* at 852 (defining "student support services" as "... salary, benefits, supplies, and contractual fees for staff providing attendance and social work, guidance, health, psychological services, speech pathology, audiology, and other support to students.").

448 *Ibid.* at 842 (defining "institutional support" as: "[t]he category of higher education expenditures that includes day-to-day operational support for colleges, excluding expenditures for physical plant operations. Examples of institutional support include general administrative services, executive direction and planning, legal and fiscal operations, and community relations.").

449 Vedder, *Restoring the Promise*, *supra* note 172, at 170 (providing a list of examples of what these categories mean in practice, whereas the definitions within the statistics sometimes tend to be broad or imprecise).

450 Snyder, *Digest of Education Statistics*, *supra* note 43, at Table 334.10.

451 *Ibid.* at Table 334.10.

452 *Ibid.* at Table 334.30.

453 *Ibid.*

454 *Ibid.* at Table 334.50.

tution. The institutions continuing to focus primarily on instruction are the public community colleges, for-profit universities and small liberal arts colleges.[455] Even their curricula have become increasingly focused on professional training. Although, as the name suggests, liberal arts colleges and public universities still do offer liberal education or humanities programs focused on learning purely for the sake of learning.[456] A liberal, humanities-based education, as opposed to profession training, seeks to provide students "self-knowledge, wisdom, and the judgment to be a responsible citizen."[457] The means for providing a liberal education differ somewhat among the various traditions—i.e. the traditions of ancient Greece, Rome, post-Enlightenment Europe and the US—but the newer variations are nonetheless rooted in the previous ones.[458]

The humanities, home to philosophy, language studies, literature, history and the arts, are the traditional core of the university and are defined by inquiry and criticism.[459] A course of study in the humanities should act to strengthen students' reasoning and communication abilities, leading to a broad, transferrable skill set. The humanities contribute to individual growth, leadership skills and human development. This system of

455 Vedder, *Restoring the Promise*, *supra* note 172, at 26 (noting the uniquely American nature of liberal arts institutions with low student enrollment and "high quality bachelor's degrees").

456 Shapiro, Harold T. *A Larger Sense of Purpose: Higher Education and Society: Non Nobis Solum*. Princeton University Press, 2005, p. 92.

457 *Ibid.*

458 *Ibid.* at 93.

459 For the purposes of this dissertation, the "humanities," refers to the categories that are mentioned in the text above and any mention of the "liberal arts" or "arts" are meant to have the same meaning. The humanities are derived from the classical Trivium (grammar, logic and rhetoric) and Quadrivium (arithmetic, geometry, music and astronomy), which were the basis of philosophical or theological studies in the Middle Ages. "Humanities" was a surprisingly difficult term to define throughout the course of my research due to many sources' broad usages or lack of consideration as to what the purposes of the humanities are. For example, there is often little delineation made between political theory, which has been studied for thousands of years, and political science, which can be traced back to the nineteenth century. Many sources still distinguish the humanities from law, politics and the other social sciences, at least in terms of disciplines, but tend to conflate their purposes together. *See e.g.*, Cole, *Toward a More Perfect University*, *supra* note 142, at 68, 91 (discussing the separation between the liberal arts and humanities, stating that "the objectives of the sciences, humanities, and the behavioral and social sciences are not as different as they are often made out to be.").

cultivating values should aid graduates in promoting civil society.[460] If the humanities are a litmus test of universities' health, then all interested parties should be concerned. Students are not studying the humanities at the same rates as in the past. Despite the explosive growth of overall enrollment and degree issuances since the 1970's, the number of degrees being conferred for the humanities, hovering around 150,000 per year, has remained essentially unchanged.[461] At the same time, the conferral of professional degrees has grown exponentially, greatly outnumbering degrees in the humanities.[462]

Declining rates of study in the humanities may be related to slightly higher under- and unemployment rates of graduates in the area as well as students' parents and college counselors' aversion to the field of study.[463] Another factor dissuading students from this path is likely their fear of taking on student debt in light of these employment prospects. Many pragmatic onlookers see the liberal arts and humanities programs as being entirely "irrelevant" and "superfluous."[464] When faced with growing demand for professional training from students and their advisors, universities typically respond in kind by cutting down and eliminating support for the humanities, usually in favor of more financially beneficial programs.[465] However, graduates of the humanities are just as likely as their peers to at-

---

460 Keohane, Nannerl. "The Liberal Arts and the Role of Elite Higher Education." In *In Defense of American Higher Education*. Johns Hopkins University Press, 2001, pp. 182, 187–88.

461 Snyder, *Digest of Education Statistics*, *supra* note 43, at Tables 322.10, 318.30; *but see* Vedder, *Restoring the Promise*, *supra* note 172, at 99 (including the social sciences in his definition of the humanities, which tends to double the number of degrees conferred).

462 Snyder, *Digest of Education Statistics*, *supra* note 43, at Table 322.10.

463 *Ibid.* at Table 505.10; Vedder, *Restoring the Promise*, *supra* note 172, at 69.

464 Crow & Dabars, *supra* note 12, at 140.

465 Pinker, *supra* note 6, at 372, 405–06 (suggesting that potential students may be second-questioning university disinterestedness, due to political polarization and non-disinterested faculties; within the humanities professors are overwhelmingly left-leaning, with around sixty percent identifying as "far left." The disparity between liberal- and conservative-identifying professors has increased significantly over the past three decades and that, especially within the liberal contingent, the ideology has moved increasingly further left); *but see* Vedder, *Restoring the Promise*, *supra* note 172, at 284 (recognizing that political-polarization is nothing new and that the pendulum has merely swung to the opposite extreme of the political spectrum; where anybody in the 1950's supporting Marxism or Communism would have been shunned and blacklisted, the same happens today to conservative ideologues).

tain management positions. Humanities graduates also enjoy an additional degree of post-graduation flexibility that would not be available to those with degrees from majors such as fitness studies or criminal justice.[466] Furthermore, graduates of the humanities tend to be just as satisfied with their employment and general well-being as graduates from other fields.[467]

Professional training programs could be considered quite successful in terms of graduating individuals who are prepared to work in various vocations, but the outcomes are still likely to be highly dependent on which university that the graduates are coming from. Graduates from more-elite universities tend to find work in their fields, but those coming from the lower-ranked universities are more likely to be underemployed and may even find themselves competing for jobs with high school graduates.[468] Graduates of professional training programs can also enjoy better chances of career advancement. An interview with a mechanical engineer confirmed so much; while many of his talented colleagues were trained as machinists, his movement to management was clearly connected to having a college degree.[469] Professional training is the field in which for-profit universities have been most effective, and their methods have been adopted elsewhere. For-profit leadership in the area of distance learning has taken root in many of these programs, offering various courses online.[470]

The outcomes of university education are also highly dependent on students and their contributions to their own development. Recall the different pathways described above. Today's students, especially those on the social pathway, commit significantly less time to their studies than students did in the 1950's and 1960's. These "full-time students," instead of being in class, preparing for class, studying for examinations or working on projects, actually spend more time "partying, working out at the gym, watching television or movies."[471] It has been shown that overall knowl-

---

466 "The State of the Humanities 2018: Graduates in the Workforce & Beyond." *Humanities Indicators*, American Academy of Arts & Sciences, Feb. 2018, www.amacad.org/publication/state-humanities-2018-graduates-workforce-beyond, p. 16; Vedder, *Restoring the Promise*, *supra* note 172, at 83.

467 *Ibid.* at 3, 20–24.

468 Vedder, *Restoring the Promise*, *supra* note 172, at 74–75.

469 Telephone interview with Richard Allen, Mechanical Engineer, Perryman Company (Mar. 26, 2019).

470 Angulo, *supra* note 104, at 147.

471 Vedder, *Restoring the Promise*, *supra* note 172, at 49, 64; *see also* "American Time Use Survey--2018 Results." *Bureau of Labor Statistics*, U.S. Dep. of Labor, 2019, https://www.bls.gov/news.release/pdf/atus.pdf.

edge of civics, the study of American history, political institutions and the rights and duties of citizenship, is barely different between the freshman and senior students of many universities.[472] Furthermore, many college graduates have difficulties in reading simple charts.[473] Corresponding with declining expectations by universities and student inputs, grade inflation has led to noticeably higher Grade Point Averages.[474] This suggests that there are more students now on the social pathway than ever before.[475]

3. Free Speech Protections on Campus

Meaningful education is also dependent on there being a culture of openness and systematic protection of free speech, allowing for inquiry and debate on controversial issues. Even if students are enrolled in the humanities, their ability to inquire without fear of repercussion is dependent on their campus environment. Considering that academic freedom, protections for the expression and analysis of heterodox ideas, is one of the traditional university privileges, it is concerning to see many university policies, albeit well intentioned, that place a heavy burden on free speech. Oftentimes, when policies against true threats, incitement, obscenity, harassment, bullying, bias, hate speech, and those for tolerance, respect and civility are created and implemented, they have a tendency to be overprotective, broad or vague enough to violate First Amendment free speech principles (in cases where the First Amendment applies).[476] A professor with decades of experience in academia reminds readers that:

> [t]he goal of academic discourse is not merely to teach students to think and provide them with the intellectual and analytical tools that will enable them to think well. Great teachers challenge their students' and colleagues' biases and presuppositions. They present unsettling ideas and dare others to rebut them and to defend their own beliefs in a coherent and principled manner. The American research university

472 Vedder, *Restoring the Promise*, *supra* note 172, at 66.

473 Brint, *Two Cheers for Higher Education*, *supra* note 75, at 15.

474 Vedder, *Restoring the Promise*, *supra* note 172, at 98.

475 Another question beyond the scope of this dissertation, but nonetheless deserving of further study is: whether student loans act to recreate familial wealth, thereby placing more students onto the social pathway?

476 "Spotlight on Speech Codes 2019." *FIRE*, 2019, www.thefire.org/resources/spotlight/reports/spotlight-on-speech-codes-2019/; U.S. Const. amend. I.

> pushes and pulls at the walls of orthodoxy and rejects politically correct thinking. In this process, students and professors may sometimes feel intimidated, overwhelmed, and confused.[477]

There has also been a tendency—mainly by students—to conflate offensive or "triggering" messages with physical violence, thus, leading to calls for prohibition of otherwise constitutionally protected speech. In response, some universities have implemented campus Internet usage policies, security fees for campus events, prior restraints, the creation of limited free speech zones and highly restrictive viewpoint-based limitations on who may speak, accompanied by excessive time, place and manner restrictions.[478] Furthermore, many professors have been requested to offer *trigger warnings* before discussing controversial topics. Accusations of *microaggressions*, small slights or insults in discussion as subjectively observed by the listener regardless of the speaker's intentions, are surely not in line with academic inquiry. Due to student outcry, speakers are now routinely *disinvited* from campus events, and those with heterodox ideas that still participate are frequently *shouted-down*.[479] There have also been instances of extreme physical violence and threats to some campus speakers.[480]

The Foundation for Individual Rights in Education (hereinafter, FIRE) conducts routine surveys on the state of free speech on university campuses. In a 2019 survey of 466 mostly middle- to top-ranked universities, FIRE reported that nearly twenty-nine percent of universities "have at least one policy both clearly and substantially restricting freedom of speech...."[481] Of the public and private universities included in FIRE's study, the private universities were more than twice as likely to have such policies; about forty-seven percent of the private universities in their study did so.[482] Speech codes, first arising during the 1980's and 1990's were, as FIRE points out, a product of university administrators desire to create policies against discrimination and harassment, but without "fully consider[ing] the philosophical, social, and legal ramifications of placing restrictions on speech, particularly at public universities."[483]

---

477 Cole, *Who's Afraid of Academic Freedom*, *supra* note 140, at 50.

478 *Spotlight on Speech Codes*, *supra* note 476.

479 Vedder, *Restoring the Promise*, *supra* note 172, at 51.

480 *Ibid.* at 284.

481 *Spotlight on Speech Codes*, *supra* note 476.

482 *Ibid.*

483 *Ibid.*

A university's status of being public or private is highly determinative as to whether its speech codes are constitutionally permissible and, thus, likely to be upheld in the courts. Public universities, for the purposes of free speech analysis, are treated as state-actors, therefore requiring them to protect students' First Amendment rights under the US Constitution. Private universities, on the other hand, are not state-actors and, thus, are not bound to guarantee First Amendment protections on campus. Although, acceptance of federal funding binds almost all universities to federal antidiscrimination laws and their nonprofit statuses require that they abstain from electioneering, i.e. promoting or opposing particular political candidates, and substantial lobbying.[484] Sometimes private universities' speech codes are struck down on free speech grounds due to free expression recitals in student handbooks; these protections, though, arise under a contract-theory.[485] A university's role as a forum for free speech is perhaps one of the most essential roles that it can play, allowing an atmosphere for meaningful education in the humanities. Meaningful education also is a means of knowledge dissemination. The public stands to gain from graduates who are more critical in their thinking and curious about the world and its inhabitants. If universities do not provide this kind of forum, the substantial privileges that they are afforded could be reconsidered by Congress.

4. How the University Types Influence Each Other

When universities are primarily concerned with revenue streams or their financial competition with other institutions, they inevitably begin to mimic their for-profit competitors. This draws them into the fray with "the kinds of violations, predatory behavior, government aid abuse, and poverty profiteering" that is intrinsic to them when the massive pot of federal financing is available.[486] The drive to maximize profit, *via* higher student enrollment and lower standards, abandons "academia's traditional system of trust" where nonprofit universities should prioritize academic performance and reputation of the institution, not allowing their finances to become a consideration in the quality of student admissions or pun-

484 *See generally* 20 U.S.C. § 38 (1986).
485 *Spotlight on Speech Codes*, *supra* note 476.
486 Angulo, *supra* note 104, at 147–48.

ishment for academic dishonesty.[487] One professor points out that the incentives for all universities to prioritize their revenues, at the expense of their core missions, has swapped traditional university aims for "ignorance production."[488] This drive to do so is a result of the extreme competition between universities. Furthermore, the adoption of for-profit features in a nonprofit setting blurs the boundaries between the university types.

Is the public benefiting from universities' education efforts? On one hand, the sheer volume of institutions and the number of students that they admit has exposed many postsecondary students to fields that they, otherwise, might not have encountered. The maximum-exposure approach, pushing as many students as possible into colleges and universities, has succeeded in some regards, while setting many graduates behind. Focusing in more narrowly, one sees that open access public and for-profit universities could be described in this manner. On the other hand, private nonprofit universities are regarded as providing good high-quality education, particularly benefiting from low student to instructor ratios. Although, their academic standards are still bound to the fate of the studies of the humanities; there must be challenging classroom experiences and students must have access to their professors. This has never been truer than today, where the Internet provides unprecedented access to knowledge and students need to be equipped to competently navigate it.

When nonprofit universities offer professional training programs, they are venturing into areas that can just as easily be taught to lecture halls full of hundreds of students, as state universities tend to do, or streamed over the Internet, as is normal for for-profit universities. Recall that the medieval universities that survived did so because they did not follow many professional training trends, and, rather, persisted in their core mission of promoting a meaningful *studium*. Students may hesitate to study in the humanities because it rarely illuminates a clear career path, but those that do have received an education that no series of mass-lectures or streamed-videos can recreate. Universities may also fail to see the short-term benefits of directing resources toward such areas of study, but those that have persisted through the centuries prove that humanity studies are an irreplaceable cornerstone of the university curriculum. America's private, nonprofit universities are the biggest beneficiaries of this formula for longevity; conversely, the US has benefited greatly from leaders, writers, inventors and many other upright citizens that these institutions

487 Best & Best, *supra* note 23, at 117.
488 Angulo, *supra* note 104, at 147–48.

have produced. Whether the nonprofit universities will continue in this direction is yet to be seen.

III. Research

1. Research Statistics

Research in higher education is led by the largest public research universities, but still well represented by a small group of highly funded private institutions. Community colleges and for-profit universities that exist solely for education through instruction do not engage in research. Public universities invest around $36 billion into research annually, whereas private universities' expenditures are a somewhat smaller $19 billion.[489] The majority of university expenditures on research are not derived from students' tuition fees, but, rather, from federal grants.[490] Universities fight to secure funding grants by presenting themselves as quality institutions; this in turn fuels the competition for top faculty, graduate students and facilities.[491] A side-effect of the competition for prominence in research is that if a university could be distinguished for having a quality research program, this is used as a proxy for determining the quality of undergraduate instruction within the same university for the purposes of name-recognition and rankings.[492] In trying to determine what universities' priorities are, it is useful to look at their shares of research expenditures; where private and public universities invest in the range of twenty-five to, sometimes, nearly fifty percent of their revenue into research, for-profit universities invest a measly 0.001 percent or eighteen dollars per student.[493] In other words, the university form is highly determinative as to how extensive their research efforts are.

489 Snyder, *Digest of Education Statistics*, *supra* note 43, at Tables 334.10, 334.30.
490 *Ibid.* at Table 335.50.
491 Crow & Dabars, *supra* note 12, at 261.
492 *Ibid.*
493 Snyder, *Digest of Education Statistics*, *supra* note 43, at Tables 334.10, 334.50.

2. Research Universities

Research universities are particularly well designed to create new knowledge and transmit it to the professions, academia and society.[494] Investing taxpayer money into university research is often based on the premise that it will promote economic growth and eventually scientific development through the "positive spillover effects" of basic research.[495] The Association of American Universities (hereinafter, AAU) is representative of top research universities in the US as well as the largest recipients of federal research financing.[496] It is an exclusive association of the top sixty-two, primarily US, research universities and was founded to "advance society through education, research and discovery."[497] AAU universities seek to offer high-quality education and research in a broad array of disciplines.[498] Other important factors for admission to this club of elites are overall federal research funding, memberships in national academies, faculty awards, fellowships, frequency of citation to faculty research, PhD output, postdoctoral education as well as the quality of an institution's undergraduate education.[499]

The traditional hallmarks of university research were built "around the norms of communal sharing and responsibility, disinterestedness, and organized skepticism," but government and industry have had an influence.[500] University research spending is well over $50 billion annually, but it is only a fraction of the estimated $500 billion spent yearly on research in the US, also including substantial private investment into basic research.[501] The majority of funding for university research comes from federal agencies and has generally allowed university researchers to define

494 Walshok & Yankelovich, *supra* note 18, at 3.

495 Vedder, *Restoring the Promise*, *supra* note 172, at 237.

496 The AAU is similarly founded as a 501 (c)(3) nonprofit, charitable organization. *See* "Association Of American Universities – Nonprofit Explorer." *ProPublica*, 9 May 2013, projects.propublica.org/nonprofits/organizations/521947112.

497 "Who We Are." *Association of American Universities (AAU)*, www.aau.edu/who-we-are.

498 "Membership Policy." *Association of American Universities (AAU)*, Oct. 2016, www.aau.edu/who-we-are/membership-policy.

499 *Ibid.*

500 Brint, *Two Cheers for Higher Education*, *supra* note 75, at 91.

501 Snyder, *Digest of Education Statistics*, *supra* note 43, at Tables 334.10, 334.30; *see also* Brint, *Two Cheers for Higher Education*, *supra* note 75, at 206 (noting that the largest percentage of research expenditures in the US are made by the defense industry).

their own projects, at least when the financing is not defense-related.[502] Despite the discretion given to researchers, funding allocations steer the general areas of research to those that are prioritized by the federal government.[503] In addition, only a small portion of universities even engage in research, less than five percent of all universities do so.[504] University inventions are greatly outnumbered, in fact, by private entrepreneurs, for-profit research departments and government researchers.[505]

3. The Types of Research

Universities focus on basic research more than any other type of institution, but they now are nearly equally engaged in applied research.[506] This systematic shift toward applied research, both in the US and abroad, demonstrates the negative correlation between outside commercial funding and universities' basic research.[507] In other words, it is likely that, as commercial funding increases, basic research will decline. This proportional drop in basic research is related to a general misunderstanding of what universities have to offer through their research efforts. These institutions, rather than developing inventions, i.e. patentable technology, make their greatest contributions through massive amounts of peer-reviewed publications, accounting for at least eighty percent of all peer-reviewed articles.[508] Above all else, scientific articles serve as verification mechanisms to analyze critically, provide feedback and do so with the world's leading scientific authorities. When patents are filed, they most often include a list of key citations to related research; academic sources dominate with around twenty-five percent of all patent citations to articles.[509] Universities also make very valuable contributions to innovation through outside collaborations, student training and knowledge sharing.

---

502 Snyder, *Digest of Education Statistics*, *supra* note 43, at Tables 333.10, 333.40.

503 Johnson, Rob. "The STM Report: An Overview of Scientific and Scholarly Publishing." *STM*, Oct. 2018, www.stm-assoc.org/2018_10_04_STM_Report_2018.pdf, pp. 69–70.

504 Brint, *Two Cheers for Higher Education*, *supra* note 75, at 39.

505 *Ibid.* at 92.

506 Bentley, Peter James, et al. "The Relationship between Basic and Applied Research in Universities." *Higher Education*, vol. 70, no. 4, 2015, p. 699.

507 *Ibid.* at 703.

508 Brint, *Two Cheers for Higher Education*, *supra* note 75, at 39.

509 Johnson, *The STM Report*, *supra* note 503, at 75.

There are still plenty of instances of universities developing patented technology and other trademarked products, which have proven to be extremely lucrative.[510] Congress' 1980 passage of the *Bayh-Dole Act* allowed for university ownership of patents and retention of profits resulting from federal research funding.[511] *Bayh-Dole* clearly affected the rate of university patenting. When it was adopted, universities in the US filed around three hundred patents per year, in recent years it has increased to over six thousand filings per year.[512] Their extensive research efforts have led to these universities creating technology transfer offices as well as retaining the services of patent attorneys to ensure compliance with patent laws and marketability. Controversy is also stirred up by the fact that these universities are using public money to compete with for-profit firms and, when they generate profits, the proceeds will likely be reinvested into further patent research, not necessarily classroom instruction.[513] Similar to the comparative rates of patent filing, universities also lag far behind the other sectors in terms of revenue-generating licenses.[514]

Some universities aim to promote research not just because of their higher ideals of knowledge production, but they may also be seeking new revenue sources, usually coming in the form of massive government research grants. With government funding for research tapering in some areas, universities became friendlier to outside corporate funding.[515] These partnerships have also benefited outside corporations, who either become co-owners on patents or, more generally, beneficiaries of university labor for their products. Outside partnerships also lead to massive sponsorships. In 1989, Shiseido, Co., a Japanese skincare business paid Harvard University eighty-five million dollars for the exclusive right to sell products developed by Harvard scientists.[516] Many agreements of this sort were made since, one particularly large one being the University of California-

---

510 Rooksby, Jacob H. *The Branding of the American Mind: How Universities Capture, Manage, and Monetize Intellectual Property and Why It Matters*. Johns Hopkins University Press, 2016, pp. 64–177.

511 35 U.S.C. § 212 (1984).

512 Brint, *Two Cheers for Higher Education*, *supra* note 75, at 100 (noting that, despite this great increase in university patenting, their patents comprised only four percent of all new patents in 2014).

513 Hansmann, *Why Are Colleges and Universities Exempt*, *supra* note 174, at 20.

514 Brint, *Two Cheers for Higher Education*, *supra* note 75, at 101 (observing that university technology transfer offices oversaw only about sixteen-thousand licenses as of 2014).

515 Rubin, *supra* note 319, at 1071.

516 *Ibid.* at 1072.

Berkley's 2007 ten-year contract with British Petroleum, for five hundred million dollars, to develop biofuels and alternative energy sources.[517] Critics point out that these arrangements promote secrecy for research findings, excessive corporate influence over research findings and excessive influence over research agendas in general.[518] Furthermore, such agreements tend to "rent out" private university laboratories to corporations, which may also end up acquiring patent rights based on the research.[519] When research efforts do not succeed in producing patents and licensing revenues, they act as a drain on university resources that could have otherwise been spent on instruction.

Beyond the type of university research that results in patents, it should also be expected that professors and PhD candidates are writing substantially in their fields, creating copyrightable material. One professor has described the past decades as being a "true golden age" for universities based on their massive research expenditures, numerous inventions and output of high-quality publications.[520] Not only has the number of scholarly articles and materials skyrocketed since the 1970's, but, at the same time, the number of periodicals, journals and other field-specific publications has also grown greatly.[521] This growth of publication in nearly every discipline is likely due to requirements that faculty publish in order to be qualified for tenure.[522] As the number of publications and journals increased, the number of citations, often used as the measure of an article's success, to these academic publications also ballooned.[523] This aspect of university research, resulting in copyrightable publications, is perhaps one

---

517 *Ibid.* at 1073; Brint, *Two Cheers for Higher Education*, *supra* note 75, at 108–09 (noting that BP did not renew this funding).

518 Rubin, *supra* note 319, at 1073.

519 Hansmann, *Why Are Colleges and Universities Exempt*, *supra* note 174, at 20.

520 Brint, *Two Cheers for Higher Education*, *supra* note 75, at 9–10; *see also* Cole, *Toward a More Perfect University*, *supra* note 142, at 220 (listing the following factors for the prestige and quality of research universities: publication of high-impact books and papers, research dollars obtained, library quality and the quality of other information services).

521 Johnson, *The STM Report*, *supra* note 503, at 25–29.

522 Vedder, *Restoring the Promise*, *supra* note 172, at 236 (noting that the focus of "research in academia is not just working in laboratories, it is interpreting Shakespeare and composing symphonies, assessing the past, analyzing the present political, economic, social, and cultural milieus—and engaging in scientific discovery.").

523 Johnson, *The STM Report*, *supra* note 503, at 64–69.

of higher education's single-most important contributions to the progress of knowledge.[524]

While private, nonprofit universities have shown some success in their research endeavors, it should be recognized that these successes come at the cost of universities coming to mirror many of the outside governmental and for-profit counterparts. Success in terms of university research ought to be considered synonymous with peer-reviewed publications; most other research successes, resulting in profitable patent licenses, are statistical outliers and, nevertheless, often fruits of the published research.[525] This type of university research, i.e. publication, has contributed greatly to all of humankind, not just the American public. University attempts to compile valuable patent portfolios will invariably direct funding away from this and other valuable university missions. Other countries concentrate their research efforts in outside foundations, institutes and academies like the German Max Planck Institutes, for example. This demonstrates that there are viable alternatives for promoting innovation beyond the university campus.[526] Therefore, certain university forms do contribute greatly to knowledge dispersion, but all interested parties must proceed carefully to avoid wasting public resources as well as the commercialization of publicly funded research.

---

524 Cole, *Toward a More Perfect University*, *supra* note 142, at 15.

525 Marginson, Simon. "The New World Order in Higher Education." In *Questioning Excellence in Higher Education: Policies, Experiences and Challenges in National and Comparative Perspective*. Sense Publishers, 2011, p. 8 (stating that:
[t]here are normally several steps that must occur before ideas become enfolded into commodities, and by that stage the ideas have long been transformed by other economic processes in which the commercial value is created. It takes deep pockets to hold onto private ownership of the idea in itself all the way down the commercial value-creating chain. From time to time there are rare cases of lucrative research programs, especially in pharmaceutics, other branches of biotechnology and electronics, in which research-generated knowledge owned by universities and / or their scientists feed directly into a new product. But high income earning patents are not the norm in research. Only a small proportion of research results in specific fields turns out to be commercially patentable.... When universities try to lock up research results as patents they have difficulty sustaining the costs of worldwide protection...).

526 "Annual Report 2018." *Max-Planck-Gesellschaft*, www.mpg.de/13594766/annual-report-2018.pdf.

IV. Certification

Certification refers to the university gatekeeper function, whereby they grant degrees that show competence in particular areas. If not demonstrative of competence, degrees in many fields serve as a prerequisite to the undertaking of certain types of work or, at the very least, indicators that somebody is "relatively bright, disciplined and hard-working and also relatively knowledgeable about the world."[527] Certification is a short-cut method of judging whether somebody is capable of particular tasks and is, to a certain extent, rightfully relied upon by customers, potential employers and peers to make quick assessments as to a person's abilities. Depending on the institution making a certification, it may also be a mark of quality. In the competition to position themselves for prestige, i.e. perceived quality, universities become more selective in their admissions processes and increase funding for "high status activities" such as graduate programs and faculty research.[528] Regardless of whether their programs are of a higher quality or contribute to social mobility, such things must minimally be signaled to maintain institutional reputation and to secure private donations.[529] Assuming that university degrees really do certify that a meaningful course of study was successfully undertaken, this certification helps everybody from students to employers and society. This, though, requires that rigorous admission and academic standards are maintained.

The hierarchy of university rankings, prestige and graduates' outcomes is highly observable in the context of certification.[530] The perceived prestige gap between the most elite universities and middle- and low-ranked universities is wide and continuously growing and is directly traceable to their admissions standards. Universities' admission standards have polarized in their attempts to attract particular tiers of high school graduates to their institutions. While the admissions criteria at the elite private universities have become stricter, other less-selective universities have increased

---

527 Vedder, *Restoring the Promise*, *supra* note 172, at 98–99.

528 Armstrong & Hamilton, *supra* note 210, at 20 (noting that universities mostly want to attract students who can pay tuition fees and that have excellent academic credentials. Diversity is also a valuable consideration).

529 *Ibid.*

530 *See generally* Van der Wende, Marijk. "Towards a European Approach to Ranking." In *Paths to a World-Class University: Lessons from Practices and Experiences.* Sense Publishers, 2011 (describing how even European universities are increasingly being added to ranking lists).

their enrollments and lowered their standards.[531] In terms of perceived prestige, the most selective universities leave the rest behind. Although, this was not the case in the 1950's or 1960's, for example, when students from middle-tier public universities were also "considered unusually talented relative to the general population."[532] Furthermore, considering that such a broad swath of Americans have college degrees, it is questionable as to whether they can continue to serve as effective certification mechanisms.

If certification is the means of acquiring jobs, then it should be brought to the forefront that college degrees are now overly abundant, especially relative to the types of jobs that require candidates with a university degree.[533] The rates of college graduate employment far surpass the number of jobs requiring this type of certification, leading to the conclusion that college graduates are considerably underemployed.[534] Which graduates, then, are most likely to be underemployed? The most obvious connection to underemployment is the perceived prestige of a university; is it a highly selective institution or a university with generally open admission standards? Graduates of the most selective universities will have not only better employment prospects than those from lower-ranked and less-selective universities, but they also stand to earn much more throughout their careers.[535] Secondly, where did the graduates' academic performance rate them alongside their peers? It has been observed that graduates in the bottom quartile of their class have very similar employment and wage prospects to high school graduates.[536] Note, however, that many elite universities overcome this second proviso, weaker employment prospects for lower-ranked students, by eliminating grading altogether. Third, graduates' areas of study are also a major determiner for their career prospects;

531 Hoxby, Caroline. "The Changing Selectivity of American Colleges." *Journal of Economic Perspectives*, vol. 23, no. 4, Oct. 2009, pp. 1–7.

532 Vedder, *Restoring the Promise*, *supra* note 172, at 98–99.

533 Roth, Gary. "The New Underemployed, Educated Working Class." *New Labor Forum*, vol. 28, no. 3, 18 July 2019, pp. 88–91.

534 *Ibid.*

535 Vedder, *Restoring the Promise*, *supra* note 172, at 77, 80 (explaining that graduates from the top twenty-five universities will have average earnings of nearly eighty percent greater than students from the bottom-ranked universities. Graduates from mid-ranked universities, predictably, earn in the middle-range).

536 *Ibid.* at 72 (discussing generally the difficulty for high school graduates to compete with college graduates for jobs that do not require degrees; it is likely that, even for bartenders, that if there are enough applicants, the degrees will act as a weeding-out mechanism).

science, technology, engineering and mathematics (STEM) areas are likely to be better for employment and compensation than majors in the humanities.[537]

The monopoly that universities hold over the issuance of degrees could be the most important privilege that they enjoy. Despite university shortcomings in scientific research, professional training and the development of students' cognitive and critical thinking skills, it may be that the "exchangeable currency of accredited degrees" at least serves as an economic driver.[538] Beyond economic utility, degrees still signal job-candidates' qualifications to the rest of the world. Universities awarded degrees to students in the past and, now that these graduates are the business leaders, they are the ones looking to hire the next generation. Graduates of prestigious universities will likely project their own positive characteristics onto applicants from the same or similar universities, trusting that the institutions put out good-quality candidates. The value of any certification is most likely to be dependent on the institutions' reputations for selectivity; the presumption being that the more selective the university, the better quality the admitted students. Selectivity is, of course, bolstered by the factors that form university rankings, such as alumni salary, alumni achievements and, perhaps, awards conferred to alumni or faculty. Thus, the actual value of any individual university's certification might have more to do with their admission criteria, rather than being any indicator of the institution's educational quality. Entrusting universities with the power to certify graduates ought not to be taken lightly; when university degrees really are indicators of rigorous academic programs, and not just perceived prestige, everybody wins.

V. Social Mobility

Pre-industrial innovation was not particularly democratic. A very small portion of the population, which was likely to have been literate and trained in particular areas, would have made major advances.[539] Gradual advancements were generally made by craftsmen, but these skills or techniques would have likely been confined to the closed networks within

537 *State of the Humanities*, *supra* note 466, at 6, 12.

538 Brint, *Two Cheers for Higher Education*, *supra* note 75, at 59, 372.

539 Mokyr, *Culture of Growth*, *supra* note 13, at 119.

various trades or guilds.[540] Meanwhile, elites, those with access to printed materials and education, led industrialization.[541] Contributions to overall human capital were made through education and training, but the outcomes were significantly different depending on one's social class. Whatever education would have been available to the poor or working masses would have been to provide basic literacy and religious studies, whereas wealthier students were likely to receive a more thorough, richer education in the humanities.[542]

Participation in the innovation process not only entails having access to knowledge, but also invokes the degree to which one can disperse their ideas. At the time of the American Revolution and later during the ratification of the Constitution, the Republic of Letters was an ongoing international discourse of ideas by some of the greatest thinkers of the era.[543] Although these men, Voltaire, Rousseau, Franklin and Jefferson to name a few, were all brilliant individuals, their access to the public debate was increased by being born into families that could either afford to provide formal education or otherwise make books available.[544] Despite the fact that many were excluded because they had poor access to knowledge, the Republic was meant to be merit-based and egalitarian.[545] Even with its shortcomings, participation in something as progressive as the Republic of Letters would have been unheard of in Europe during the Middle Ages, where social standing was determined by family name, wealth, income, and possibly by acquiring a doctoral degree that could elevate one's status parallel to nobility.[546] Universities gradually opening up to new students and improving technological platforms, as will be discussed in Part II,

540 Kostylo, Joanna. "From Gunpowder to Print: The Common Origins of Copyright and Patent." In *Privilege and Property, Essays on the History of Copyright*, edited by Ronan Deazley, Martin Kretschmer, and Lionel Bently, Open Book Publishers, 2010, pp. 41–44.

541 Mokyr, *Culture of Growth*, *supra* note 13, at 120.

542 *Ibid.* at 124–26. (noting that, being the leading technological leader in Europe, Britain had a mediocre schooling record, whereas Prussia and Scandinavian countries excelled in their literacy rates, but still lagged in economic improvement).

543 Darnton, Robert. *The Case for Books*. PublicAffairs, 2009, pp. 4–5.

544 *See e.g.*, Serena, Jeff, editor. *The Autobiography of Benjamin Franklin the Complete Illustrated History*. Zenith Press, 2016, pp. 19–28.

545 Darnton, *supra* note 543, at 5.

546 Rüegg, *Themes*, *in* VOLUME I, UNIVERSITIES IN THE MIDDLE AGES, *supra* note 155, at 3, 22.

both provided significant new structures for individual participation in the innovation process.

Today, upward social mobility in the US can be partially realized through graduates' credentials; a degree from an elite university will open many employers' doors, whereas students graduating from average-ranked universities will not experience this same advantage. A university degree is a certification that can better employment opportunities; this is, of course, complimented by the socialization factor.[547] Socialization comes into play, especially at the most selective universities, in terms of student's learning environments. There they are surrounded by other highly intelligent and creative students. Being surrounded by such peers contributes to greater academic growth, creativity and inventiveness of the individual students.[548] Personal relationships will also be formed, opening the doors to a broad array of advantages. Students of the most elite universities can expect to meet highly successful alumni, which is invaluable for their internship and job searches. With admission being the greatest hurdle, students need not expend great effort in achieving the highest grades, because even with a "gentleman's C" from these institutions, finding employment would not be a problem.[549] A former president of Princeton University even referred to his university as the "finest country club in America."[550]

Some students on the mobility pathway may not be able to make their climb through social interaction because of factors relating to the type of institution being attended and the attitudes of students and faculty within the institutions. Recall from the access section above that university selectivity has a strong correlation with students' family wealth. Even for elite universities' modest success in diversifying their student bodies in terms of race, their students are overwhelmingly out of the upper-middle-class and higher.[551] Students out of low-income families are the smallest and least-apparent minority at the most prestigious universities and the prevailing attitudes toward them and their upward mobility are not particularly welcoming. One such student described in his memoir that he and his low-income peers were "newcomers who don't quite belong."[552]

547 Johnson, *The Uncertain Future*, *supra* note 73, at 147.

548 *Ibid.* at 14.

549 Karabel, *The Chosen*, *supra* note 256, at 177.

550 *Ibid.* at 74.

551 Vance, *supra* note 229, at 202 (observing that "but for all of the Ivy League's obsession with diversity, virtually everyone—black, white, Jewish, Muslim, whatever—comes from intact families who never worry about money.").

552 *Ibid.* at 205.

The most elite universities' acceptance of Jews, Asians, African Americans and less-affluent students was begrudging, but, nonetheless, necessary for their own survival in a changing society.[553] A failure to admit the most meritorious of any group would, rightfully, call the institutions themselves into question. More-open admissions have contributed to a better "distribution of opportunity" as well as an improved public perception regarding the fairness of America's systems for rewarding hard work and merit.[554] As seen above with the other university goals, the institution type makes a difference; the greatest social benefits coincide with the most selective universities and diminish as universities become less selective.

Today's expansive access to higher education has served to democratize individual education and collective innovation. Women have certainly bettered their lot over the past decades, now enrolling at higher rates than men, graduating at higher rates than men do and with better grades.[555] Universities' doors have been similarly opened to many other historically marginalized groups. Admissions processes have clearly improved over the last decades to reward merit, but the system has fallen short of being a pure meritocracy; students' social backgrounds still weigh heavily.[556] Despite these shortcomings, American universities still play a major role in keeping the "American dream" alive.[557] Universities primarily promote the American dream by providing a means for social mobility. Modern technology has also altered access to information and, thus, mobility; university outsiders of all stripes now have unprecedented access to a wide array of online materials, which will be covered extensively in Part II.[558] Massive open online courses (hereinafter, MOOCs) may now be changing the dynamic away from requiring university attendance and, instead, toward self-disciplined individuals using readily available online materials to train themselves in any number of fields.[559] Technologies such as these have facilitated the extensive access to higher education that today's students enjoy, but as long as the universities maintain their monopoly on

---

553 Karabel, *The Chosen*, *supra* note 256, at 541.

554 *Ibid.* at 548.

555 Armstrong & Hamilton, *supra* note 210, at 7.

556 Karabel, *The Chosen*, *supra* note 256, at 548–49; Crow & Dabars, *supra* note 12, at 45.

557 Trow, Martin. "From Mass Higher Education to Universal Access, the American Advantage." In *In Defense of American Higher Education*. Johns Hopkins University Press, 2001, p. 121.

558 Darnton, *supra* note 543, at 10.

559 Cole, *Toward a More Perfect University*, *supra* note 142, at 148.

certification, they will continue to exercise the largest influence on social mobility.

VI. Conformity with Nonprofit Principles

Many of the authors writing on "multiversities" comment on organizational size, range of activities and entanglement with the other sectors.[560] One point that is generally left unexplored is the fact that these "multiversities" are founded as "universities," registered with state and federal governments as nonprofit, charitable organizations and must operate under nonprofit law for a *uni*tary purpose: education. This issue is likely left aside because, despite constantly expanding university activity, nonprofit law has been substantially weakened by lax enforcement and substantial safe-harbors within the law itself. The largest universities have bitterly competed and drawn most other universities into the competition as well. Their competition has resulted in universities undertaking substantial commercial operations, compensating administrators millions of dollars as well as accumulating massive endowments. Could it be that they do these activities to the detriment of their obligations as nonprofits? Asking whether private, nonprofit universities are complying with the IRC's tests, whether the non-distribution constraint works to prevent rent-seeking and what implications this has for the public benefit, this section discusses universities' commercial operations, administrative compensation and capital accumulation.

1. Commercial Operations

Perhaps the most apparent and flagrant area of university intrusion into commercial activity is in the areas of athletics. College athletics have become a vortex, consuming massive amounts of university resources and drawing many institutions into the mix that have neither a desire to

560 Kerr, *supra* note 106, at 31 (coining the of phrase "multiversity," which has come to be frequently used in literature on higher education. Kerr also uses the metaphor of traditional universities or colleges being like small monastic villages in comparison to "modern universities" that have the complexity, perhaps, of a small town with one industry. Multiversities, on the other hand, would be more comparable in their complexity to a burgeoning metropolis with a tremendous amount of interested parties and interactions among them).

compete nor the internal infrastructure to do so. Nonetheless, in order to attract potential students, most universities spend extensive sums of student-subsidized money on sports programs, which are mostly financial liabilities and contribute to universal cost increases throughout higher education. A former university president notes, "... there are many more financial losers than winners among intercollegiate athletic programs."[561] Some further outcomes of universities' involvement in sports-entertainment have been the lowering of academic standards and a rash of scandals, requiring that these educational institutions activities be called into question.[562]

The National Collegiate Athletic Association (hereinafter, NCAA), also a nonprofit organization, is the organizational and regulatory body for North American intercollegiate sports, presiding over more than 1,200 member institutions and conferences.[563] Using factors such as "competitiveness" and "investment into sports programs," the NCAA divides all member universities into the following three categories: Division I, Division II and Division III. Although most university athletic programs at most universities are not profitable, top-tier athletics at Division I schools, some of which are nonprofit institutions, can generate tremendous amounts of revenue. Division I, though, is mainly represented by large state universities that pour extensive resources into sports programs, thereby attracting top-recruits and perpetuating success in athletics by maintaining their rosters of talented players and extensive athletic facilities.[564] The biggest incentives for student-athletes to attend any particular university, in addition to the fanfare, pageantry and reputation, are scholarships, which may be either full or partial. Division II is an intermediary grouping; small liberal arts institutions mainly represent Division

561 Shapiro, *supra* note 456, at 28.

562 Johnson, *The Uncertain Future*, *supra* note 73, at 109; *see also* Vedder, *Restoring the Promise*, *supra* note 172, at 228–29 (noting, in terms of lower academic expectations that the University of North Carolina at Chapel Hill offered its student-athletes "phantom courses" over a period of eighteen years with essentially no requirements at all and high grades. In terms of non-academic scandals, a football coach at The Pennsylvania State University was arrested for sexually-abusing young boys on campus, while his superiors did not act to remove him and the University of Louisville entertained high school athletic recruits with strippers and prostitutes, just to name a few instances).

563 The NCAA is also filed as a 501 (c)(3) nonprofit charity; "National Collegiate Athletic Association – Nonprofit Explorer." *ProPublica*, 9 May 2013, projects.propublica.org/nonprofits/organizations/440567264.

564 Rubin, *supra* note 319, at 1068.

III.[565] Student-athletes at Division II universities may be able to receive partial-scholarships, but most will still be reliant on academic scholarships, student loans and other employment.[566] Division III universities are not permitted to provide athletic scholarships to their student-athletes.

Despite twenty-three of college football's twenty-five most lucrative teams being from massive state universities, teams from private nonprofits such as the University of Southern California and Notre Dame University share in these top sports programs' combined $1.4 billion annual profits.[567] The Notre Dame University football team generated around $112 million in revenue and $72 million in profits in 2017.[568] As a bloc, all of these universities usually end up reinvesting profits from their football programs into other athletics programs and facilities.[569] The large state schools, from 2014 to 2016, paid out an average of $239 million per year for football coaches' salaries and severance packages, although, only $90 million per year went towards scholarships for football players.[570] State universities, from 2016 to 2017, expended $800 million on athletic facilities and $250 million, servicing previous debts. Furthermore, investment back into academic programs was a relatively small $65 million, especially as compared to the amount spent on athletic facilities.[571]

Football coaches at large state universities are by far the highest-paid public employees in the US; Nick Saban, head coach of the University of Alabama's football team, was paid $11.7 million in 2017, totaling $64 million in compensation since 2010.[572] Saban's prior move from professional football to The University of Alabama was hardly a demotion to an "amateur" league, which the NCAA purports to be. Notre Dame, in comparison, paid its head coach Brian Kelly a salary of $2.1 million in

565 *Ibid.*

566 "Division II Partial-Scholarship Model." *NCAA*, 2019, Division II partial-scholarship model.

567 Smith, Chris. "College Football's Most Valuable Teams: Texas A&M Jumps To No. 1." *Forbes*, 11 Sept. 2018, www.forbes.com/sites/chrissmith/2018/09/11/college-footballs-most-valuable-teams/#4c1eb8906c64.

568 *Ibid.*

569 *Ibid.*

570 *Ibid.*

571 *Ibid.*

572 Andrezejewski, Adam. "Heaven Helps Notre Dame Football While Taxpayers Subsidize Alabama, Clemson, Oklahoma." *Forbes*, 27 Dec. 2018, www.forbes.com/sites/adamandrzejewski/2018/12/27/heaven-helps-notre-dame-football-while-taxpayers-subsidize-alabama-clemson-oklahoma/#20bd19a775ae.

2017.[573] Notre Dame is a terrific university, but they are an outlier in the sense that they are so academically and athletically successful at the same time. Most Ivy League and other prestigious universities invest far fewer resources into their athletics programs.[574] For the largest and most successful programs, investments into their coaching staffs and facilities do seem to presently pay off, although these programs' financial futures are already based on "crippling debt" that will have to be paid off by increased student tuition fees.[575] One estimate has about sixty-four universities at the top of the athletics hierarchy, with nearly so many pouring massive resources into their programs to join the ranks. Lower on the pyramid are approximately 135 programs similarly trying to improve their lot; even these striving programs are known to spend over $20 million per university, per year on their athletics programs.[576]

College sports are very exploitative of student-athletes. The NCAA, its constituent conferences and the member universities are registered as charitable nonprofits and claim to be supporting the "educational and athletic opportunities of [their] student-athletes," so all of them go untaxed while the student-athletes go unpaid.[577] There are countless examples of student-athletes being punished for accepting compensation. Further, the NCAA and member universities have monopolized sports for pre-professional athletes and capitalize off ticket sales, broadcast licensing, video game licensing, merchandise sales and other major sponsoring and advertising revenue. The largest sports programs have generated hundreds of millions of untaxable dollars in commercial sponsor licensing.[578] Beyond the issues with tax-exemption, this unrestrained corporate involvement in higher education has exposed universities to numerous corruption scandals.[579]

---

573 *Ibid.*

574 Vedder, *Restoring the Promise*, *supra* note 172, at 219, 231 (explaining that the most prestigious Ivy League schools, along with not granting athletic scholarships, abstain from bowl and championship games for academic reasons).

575 Andrezejewski, *supra* note 572.

576 Vedder, *Restoring the Promise*, *supra* note 172, at 218.

577 Mcintire, Mike. "The College Sports Tax Dodge." *The New York Times*, 28 Dec. 2017, www.nytimes.com/2017/12/28/sunday-review/college-sports-tax-dodge.html.

578 *Ibid.* (mentioning that the Atlantic Coast Conference, an athletic conference with fifteen member universities, generated over $250 million untaxable dollars in 2015 from corporate sponsors such as Toyota, Gatorade and Geico).

579 *See e.g.*, O'Brien, Rebecca Davis. "Ex-Adidas Executive Gets 9-Month Sentence in Basketball Bribery Case." *The Wall Street Journal*, 5 Mar. 2019, www.wsj.com/articles/adidas-executive-gets-9-month-sentence-in-college-basketball-bribery-cas

Despite the poor financial prospects for most college football teams, at least fifty-seven universities have created teams and joined the NCAA over the last ten years while students elsewhere have voted down such initiatives.[580] It is very common that program expenses exceed revenues, thus often leading to increased tuition fees.[581] Many universities opaquely charge mandatory athletic fees, which total up into thousands of dollars per student over the course of their studies, regardless of whether students even participate.[582] Smaller schools, whose football programs are not nationally competitive, usually justify investments into these programs by suggesting that they drive alumni donations, increase the universities' name recognition and spur local community activity.[583] Although, this is hard to believe since most universities raising over $500 million per year from alumni gifts, such as Harvard, Princeton and Johns Hopkins, are hardly competitive on the football field.[584] When college football does not present good financial prospects or an opportunity to be competitive, it is normal for universities to, instead, turn to college basketball. Universities such as Gonzaga, Marquette and Xavier have commanded strong national reputations on the basketball court, which has undoubtedly contributed to broader name-recognition.[585]

Sports programs are universally expensive and, in the quest to attract new students, many small universities are sucked into the competition. At least Division I programs are justifiable in that they can provide extensive scholarships for student-athletes, but, student-athletes in Division III programs, at mostly private liberal arts colleges, which are all private nonprofit universities, usually end up playing only "for the love of the sport." On the plus side, their amateur ambitions do create a more energetic campus atmosphere, but they will likely never go on to compete in the professional leagues and will, nonetheless, endure many sports injuries along the

---

e-11551821093 (discussing the sentencing of a former Adidas executive in 2019 to nine months in prison for bribing top-ranked high school basketball players and their families to attend universities that were sponsored by Adidas).

580 Novy-Williams, Eben. "College Football Teams Are Risky and Expensive—and Schools Keep Adding Them." *Bloomberg*, 6 Jan. 2017, www.bloomberg.com/news/features/2017-01-06/college-football-teams-are-risky-and-expensive-and-schools-keep-adding-them.

581 Johnson, *The Uncertain Future*, *supra* note 73, at 108-09.

582 *Ibid.* at 112.

583 Novy-Williams, *supra* note 580.

584 *Ibid.* (noting that, of the universities with the highest rates of alumni giving, only Princeton University and Davidson College compete in Division I football).

585 *Ibid.*

way.[586] This excitement, though, detracts from the focus on academics and resources for research. Considering the astonishing investments made by universities into athletics programs, it may surprise some to learn that a mere three percent of students participate in NCAA sports.[587]

Many student-athletes in most NCAA sports are quite successful in their studies, but those in the most commercialized of college sports, such as football and basketball, are often subject to favoritism, relaxed standards and appallingly low academic expectations.[588] The lower academic standards for the admission of athletes to university programs was highlighted by the 2019 college admissions fraud case, where coaches at prestigious universities had the discretion to admit student-athletes who would have otherwise not been admitted on their academics alone. Applicants were caught faking athletic credentials to qualify as recruits for sports teams, as well as paying stand-ins to take standardized college admissions tests.[589] Those undertaking these schemes are universally wealthy and well connected; this is at the expense of institutions' merit-based admissions, which tend to admit the most talented students from the middle-class.[590] The fact that the coaches and administrators were being bribed to aid in the

---

586 As of early 2019, the NCAA was facing more than three-hundred lawsuits from former college football players claiming to have serious neurological damage, such as effects from Alzheimer's disease or Chronic Traumatic Encephalopathy, because they were either misled about the risks of the sport or mistreated once injured. Although former student-athletes are unable to sue public universities, due to state sovereignty, they have, rather, redirected their lawsuits towards private universities, athletic conferences and the NCAA. Russo, Ralph D. "Wave of Concussion Lawsuits to Test NCAA's Liability." *USA Today*, 7 Feb. 2019, eu.usatoday.com/story/sports/ncaaf/2019/02/07/wave-of-concussion-lawsuits-to-test-ncaas-liability/39022587/.

587 Brint, *Two Cheers for Higher Education*, *supra* note 75, at 187.

588 Vedder, *Restoring the Promise*, *supra* note 172, at 226.

589 In one particularly well-known case, a celebrity's daughter was admitted to the University of Southern California— a highly regarded nonprofit university— and explained to followers on her YouTube channel:
With work it's going to be hard, like my first week of school I'm leaving to go to Fiji for work.... I don't know how much of school I'm gonna (*sic.*) attend but I'm gonna go in and talk to my deans and everyone, and hope that I can try and balance it all, the whole college thing.... But I do want the experience of like game days, partying. I don't really care about school, as you guys all know.
Jade, Olivia. "Basically All the Tea You Need to Know about Me (Boys, College, Youtubers) – Dailymotion Video." *Dailymotion*, 15 Aug. 2018, www.dailymotion.com/video/x6s0tqn; *see also* United States v. Sidoo, No. CR 19-10080-NMG, 2020 WL 3440990 (D. Mass. June 23, 2020).

590 Karabel, *The Chosen*, *supra* note 256, at 540.

admission of particular students is fraudulent and unfair to the other worthy student applicants. It seems that the universities had no knowledge of this criminal behavior, but they were still complicit through their relaxed standards, prioritization of athletics and for having deviated from their core academic missions.

The most commercialized sports programs are to be found at large state universities, while the overwhelming majority of private, nonprofit universities do not maintain highly competitive programs. Nonetheless, private, nonprofit universities are drawn into the competition because of the normalization of NCAA sports and universities' drive to attract students, whose expectations are driven by the more general sports culture. Due to the safe-harbors, most private, nonprofit universities are likely not violating the prohibition of excess benefit through excessive compensation to their football coaches but continue to divert resources to non-financially sustainable sports programs that could have otherwise been spent on education or lowering student costs. The commerciality doctrine and operational tests also must be taken into consideration.

Are universities with major sports programs undertaking substantial commercial activity? The test for commerciality is different in essentially every jurisdiction, but, in a general sense, one must inquire into whether there are substantial non-exempt activities, to what extent they go, whether it puts the nonprofit into competition with for-profits, the pricing for services, the use of advertising, among many other potential factors.[591] In many instances, athletic programs are substantial, even in relation to other massive amounts of university expenditures. Competition with for-profits is paradoxically difficult to demonstrate because the NCAA programs have monopolized all the talented athletes, making it impossible for for-profit alternative leagues to compete. Spectators would notice that ticket pricing for top college sports programs could be just as expensive as that for professional sports. Finally, advertising has become commonplace. Like an application of the commerciality doctrine, a court's application of the operational test would inquire into the substantiality of a non-exempt activity. If courts found substantial commercial, non-exempt, activity, universities could lose their tax-exemptions.

Universities' investment into intercollegiate sports mirrors the other forms of accentuation that occur on college campuses; it is not inherently necessary but becomes necessary through universities' drive to attract students. Financing these eccentric programs is only made possible through

---

591 Cafardi & Cherry, *supra* note 352, at 97–98.

the availability of massive student loans, the borrowing culture and students' lack of sensitivity to price increases, especially for non-educational programs. It seems that due to a lack of financial resources, cultural complacency and the normalization of college athletics, these activities have avoided the scrutiny of states' attorneys general. College athletics has become one of many eccentricities subsidized by the American taxpayer, as well as becoming a factor in the rising tide of student tuition fees. These commercial activities, going unchecked, are symptomatic of nonprofit law being influenced by its linkages with the other sectors, there being very little attempt to enforce the commerciality and operational tests and the insufficiency of the non-distribution constraint to redirect revenues back to the universities' core educational purposes.

2. Compensation

In 2014, there were thirty-nine presidents of nonprofit universities receiving over $1 million in compensation.[592] By the next year, 2015, that number jumped up to fifty-eight.[593] Leading the pack, in terms of highest compensation, was President Nathan Hatch of Wake Forest University, receiving more than $4 million in compensation.[594] As a juxtaposition, Wake Forest's full-time undergraduate tuition and other fees, in 2019, were $53,300.[595] If a student were to study law, the full-time tuition and other fees would be about $45,000 per year.[596] Assuming that these rates remained constant over the number of years that it would take a student to finish an undergraduate degree and then graduate from Wake Forest School of Law, the total costs to the student would be around $350,000. In

---

592 Strauss, Karsten. "The Highest-Paid Private College Presidents." *Forbes*, 13 Dec. 2017, www.forbes.com/sites/karstenstrauss/2017/12/13/the-highest-paid-private-college-presidents-2/#eec628f6e67 b.

593 *Ibid.*

594 Kamenetz, Anya. "More College Presidents Join The Millionaires' Club." *NPR*, 13 Dec. 2017, www.npr.org/sections/ed/2017/12/13/569943593/more-college-presidents-join-the-millionaires-club (noting that his yearly compensation was more in the range of $1 million, but deferred compensation from previous years inflated the total to over $4 million).

595 These numbers do not account for room and board, books, other supplies, and additional expenses which may exceed $15,000 per year; "Wake Forest University 2019 Tuition." *Univstats*, www.univstats.com/colleges/wake-forest-university/cost-of-attendance.

596 *Ibid.*

fairness to Wake Forest University, about fifty percent of their students do get substantial grants from the university, but those with an undergraduate degree are still, on average, saddled with $24,000 in student debt.[597] Law graduates face a much more substantial debt average of around $97,000.[598]

Such high university administrator earnings substantiate criticisms that universities have become corporatized in their missions and university presidents have essentially become corporate executives.[599] Managing non-profit universities in a corporate manner shifts internal power away from the traditional faculty and more toward administrators. Curricula, how courses are taught and the aims of research are now subject to administrative agreement.[600] Relevant to the universities' nonprofit filings is the determination of whether universities' massive compensation packages privately inure or are an excess benefit to their presidents and other administrators. Since the universities are nonprofit organizations, all interested parties should be protected by the non-distribution constraint, but, as will be demonstrated below, this might not be the case.

In the for-profit world, executives could earn millions of dollars per year, whereas nonprofit administrators will earn substantially less on average. Private university presidents earned an average of $365,000 in 2015.[601] While the relative amounts of compensation may not be particularly shocking, their rates of growth are. From 1998 to 2007, the average university president pay increased by fifty percent, whereas most for-profit executive compensation outside of higher education was essentially unchanged.[602]

The leading theory on how nonprofit administrative compensation is determined suggests that administrative compensation is not determined at an arm's length, but rather that high-level administrators have substan-

---

597 "Wake Forest University Is #98 on Money's 2019-20 #BestColleges List." *#98 In Money's 2019-20 Best Colleges Ranking*, money.com/best-colleges/profile/wake-forest-university/.

598 "These Law Schools Leave Students with the Most Debt." *U.S. News & World Report*, www.usnews.com/best-graduate-schools/top-law-schools/grad-debt-rankings?name=Wake Forest University (noting that this debt statistic represents seventy-six percent of graduates).

599 Brint, *Two Cheers for Higher Education*, *supra* note 75, at 257.

600 *Ibid.* at 270–71.

601 For-profit university presidents can avoid publically reporting their compensation, leaving the amounts up to speculation; Galle, Brian D., and David I. Walker. "The Problem of Nonprofit Executive Pay?: Evidence from U.S. Colleges and Universities." *Boston College Law School Faculty Papers*, 2015, p. 22.

602 *Ibid.* at 2, 5.

tial power in influencing their compensation.[603] These high-level administrators may have an advantage because of their ability to influence boards, to garner sympathy or simply capitalize on a lack of oversight.[604] Outrage by interested parties may negatively affect their compensation in that the board of directors would be less willing to approve of the compensation package, both directors and administrators may fear reputational harm and the university's image may be damaged in the eyes of students, alumni and other community members. The outrage experienced by individuals tends not to substantially affect top administrators enough to make a noticeable change, but there is evidence to suggest that material change can be made when such outrage is expressed by "institutional investors *en masse*, the media, and / or social and professional groups—about whose views the [administrators] and directors care."[605] As a result, administrators are likely to have complicated and opaque compensation schemes to, in essence, camouflage the true value of their compensation.[606]

Compensation is often camouflaged through either stealth compensation or gratuitous severance payments. So-called stealth compensation is mostly made through deferred payments, consulting contracts and highly gratuitous pension plans. Similar to their for-profit counterparts, univer-

603 The majority of research on how executive compensation is determined is conducted in the for-profit sector, which is dominated by two major hypotheses: the "optimal contracting" hypothesis and the "managerial power" hypothesis. The more common approach, the optimal contracting hypothesis, suggests that executive compensation is best determined by boards of directors, because they are obliged to maximize shareholder revenue, which is the ultimate goal. The premise is that shareholders would react to excessive executive compensation by voting, selling their shares or suing for a breach of duty, thus, playing an oversight role. Of course, though, shareholder ire will not restrain executive compensation at nonprofit universities because of the non-distribution constraint, i.e. there are no equity shareholders and excess revenues must be re-invested back into the organization. Due to this aspect of nonprofit governance, the managerial pay hypothesis is more effective for explaining how nonprofit executive compensation is determined; Bebchuk, Lucian Arye, et al. "Managerial Power and Rent Extraction in the Design of Executive Compensation." *The University of Chicago Law Review*, vol. 69, no. 3, 2002, pp. 845–46.

604 *Ibid.* at 754.

605 *Ibid.* at 788 (noting that firms receiving negative media coverage on the topic of executive compensation from outlets such as Forbes, Fortune, etc. during 1992–1994, had lower growth in compensation that similar firms during 1993–1994).

606 *Ibid.* at 788.

sity presidents may also receive golden-parachute severance packages.[607] Additional benefits enjoyed by university presidents sometimes include annual retention bonuses, personal vehicles, country club memberships and even, in some instances, access to private jets.[608] Furthermore, comparative *benchmarking* has become ubiquitous in practice; this occurs when boards or compensation committees guide their consultants to target compensation levels at or, often, above the fiftieth percentile for similar institutions.[609] This tendency for executives, such as university presidents, to be compensated at or above the median of their peers has resulted in a continuous ratcheting-up of compensation.[610] The universities with the largest compensation packages are also highly likely to use consultants to put a positive public-relations spin on the compensation, invariably leading to camouflaged compensation packages.[611]

Like for-profit corporations, nonprofits task their boards of directors and trustees with determining executive pay. Nonprofit boards of directors and trustees are subject to the same general weaknesses as their for-profit counterparts. One weakness arises from the fact that trustees are part-time and, accordingly, commit less time to oversight of the nonprofit.[612] Of the numerous types of directors, the "figure head" directors, who are typically included because of their public personalities, provide the least oversight over nonprofits; their inactivity allows for employees, executives

607 Bebchuk, Lucian Arye, and Jesse M Fried. "Executive Compensation as an Agency Problem." *Journal of Economic Perspectives*, vol. 17, no. 3, 2003, pp. 71–82 (rationalizing such generous severance payments through the smoother transition of leadership that they provide).

608 Vedder, *Restoring the Promise*, *supra* note 172, at 194.

609 Bizjak, John M. & Lemmon, Michael L. & Naveen, Lalitha, *Does the Use of Peer Groups Contribute to Higher Pay and Less Efficient Compensation?*, 90(2) Journal of Financial Economics, 152, 153 (2008).

610 Bebchuk et al., *Managerial Power and Rent Extraction*, *supra* note 603, at 791.

611 *See generally* Wade, James B., et al. "Worth, Words, and the Justification of Executive Pay." *Journal of Organizational Behavior*, vol. 18, 1997, p. 657.

612 Fishman, James J. "Standards of Conduct for Directors of Nonprofit Corporations." *Pace Law Review*, vol. 7, 1987, p. 397 (distinguishing differing types of board members where *monitoring directors* are outside, disinterested members charged with oversight of the organization; they are considered to be the best type for the interests of all interested parties. *Executive directors* may be outside individuals brought in for their reputation in the community or a specialty in a particular area. These may also be inside individuals such as former employees, family members or others directly involved in the nonprofit. And, finally, *Instrumental directors* are typically "legal counsel, accountants, consultants, fundraising professionals, or public relations professionals.").

and other directors to exercise much more control.[613] A second point is that nonprofit trustees, like the administrators, are prohibited from having an economic interest in the enterprise. This removes an incentive for a board member to consent to high compensation, where they would otherwise have a personal economic incentive to object.[614] Moreover, there are usually, just as in the for-profit world, close business and personal ties between trustees and administrators, often leading to deference toward the administrators.[615]

A 2015 study set out to better understand how outrage by interested parties works to constrain private, nonprofit universities, especially regarding compensation for administrators.[616] Private universities were selected for the study due to their trustees' relatively straightforward agency relationship to nonprofits' interested parties. In contrast, state governors or other politicians may elect public university trustees. Further, public universities tend to be substantially controlled by state actors; this entanglement with the state also creates the possibility of there being statutory pay-caps, thus making public universities less-than-optimal subjects for an analysis of agency relationships.[617] The authors drew their data from 341 private, nonprofit universities between the years 1999 and 2007 to study whether the *outrage constraint* was significant with respect to a number of variables related to administrative compensation at private nonprofit universities. One of the variables was the "exposure to current donations."[618] It was hypothesized that the "warm glow" of giving, i.e. the enhanced personal satisfaction of giving to organizations with which the donor identifies, may encourage overall giving. The variable of exposure to current donations was hypothesized to show that donors who are motivated by an

---

613 *Ibid.*

614 Galle & Walker, *supra* note 601, at 14.

615 Johnson, Danné L. "Seeking Meaningful Nonprofit Reform in a Post Sarbanes-Oxley World." *Saint Louis University Law Journal*, vol. 54, no. 1, 2009, pp. 203–04 (stating that the typical "incestuous director relationship" from the for-profit sector is often replicated in the nonprofit sector).

616 Despite the universities in the study being private, the reported income of their highest compensated administrators is publicly available through mandatory filings. Galle & Walker, *supra* note 601, at 17.

617 *Ibid.* at 17–18 (citing to James Monks, *Public Versus Private University President Pay Levels and Structure*, 26 Econ. Of Educ. Rev. 338, 45 (2007)) (noting that public university presidents earn about fifty percent less salary than their private university counterparts; note, though, that Monks' calculation is of salary, not total compensation).

618 *Ibid.* at 18–21.

institution's "warm glow" are more sensitive in their giving than are other revenue providers such as tuition fee-paying students or grant-making institutions.[619]

The authors of this study concluded that the exposure to current donations variable was the most significant in correlating stakeholder outrage with executive compensation; they labeled it "statistically significant" as well as "economically substantial in magnitude."[620] They noted that every nineteen percent, i.e. one-standard deviation, increase of donation revenue corresponded with around $111,426 less in executive compensation.[621] The authors make clear that donors change their giving based on executive compensation and that "[a]s a result, it is certainly plausible that at schools where donations contribute relatively more to overall revenues, presidents and trustees would have a stronger incentive to hold down reported compensation."[622]

Universities that are heavily reliant on donations may also operate differently than those with their revenue derived from tuition fees and endowments. Where the relationship between *donations* and presidential pay had a negative correlation—i.e. the more that a president is paid, the fewer donations will be given—*tuition fees* and presidential pay share a significant positive correlation.[623] The data also indicate that schools with larger endowments correlate with greater presidential compensation, but, as will be discussed below, the causality regarding endowments is not quite so clear. The authors, in these cases, were only able to demonstrate

---

619 *Ibid.* at 19.

620 *Ibid.* at 27.

621 *Ibid.* at 27 (noting that this calculation was made in 2007-dollar amounts).

622 *Ibid.* at 27, 29, 33 (finding a statically significant relationship between religious affiliation and lower executive pay; presidents at these universities were paid around $88,000 less per year. Although religious affiliation could be connected to the outrage constraint, it seems most likely that presidential compensation at religious affiliated universities is lower due to the "warm glow," that is the personal satisfaction and positive recognition, that the presidents get from working at such institutions. The satisfaction that they receive for working at these institutions serves as a substitution for the greater compensation that they could receive elsewhere).

623 *Ibid.* at 32 (explaining that for every one-standard deviation uptick in tuition fees, university presidents would receive about $94,000 more yearly. This phenomenon may be explained with the following three hypotheses: 1) weak student and parent monitoring results in fewer constraints, 2) tuition fees and high presidential pay may be the "result of high agency costs for the university's principals" or 3) high tuition fees are perceived to be related to high institutional quality).

that executives in charge of larger pools of money are better-compensated, not that there was any correlation with the agency-cost relationship.[624]

University presidential pay increased significantly between the years 1997 and 2007. While for-profit CEOs generally receive much greater absolute amounts, the rate of increase for their compensation is dwarfed by that of university presidents. There is no definitive answer as to why university presidents' compensation increased so rapidly during this period, but there are some well-founded arguments to explain the phenomenon. In line with the above-mentioned correlation between higher tuition fees and greater presidential compensation, it should be recognized that, while average tuition fees increased by forty percent, presidential pay went up by fifty percent.[625] There is also a possibility, following the IRS's 2002 creation of intermediate sanctions, that benchmarking executive pay with that of their peers compensated at median and higher levels led to an inevitable ratcheting-up in compensation throughout academia.[626] Seeing that a university president is receiving compensation in the fiftieth to the seventy-fifth percentiles is likely to mitigate stakeholder outrage.[627]

The pressure on nonprofits to generate income is continuously increasing, putting boards and administrators into the difficult position of trying to achieve the organizations' stated legal and social goals while simultaneously raising tuition fees to increase their revenue streams.[628] Universities with the greatest amounts of donations and endowments seem to retain the warm glow, trust with alumni and, thus, seem to be restrained by the non-distribution constraint. On the other hand, reliance on tuition fees acts to supplant warm glow, allowing for outrageous administrative compensation. Although, since the universities have massive streams of tuition fee-based income at their disposal, outrage from interested parties may no longer be their first concern. Paradoxically, the growth of nonprofits through government subsidies has resulted in the reduction of educational

---

624 *Ibid.* at 32.

625 *Ibid.* at 33.

626 26 U.S.C. § 4958 (1996); Elson, Charles M., and Ferrere, Craig, Executive Superstars, Peer Groups and Overcompensation: Cause, Effect and Solution p. 9 (August 7, 2012). https://lerner.udel.edu/sites/default/files/pdfs/Elson_Ferrere_Paper.pdf.

627 Galle & Walker, *supra* note 601, at 34.

628 Bovens, *supra* note 393.

initiatives and the loss of organizational vitality and character.[629] This trend also coincides with greater focus on profit optimization and less focus on their exempt purposes.

It is the decision of the state and federal governments, as well as numerous interested parties to inquire into nonprofit universities' compensation of their administrators.[630] Recall that the interested parties of nonprofit universities could be as diverse as students, donors, directors, members of the community and the local, state and federal authorities, none of whom possess an equitable interest in the universities. These interested parties should at least minimally demand transparency regarding camouflaged compensation, because, due to the extensive privileges given to the private universities, their compensation is of public concern. Finally, as in all other areas, state and federal officials should scrutinize administrators' compensation for private inurement and excess benefit. Although it is unlikely that an attorney general could demonstrate that a university president's influence over the board of directors so that he is privately inured, it may be possible to demonstrate excess benefit. This still comes into conflict with the safe-harbor provisions tied to benchmarked presidential pay; the presidents will be able to claim safe-harbor by just showing that most other similarly situated presidents are paid within the same range.

3. Capital Accumulation

Considering privileges such as extensive tax-exemptions and subsidized student loans, some universities have, at least over the last decade, moved into very questionable territory in terms of how they manage their endowments. In total, university endowments nationwide have far surpassed $500 billion, with about three-fourths being held by the most prestigious, eleven percent of universities.[631] Traditional investments for those managing endowments would include US government bonds and other equities, but, in the hunt for more lucrative investments, endowment managers

---

629 Smith, Steven Rathgeb, and Michael Lipsky, *Nonprofits for Hire: The Welfare State in the Age of Contracting* 26 Cambridge, MA: Harvard University Press (1993).

630 Roomkin, Myron J., Burton A. Weisbrod. "Managerial Compensation and Incentives in For-Profit and Nonprofit Hospitals." *Journal of Law, Economics and Organization*, vol. 15, 1999, p. 750–51.

631 Snyder, *Digest of Education Statistics*, *supra* note 43, at Table 333.90; *see also* Saul, *supra* note 175.

have looked toward private equity and hedge funds.[632] These sorts of investments could subject nonprofit universities to UBIT, intermediate sanctions and even, revocation of their tax-exemptions, but universities have made extensive use of "blocker corporations," which are set up in offshore jurisdictions with little or no taxation.[633] Needless to say, universities also provide little or no transparency into their offshore investments. While overall student debt continues to grow at an alarming rate, these endowments are being stockpiled, sometimes even to the extent that they "exceed the gross national product of entire countries."[634]

A 2001 study investigated the relationship between presidential compensation and excess university revenues. Nonprofits derive revenue from funding streams such as individual contributions, grants, fees for the provision of services, government contracts and endowments; nonprofit law is primarily concerned about how these funds are used to compensate employees and others who are close to the organization.[635] Determining whether there is some type of variable pay arrangement for nonprofit administrators is essential in deciding whether there is a violation.[636] Theoretically, both the non-distribution constraint and limitations on funds, such as the restrictions that may be placed on endowments, should serve to keep the executives from being privately inured. The authors of the study, though, found a significant relationship between the size of excess revenue, investments and administrative compensation.[637] If overall revenues were to increase by one percent, their study indicates that an administrator would likely receive an extra $320 in compensation.[638] Further, this trend was even stronger regarding investments; for every one percent uptick in investments, administrators are compensated an additional $626.[639] The authors state that administrative compensation, particularly at nonprofit

632 *Ibid.*

633 *Ibid.*

634 *Ibid.*

635 Frumkin, Peter and Elizabeth Keating. "The Price of Doing Good: Executive Compensation in Nonprofit Organizations." *Hauser Center Working Paper*, 2001. p. 11.

636 "Compensation for Nonprofit Employees." *National Council of Nonprofits*, 23 July 2019, https://www.councilofnonprofits.org/tools-resources/compensation-nonprofit-employees.

637 Frumkin & Keating, *The Price of Doing Good*, *supra* note 635, at 18.

638 *Ibid.*

639 *Ibid.*

universities, is "significantly associated with fixed assets."[640] While the absolute numbers, in terms of variable pay for administrators, are not exactly shocking and the investment of university endowments is not *per se* problematic, the resulting variation in administrators' compensation can open the door to courts questioning potential excess benefit or private inurement.

I. Private, Nonprofit Universities and the Public Benefit

In this part, I described the access issues surrounding private, nonprofit universities in relation to overall access to higher education. Today's level of access is tied directly to the availability of student loans, which can essentially be borrowed by anybody. Thus, access is more a question of affordability. Private, nonprofits were traditionally a more expensive option, leaving public universities as a viable, more cost-effective alternative. Since student loans have lowered the boundaries between institution types, all universities have become more expensive, thus, being less accessible. The number of degrees being issued has certainly increased, but this metric alone is insufficient to say whether the public is benefiting. The public benefit must also be considered in the long-term; today's massive tuition fee bills will eventually come due in the form of massive public debt and a significant part of the population being marginalized by their private debt or both. Regarding access, the university system continues to benefit the public by admitting large swaths of society, but this benefit is limited by the astronomical costs of admission and individual outcomes, depending on which type of institution was attended.

Next, Part I investigated universities' main goals: education, research, certification and social mobility. Private, nonprofit universities continue to provide quality *education* but expose themselves to the risks associated with having too much of a focus on professional training. Professional programs are naturally in demand and helpful for universities to attract students but do not share the same penchant for longevity as humanities-based programs. Universities' extensive focus on *research* should not be geared toward producing patents, but, rather, toward publishing and creating copyrightable content. As it stands, universities still do produce a tremendous amount of copyrightable content, which will be addressed

640 *Ibid.* at 20 (including primary schools, secondary schools, colleges and universities in their definition of "educational institutions").

in further detail in Part II. The university monopoly over *certification* has conferred the public trust upon universities and this should be approached cautiously when asking if the public is being benefited. University rankings correlate with the value of any university's certification of its graduates and how beneficial it will be to them following graduation. Unfortunately, universities' certification of graduates is becoming increasingly disassociated with guarantees of quality education or graduates' capabilities. *Social mobility* remains possible through higher education, but students should be aware of which pathway they are on and how they can develop suitable plans for their individual situations. Universities and other knowledge systems now provide an unprecedented amount of opportunities for individuals to educate themselves and to pursue the American dream but, if approached improperly, many of the interested parties can find themselves buried under crushing debt. There clearly are many variables affecting the public benefit, both negatively and positively, in relation to the university system but, overall, the public benefits from this system immensely.

J. Private, Nonprofit Universities' Legal Structuring and the Public Benefit

Nonprofits' commercial operations, administrative compensation and capital accumulation were observed in light of the non-distribution constraint and numerous tests for nonprofit compliance. Keeping in mind that all private, nonprofit universities are filed and must operate for educational purposes, the example given above of universities competing in NCAA sports raises some serious red flags concerning the commerciality and operational tests. Similarly, high compensation for administrators and variable-pay arrangements for those managing massive amounts of wealth call into question whether the private, nonprofit universities are partaking in private inurement and excess benefit transactions. Unfortunately, these concerns are now more of an academic matter; the IRC safe-harbors and lax enforcement against nonprofits have welcomed all these activities. Because the non-distribution constraint has been weakened, there is effectively no external mechanism remaining to guarantee that students will receive a quality education for a reasonable price.

From a GST standpoint, the linkages between private, nonprofit universities, the other sectors and other types of universities have introduced several incompatible, outside elements into the nonprofits' operations. Government funding has weakened the universities' dependence on endowments thereby forgoing their many positive benefits. Private universities' core goals have also been influenced by outside elements that have driven them to compete in activities that may be done more efficiently by, perhaps, the government or private, for-profit sector. Finally, there has been a large internal shift away from functioning as nonprofits, thus, risking that private, nonprofit universities may become too entangled with the other sectors and lose independence. Their longevity is also at risk. Despite this structural weakening of private, nonprofit universities, the growing number of private institutions that have rejected student lending and eliminated student fees for students from low-income families are returning to the nonprofit model. Their private return to the nonprofit model, despite the lack of external controls, contributes greatly to the public benefit. As shown in these sections, these universities continue to benefit the public but have many shortcomings, so the next section provides approaches toward how the universities can be improved.

K. How Can Private, Nonprofit Universities be Improved through the Law?

Part I demonstrated universities' purposes, their privileges, how the nonprofit sector is organized and how the public can be a beneficiary of this knowledge system. Although they benefit the public, universities are extraordinarily expensive and, thereby, exclusive. This means that there is room for improvement. Through disregard for how these institutions are meant to function, the federal government has misaligned many of the underlying economic incentives. In order to move back into the parameters set by nonprofit law, private universities should seek to cut administrative and non-instructional costs like athletic programs, discourage debt accumulation and encourage personal and family savings. Institutional longevity is best promoted through strong academics and improved student outcomes, whereas low admissions standards and profit maximization lead to the opposite result. The problems surrounding private universities inevitably permeate the rest of higher education; thus, realigning private universities to their model serves not only their interested parties, but the rest of higher education as well.

Dating back all the way to the first founding, universities have enjoyed extraordinary privileges. First, the privilege of academic freedom, i.e. tenure for professors, and right to freedom of speech ought to be protected. As long as private universities continue accepting federal funding, both students and professors should have an actionable right to the First

Amendment's free speech protections on campus. Second, all interested parties must scrutinize tax-exempt gift giving, other privileges relating to tax-exemptions and the extensive subsidies given to universities. Not only must the universities strictly follow the requirements set by law, but law enforcement needs to take a renewed role in overseeing university activities. Third, the safe-harbors written into the law, especially regarding administrators' compensation and excess benefit transactions, need to be seriously reconsidered by Congress. Such rules act to nullify the effect of the non-distribution constraint and its related economic incentives. The neutralization of the non-distribution constraint discourages university attendance and leaves a significant portion of the population unable to access higher education and paywalled first-class academic works, which is discussed further in Part II. Concerning financial support, the federal government's subsidization of higher education has been most catastrophic to those in greatest need of financial aid. If the public goals for supporting these institutions are not being met, the privileges are subject to being restructured within the legal system.

Finally, the privilege to grant degrees remains the most valuable privilege held by universities. Universities have maintained their monopoly, but rising costs and digital alternatives challenge the status quo. Allowing universities the privilege of granting degrees places a tremendous amount of the public trust into these institutions. A degree from a top private university is the gold standard for higher education certification. Prospective students, looking into lower-ranked universities, should be aware of the limited value that some degrees can offer, especially before they take on tens of thousands of dollars in debt. Realizing this, politicians can work to redirect the subsidies, i.e. privileges, to make open access education affordable, without requiring students to take out massive loans. One of many ways to do this would be to shift demand-side subsidies, i.e. student loans, to supply-side subsidies, such as federal grants to the states and municipalities, to fund institutions. Students at private universities could continue to be supported by government grants, university grants, private donations, private loans and, perhaps the most radical proposition of all; these measures, along with cuts to non-instructional spending, could lead to lower, more manageable tuition fees.

GST analyses set out to find constructs and organization at every level and Part I has brought several of them to the forefront. Longevity for university systems is promoted by sustainable financing methods, quality education, tenure and continuing to teach in the humanities. Job training ought not to be the central or sole focus. The most prestigious universities have, in part, solidified their position through extensive research. Research, though, should be a means of promoting knowledge and not seen as a means for improving universities' bottom lines. Taking on massive amounts of debt, individually and collectively, is not a permanent solution to access issues. All institutions should be strictly held to their legal obligations arising in their nonprofit charters and the IRC. Saturating higher education with federal loan money promotes behavior contrary to institutions' legal responsibilities, as federal loans may also contribute to high-risk students being enrolled in higher education to their own detriment. If a student is scholastically unqualified to be enrolled and is admitted anyway, he or she is significantly more likely to be burdened by insurmountable debt. Furthermore, massive amounts of individual debt become a collective problem. Broad access to practically unlimited student loans has already caused a bubble, inflating the costs of higher education. This may very well end up costing the US taxpayers trillions of dollars, notwithstanding the fact that most taxpayers purposefully avoided taking out such loans for themselves! A halt to the issuance of student loans coupled with an adherence to nonprofit principles, promoting both high enrollment rates and affordable tuition fees, would significantly advance the benefit to the public.

Part II: Copyright

Part II seeks to identify the goals of copyright law (*telos*) as observed in its historical and legal development. The goals are most clearly observed through primary sources of law such as the US Constitution, federal statutes, case law as well as congressional commentary. These primary sources of law are further supplemented by secondary sources such as academic books, articles and commentary, which aid in interpreting and understanding copyright law. Once copyright law's purposes are identified this information will be used in Part II's analysis regarding five factors: access to academic materials, copyright in relation to the three major sectors as well as copyright's production, structural and expressive functions.

A. *Introduction*

Copyright is quite difficult to categorize as any particular type of law; while this system comes into constant contact with areas such as contract law, constitutional law, property law and criminal law, it is unlike the others due to its unique function.[641] Some believe that copyright is a monopoly, although that is not entirely accurate. For example, the fair use defense, allowing for certain public uses of copyrighted materials, breaks authors' absolute control over works.[642] If copyright is a monopoly, it is a limited one. Likewise, defining copyright as a property right, granting exclusive domain over creative works, similarly falls short because of the public's ability to use works *fairly*.[643] The ongoing debate leaves copyright's actual nature unsettled. Some even go further to conceptualize it as

641 Kretschmer, Martin, et al. "The History of Copyright History: Notes from an Emerging Discipline." In *Privilege and Property, Essays on the History of Copyright*, edited by Ronan Deazley, Martin Kretschmer, and Lionel Bently, Open Book Publishers, 2010, p. 6 (noting, beyond substantive areas of law, the social norms that copyright comes into contact with: "systems of ascription and control, flows of money, as well as the transfer and sharing of ideas and expression.").

642 *See generally* Bell, Abraham, and Gideon Parchomovsky. "The Dual-Grant Theory of Fair Use." *University of Chicago Law Review*, vol. 83, no. 3, 2016, p. 1053.

643 Netanel, Neil W. *Copyright: What Everyone Needs to Know*. Oxford University Press, 2018, p. 15.

a privilege or an exception to free expression.[644] Copyright is amorphous in that it contains all these qualities without any definitive delineation. Despite there being solid grounds for all of these views, the last decades have been very favorable to the large "copyright-industries" that tend to view copyright as a property right and any infringement thereof as "theft;" their influence on modern copyright legislation and litigation has been substantial.[645]

It is no coincidence that copyright law, as we perceive it, did not exist prior to the invention of the printing press. At that time, the means of recording information were neither capable of being mass-produced nor were they likely to be widely distributed. The "clay tablets, stone, metal plates, wood, papyrus, animal skins, parchment" and other traditional media upon which words were first transcribed were, to a great degree, inaccessible and could only be painstakingly reproduced by hand.[646] In addition to the difficulties with copying, transporting and preserving texts, there were also substantial challenges with regard to guaranteeing the accuracy of any given text, especially because texts were so rare.[647] Print media revolutionized this and, today, the revolution continues with the ability to digitally copy, cut, paste, make screenshots, digitally edit and share. The digital revolution originally came with the promise that the Internet would democratize access to knowledge but, as will be shown in Part II, much of this promise remains unfulfilled due to excessive copyright and technical controls over content.

Some of the oldest texts in our collective patrimony have likely survived because they were literally written in stone, but their degree of permanence was matched neither in terms of overall availability nor with regard

644 Bell, Tom W. "Copyright as Intellectual (Property) Privilege." *Syracuse Law Review*, vol. 58, 2008, p. 524; Nimmer, Melville. "Does Copyright Abridge the First Amendment Guarantees of Free Speech and Press." *UCLA Law Review*, vol. 17, no. 6, June 1970, pp. 1180–1204; Nimmer & Nimmer, *Nimmer on Copyright*, *supra* note 71, at vol. 5, §§ A. 05, 19E.02 (explaining the importance of classifications within the law in that they not only "structure our thought," but also can lead to different practical outcomes when we are working within different analytical frameworks).

645 Netanel, Neil W. *Copyright's Paradox*. Oxford University Press, 2010, p. 7.

646 Dallon, Craig W. "The Problem with Congress and Copyright Law: Forgetting the Past and Ignoring the Public Interest." *Santa Clara Law Review*, vol. 44, no. 1, 2004, p. 377.

647 *Ibid.* at 378.

to accessibility.[648] Most works from the thousands of years preceding the printing press have unfortunately been lost due to war and neglect, but some classics have survived.[649] It is likely that the few surviving works were in relatively greater circulation, which increased their chances of survival.[650] Despite the obvious differences, early works share an essential characteristic with today's print and electronic media: they are "fixed" into a tangible medium. As will be discussed below, fixation is a cornerstone of copyright, which facilitates knowledge preservation. Knowledge and innovation are also advanced with the use of new media: there were millennia between the first writings and the printing press, centuries between the printing press and Internet, seventeen years between the Internet and search engines and many leaps in the years since.[651] As soon as the printing press was invented, knowledge was fixed into the printed format far quicker than the world had ever seen. This naturally led to a greater dissemination of works, increased access to knowledge, major social advances and, eventually, the need for copyright laws.[652]

Technology and transportation have also served to democratize access to knowledge. Obvious examples of these are the printing press, improved postal services and boats, planes, trains and automobiles. More efficient communication networks were the means by which pre-Enlightenment

---

648 Take, for example, the Rosetta Stone, which was discovered in the late eighteenth century, allowing researchers to compare a Greek text with a direct translation of the same text in ancient Egyptian hieroglyphics; this text, carved into stone thousands of years before, allowed for the translation of an otherwise indecipherable ancient language. Had it not been for this engraving, this knowledge may have been lost forever.

649 Wagner, Bettina, and Marcia Reed. *Early Printed Books as Material Objects: Proceedings of the Conference Organized by the IFLA Rare Books and Manuscripts Section, Munich, 19–21 August 2009*. International Federation of Library Associations, 2010, pp. 1–3.

650 Mokyr, *Gifts of Athena*, *supra* note 12, at 8.

651 Darnton, *supra* note 543, at 23, 131; *see also* Loren, Lydia Pallas. "Fixation as Notice in Copyright." *Boston University Law Review*, vol. 96, 2016, p. 961 (noting that modern technology has caused a boom in the quantity of materials that are fixed into tangible medium and that are likely subject to copyright).

652 *See* Kretschmer et al., *The History of Copyright History*, *supra* note 641, at 3 (distinguishing the major periods in the development of copyright: "Invention of printing press (ca. 1450); Feudal regime of printing privileges (Venice late fifteenth century; imperial fairs c15-c17); Stationers' companies (Basel 1531; London 1557); First Statues (England 1710; US 1790); Author Rights (France 1791/1793; Prussia 1837; UK 1842); Berne Convention (1886).").

"associational societies" could communicate effectively.[653] The majority of rural households in the late nineteenth century, when radio, television, film, Internet and music recording were unheard of, would not have even possessed a book or newspaper.[654] Instead of being engulfed by such grueling boredom, today's rural inhabitants are in many ways just as connected as their metropolitan peers. They can access half a billion websites and read newspapers from around the world. Geography no longer is a restriction. Rather, copyright, licensing and technological controls over content are now at the forefront of the discussion regarding access issues. There is no question that general access to knowledge is better today than at any previous time, but the best access is limited to those in universities and other institutions with access to all the top databases. The public, which is meanwhile financing the lion's share of research subsidies and universities, is locked out. The reality is that even the best search engines cannot compete with paywalled databases in providing access to first-class works; those who are dependent on open search engines are left using second-class works.

Copyright, being a system meant to drive creative expression and vibrant democratic values, aided in the formation of mass-media conglomerates over the last decades in radio, television, film, music and publishing. These conglomerates tend to produce relatively "homogenous," inoffensive content, geared to the sensibilities of the largest demographics within their markets.[655] Naturally, traditional media adds value to their content through their access to resources for journalists, access to experts, higher production quality and editorial standards. Although, now with Internet communications, artists, writers, bloggers and authors have essentially no barriers to entering the collective discourse. This not only changes *who* is publishing, but *what* they are publishing and *how* they are publishing it. As a matter of course, this has created a new interplay between traditional mass-media outlets and their Internet competitors. With declining traditional media, the new voices entering the marketplace of ideas are stronger and louder than ever before, but they still are resource-dependent and require stable means of finance for their endeavors; this is not to mention the implications that their involvement will have on fair use principles.

Of all the portals within the Internet, perhaps video streaming services are one of the most revolutionary elements of the modern, digital revolu-

653 Mokyr, *Culture of Growth*, *supra* note 13, at 42.
654 Pinker, *supra* note 6, at 260.
655 Netanel, *Copyright's Paradox*, *supra* note 645, at 39.

tion. While video lectures are still often tucked away behind universities' paywalls, many websites such as YouTube, Vimeo, Dailymotion, The Internet Archive, and some MOOCs provide open access to seemingly endless amounts of video, audio and texts. Denouncing the common myth that such platforms are only useful for "cute cat videos," one professor stated that:

> … [t]here's a technological revolution; it's a deep one. The technological revolution is online video and audio, immediately accessible to everyone all over the world. And, so, what that's done, it turned the spoken word into a tool that has the same reach as the printed word. So, it's a Gutenberg revolution in a domain of video and audio. That might be even deeper than the original Gutenberg revolution, because it isn't obvious how many people can read, but lots of people can listen.... You've got a little bit of that with TV, you've got a little bit with radio, but there was bandwidth limitations that were really stringent, especially in TV where you could get thirty seconds, if you were lucky, and six minutes, if you were stellar, to elucidate a complicated argument.... Everything gets compressed to a kind of oversimplified entertainment. But, now, all the sudden, we have this forum for long-form discussion, real long-form discussion. And, it turns out that everybody is way smarter than we thought. We can have these discussions publicly and there is a great hunger for that.[656]

Perhaps this technological boom was not inevitable; technological advances have sprouted up and fizzled out throughout history in every corner of the world, but the outgrowth of technology and innovation in the West has clearly been a success due to the ability to sustain it and continue building upon past progress.[657] The university system, as discussed in Part I, and copyright, the focus of Part II, are both knowledge systems, providing a stable foundation for the growth of knowledge and innovation.

This second part will delve into the historical development of copyright in the US, its theoretical underpinnings, its inner workings, its relationship with international copyright treaties, exceptions and alternatives. Copyright is a system meant to advance societal progress through promoting authorship and, thereby, increasing overall innovation. Copyright has

---

656 "The Joe Rogan Experience #1139 Interview with Jordan Peterson, Prof. of Psychology, University of Toronto." *YouTube*, 2 July 2018, www.youtube.com/watch?time_continue=1&v=9Xc7DN-noAc.

657 Mokyr, *Culture of Growth*, *supra* note 13, at 339.

three major functions—the production function, structural function and expressive function—that will be the lynchpin for this section's analysis, answering the question: is copyright benefiting the public and, if so, is it doing so in accordance with its legal structuring?[658] Once the system is explained and its functional problems are identified, some means for improvement will be discussed. There is substantial overlap between the realms of nonprofit universities and copyright, both being GST open systems, so this section is framed in the context of that close relationship. Finally, most writing on copyright tends to focus narrowly on a select-few important cases that shed some light on very specific aspects of copyright.[659] Judges also avoid weighing copyright against the First Amendment of the US Constitution and opt rather for narrow, technical decisions within copyright.[660] Such extensive focus on narrow sub-issues usually leads to piecemeal case law and proposals for reform. In contrast to this narrow approach, which loses sight of copyright's big picture, Part II approaches copyright law more holistically in its description and assessment of the system.

B. History

Copyright protection in the US is one of Congress' constitutionally enumerated powers. Copyright law is found primarily at the federal level, is codified in the US Code and has an extensive common law development, which continues to evolve. Today's stringent copyright regime has its

---

658 Netanel elucidated these three functions. *See generally* Netanel, *Copyright's Paradox*, *supra* note 645.

659 *See e.g.*, AIME v. Regents of the University of California, No. 2:10-cv-09378-CBM (D. Ca. 2012) (dismissing plaintiffs' claims that UCLA classroom video streaming was copyright infringement); Cambridge University Press v. Patton, 16-15726 (11th Cir. 2018) (ruling that the majority of plaintiffs' claims that defendant, Georgia State University, violated plaintiffs' copyrights were, rather, protected by fair use. Defendant had various course materials saved on its electronic reserve system at the university); Kirtsaeng v. John Wiley & Sons, Inc., 568 U.S. 519 (2013) (deciding that copies of books bought abroad and then resold in the US were not a copyright infringement. The Supreme Court based their decision on the First Sale Doctrine); Authors Guild v. HathiTrust, 755 F.3d 87 (2d Cir. 2014) (permitting defendant's keyword indexing system that enabled works to be found in search engines).

660 Abrams, Howard B., and Tyler T. Ochoa. *The Law of Copyright*. West, 2018, § 1: 23.

roots in the numerous controls on publication implemented by English sovereigns, legislation by the US Congress as well as some international treaties. Throughout the course of time, differing underlying policies encouraged the implementation of copyright. Looking back at early English copyright law aids in understanding modern copyright in the US. Going even further back to study the precursors to copyright, especially those in England, contributes a fuller picture of how restrictions on publication serve sovereigns' ends, affect the creation and dissemination of knowledge and act to benefit the public.[661] These precursors to modern copyright law were in no way meant to recognize individual authors' rights or any of the other modern justifications for copyright. Instead, they were *ad hoc* grants of exclusive privilege to publishers to print and sell their books. Out of the centuries of evolution, two predominant premises for copyright protection have emerged in the West: the *authors' rights tradition* and the *public benefit tradition*.

Far from England, the first exclusive privileges for printing were granted in Venice. It was the Venetian Republic, in 1496 that granted the first privilege to a German printer for a term of five years.[662] Similar to the privileges granted to academics, as discussed in Part I, printing privileges were designed to meet specific ends. The Venetians wished to attract skilled professionals and to support new industries. Through the grants of privileges, they wished to foster innovation and entrepreneurship. If a new type of industry was sprouting elsewhere, it was likely that the sovereigns would take measures to make their cities more attractive. Privileges came in many forms; other sovereigns and popes who were envious of the Venetians may have granted privileges ranging "from the rights to immigrate and settle in the city, the cancellation of debts, granting immunity from prosecution for criminal offences, or, in the case of those holding papal office, even the promise of an absolution of specific sins."[663] Notably, the Venetian printing privileges were grants made to individuals as a means of

661 Dallon, *supra* note 646, at 371–76 (exploring the ancient Roman system of compensating authors for their manuscripts, the Jewish law tradition of encouraging accurate copying of religious texts and an early Irish dispute over the copying of a manuscript; none of these instances could be directly compared to today's copyright issues, but they do share similarities).

662 Kostylo, *supra* note 540, at 22–25 (noting that the exclusive privileges for printing were similar to privileges granted to other trades. Furthermore, as was done in many forms of merchandise, books were treated in the same way and valued by their weight).

663 *Ibid.* at 35–36, 41.

"municipal protectionism" whereas later systems, such as England's, were guild or trade monopolies made for the purpose of controlling printing and, thereby, the flow of information.[664]

The English system of printing privileges arose in the sixteenth and seventeenth centuries. Even earlier in the fourteenth century, though, when texts were copied and bound by hand, a number of related trades began to arise in London, namely the *stationers*.[665] Stationers, working alongside the other trades such as *limners* and *binders*, were generally involved in the making and trading of books.[666] Following the creation of the printing press, printers became a distinctive trade of their own; the stationers' major function then became the buying and selling of books. In 1533, the Tudors granted the stationers the oversight of all book sales and purchases.[667] This early means of regulation was very different to modern copyright law, but examining its nature is useful in understanding modern copyright, especially with its interrelationship with free speech principles.

The stationers were granted an exclusive right to "make orders, to charge fees, to settle industrial disputes, to supervise the education of apprentices, to search and destroy books printed in contravention of any statute, act or proclamation."[668] As mentioned above, the crown's goals were not to protect authors or promote the public benefit. Rather, the crown wished to "prevent publication of treasonable, seditious, or heretical books," while identifying the printers and authors of distasteful works as well as furthering other governmental objectives.[669] By granting the stationers the power to oversee the printing, binding, publishing and dealing trades, the English crown essentially outsourced its authority to this private society. Thus, all printing was required to be licensed or registered with the stationers, even in cases of printers receiving special privileges directly from the crown.[670]

The only presses permitted in England were in London, Oxford and Cambridge. In periods of political turmoil, increased scrutiny was applied

---

664 *Ibid.* at 39.

665 Fielding, David, and Shef Rogers. "Monopoly Power in the Eighteenth-Century British Book Trade." *European Review of Economic History*, vol. 21, no. 4, 12 May 2017, p. 395.

666 *Ibid.*

667 Holdsworth, W. S. "Press Control and Copyright in the 16th and 17th Centuries." *Yale Law Journal*, vol. 19, 1920, p. 842.

668 *Ibid.* at 843.

669 *Ibid.*

670 Fielding, *supra* note 665, at 395.

to the presses while the stationers were empowered to search printers' and dealers' premises for unlicensed materials.[671] The stationers protected the interests of their trade and secured "against the importation of objectionable books from abroad," while stoking concerns that unlicensed materials could be dangerous to religious and state institutions in their numerous petitions to Parliament.[672] The control of printing and dissemination of printed materials by the stationers and the crown resulted in the crown's absolute control over the public discourse on all matters concerning the state. Not only were printed materials pertaining to politics highly regulated, but, due to individual patentees holding the privileges to print other useful books, the monopolies over printing and lack of competition from abroad often led to scholars only having access to poorly printed books.[673]

Other precursors to copyright were the practices of associations such as The Republic of Letters, which sought to create a culture of exchange and openness. Once knowledge was disbursed, creators or authors would be credited with their works or discoveries, but were not allowed to exclude others from using the works.[674] Eventually, by the late seventeenth century, scientists began depositing sealed envelopes with their findings by their academies prior to publication, ensuring that they would be credited. This credit, though, led to no direct financial benefit as is contemplated by modern copyright law. Rather, authors would later benefit indirectly from their enhanced reputations.[675] Informal cultural protection of songs, myths, knowledge and artistic works also served as another precursor to copyright. Many of these cultural heritage items were and continue to be in the "common possession" of local communities.[676] It was only with the first rudimentary copyright laws that authors had legally protected interests in their works.[677]

---

671 Holdsworth, *supra* note 667, at 848.

672 *Ibid.* at 849–50.

673 *Ibid.* at 853, 56.

674 Mokyr, *Culture of Growth*, *supra* note 13, at 201 (describing that successful authors would be credited by association of their name to their idea, such as the "Boyle's Law" dyad).

675 Mokyr, *Culture of Growth*, *supra* note 13, at 201.

676 Lawrence, John Shelton., and Bernard Timberg. *Fair Use and Free Inquiry: Copyright Law and the New Media*. Ablex, 1980, p. 6.

677 Mokyr, *Culture of Growth*, *supra* note 13, at 202. (noting the difference between copyright and patent protection, where, although both put new knowledge into the public domain, patent protection strictly prohibits implementation of the knowledge).

The English Copyright Act of 1710, otherwise known as the Statute of Anne, marked a distinct moment in the history of copyright; this is generally regarded as the starting point of modern copyright law.[678] A number of Parliament's *ad hoc* privilege statutes lapsing by the year 1695 facilitated this transition.[679] Cultural changes also played a major part in this transition. England, at this time, had a rapidly developing "bourgeois public sphere," there were regular parliamentary elections, open hostility to the stationers' monopoly, distain for controls over the press and increased regard for authors and the free circulation of their ideas.[680] This is also a pivotal moment where knowledge was encouraged to be disbursed so that new theories could be developed on existing technologies. Previously, most techniques and technologies would have been kept secret by the various guilds.[681] These factors all contributed to an exponential growth in the number of printers and publications; prior to 1695, there had only been one London newspaper, and, upon the removal of the monopoly, five new newspapers were founded in that month alone.[682] Despite an orchestrated counter-campaign by the stationers and the Church of England, the Statute of Anne revolutionized printing in England.

A major feature of the Statute of Anne was that it shifted proprietary interests in literary works from the stationers and other trades to the authors.[683] Limits on the term of copyright were also a new feature, granting terms of twenty-one years for books already in print along with a term of fourteen years for new books, with the possibility of renewal.[684] Perhaps most important was that the statute listed no restraints on publication and, to the contrary, it sought to protect authors' rights which had previously not been observed.[685] This statute, with the phase for "the encouragement of learning" in its title, is a direct response to the censorship and suppres-

678 An Act for the Encouragement of Learning 1710, 8 Anne, ch. 19 (Gr. Brit.); *see also* Holdsworth, *supra* note 667, at 857.

679 Deazley, Ronan. *On the Origin of the Right to Copy: Charting the Movement of Copyright Law in Eighteenth-Century Britain (1695-1775)*. Hart Publishing, 2004, pp. 1–10.

680 Rose, Mark. "The Public Sphere and the Emergence of Copyright." In *Privilege and Property, Essays on the History of Copyright*, edited by Ronan Deazley, Martin Kretschmer, and Lionel Bently, Open Book Publishers, 2010, p. 81.

681 McSherry, *supra* note 15, at 209 (transitioning from individualism to a system where "public knowledge could be mobilized on behalf of state and society").

682 Deazley, *supra* note 679, at 11–12.

683 An Act for the Encouragement of Learning 1710, 8 Anne, ch. 19 (Gr. Brit.).

684 *Ibid.*

685 *Ibid.*; Rose, *Public Sphere*, *supra* note 680, at 83.

sion of past licensing regimes.[686] With its clear purpose of encouraging knowledge and learning, it substituted "the individual for the state as the party in need of redress."[687] Authors' ability to protect their works, though, still came secondary to the Statute of Anne's primary goal of making "useful books" available.[688] In addition to stimulating academic works and speech in the public sphere, the Statute of Anne conceptualized copyright as a right applying automatically to authors, and no longer as a special grant of permission or privilege.[689] It is also notable that it applied only to books; this is, of course, a stark contrast to the many media forms covered by modern copyright law.

The North American British colonies also engaged in a similar system of printing privilege, but the social conditions and political atmosphere created a noticeably different regime than that which arose in England.[690] The first press in the American colonies was founded in Cambridge, Massachusetts in 1638. Due to its public patronage, it was subject to the supervision of and suppression by the Massachusetts authorities.[691] The authorities, interested in promoting civil and religious cohesion, copied the English method to oversee printing, albeit in a crude manner. Despite it not being very encompassing, the Massachusetts system was the most similar colonial system to the regime in England. Even as England unraveled its system of printing privileges, the American colonies continued to implement restrictions over printing sporadically and inconsistently well into the second half of the eighteenth century. The most restrictive controls on printing were "prior restraints," either prohibiting or controlling printing before its occurrence, but the prior restraints were generally phased out in favor of post-publication sanctions by the time of the American Revolution.[692] While printing privileges were still occasionally being granted, there was no semblance of copyright law in the colonies. Furthermore,

---

686 *Ibid.*

687 *Ibid.*

688 Dallon, *supra* note 646, at 409.

689 Baldwin, Peter. *The Copyright Wars Three Centuries of Trans-Atlantic Battle*. Princeton University Press, 2016, p. 66.

690 Bracha, Oren. "Early American Printing Privileges." In *Privilege and Property, Essays on the History of Copyright*, edited by Ronan Deazley, Martin Kretschmer, and Lionel Bently, Open Book Publishers, 2010, p. 90.

691 Roden, Robert F. *The Cambridge Press, 1638-1692; a History of the First Printing Press Established in English America, Together with a Bibliographical List of the Issues of the Press*. Dodd, Mead, and Company, 1905, p. 52.

692 Bracha, *supra* note 690, at 92–95.

even once the 1710 Statute of Anne was enacted in England, it was not applicable to the colonies.[693]

There are several reasons why the privilege system never took root in the American colonies. Perhaps the simplest explanation is that there were no guilds in the English sense and therefore, the colonial governments were neither lobbied by nor aided by them in the oversight of printing.[694] Colonial governments also had very little need for intermediaries because there were so few printers for them to regulate; by 1775, there were only fifty printing houses throughout the colonies that would soon form the US.[695] It was also common practice among the printing houses to make private contractual agreements to abstain from printing each other's materials.[696] This self-regulation was furthered by an informal social norm among the relatively few printers, acknowledging that it was in all of their self-interests to abstain from directly competing with each other in their local markets.[697] Finally due to the focus at this time on printing "governmental documents, religious materials and local histories," the markets were very much localized, thus, limiting the threat of competition *via* inter-colonial trade.[698] Of the few colonial privileges that were granted, they were, like previously in England, exclusive rights to print and had nothing to do with rights of the individual authors.

The US' break from Britain following the Revolutionary War also marked a turnaround in how printed works were conceptualized in the US. Within only a few years, all the rights in particular creative works were shifted to the authors.[699] These protections for authors were first implemented in copyright statutes by state legislatures. The overwhelming majority of states passed such statutes, which were quite similar in substance to the English Statute of Anne.[700] Not long after, the US Constitution would be ratified, enshrining the protection of IP at the federal level and paving the way for a regime to facilitate the flow of knowledge in a "new industrialized market society."[701] The theoretical foundations for

693 *Ibid.* at 97.

694 *Ibid.*

695 Parkinson, Robert G. "Print, the Press, and the American Revolution." *Oxford Research Encyclopedia of American History*, 3 Sept. 2015, p. 1.

696 Bracha, *supra* note 690, at 98.

697 Parkinson, *supra* note 695, at 2–3.

698 Bracha, *supra* note 690, at 98, 100.

699 *Ibid.* at 103.

700 *Ibid.* at 110.

701 *Ibid.* at 114.

copyright law in the US, as explained below, are also substantially different from those in Europe, although the two have grown closer because of international treaties.

The continental European approach toward copyright is premised on a natural rights theory. Under this theory, authors have an inherent right over their works, like real or personal property ownership, which is not premised on the fulfillment of some prerequisite formality.[702] This is referred to as the *authors' rights tradition*. Natural rights, such as these, are not granted by copyright laws, but, rather, are separate from and preexistent

702 Continental European moral rights share a philosophical foundation with the writings of Immanuel Kant, who emphasized the inalienable personal rights of authors over their works, even being able to assert control over those who hold the economic rights. Countries such as Germany and France, representing the continental civil law tradition, allow authors to assert personality, moral, economic and natural rights. Civil law countries tend to treat creative works as an extension of authors' personalities; the French *droits d'auteur* ("rights of authors") puts authors' personal and economic rights into central focus. Moral rights, derived from the French *droit moral*, concern authors' ability to control works, once they are published for the rights of *integrity* and *attribution*. The moral right of integrity allows authors to prohibit uses of their works that negatively affect their reputations or that detract from their "artistic conception." Attribution, as a moral right, requires proper citation to authors' works and acknowledgment of their contributions. Moral rights, while attaching to authors' personalities, just as a defamation cause of action would for example, are separable from their rights to economic exploitation; even if a publisher acquires a work's economic rights, the author still may subsequently assert their moral rights. *See* Kant, Immanuel. "Von Der Unrechtmassigkeit Des Buchernachdruckes." In *Immanuel Kants Werke*, edited by Ernst Cassirer, 1913; Kretschmer et al., *The History of Copyright History*, *supra* note 641, at 4; Keyes, A.A. *Fair Use and Free Inquiry: Copyright Law and the New Media*. Ablex, 1980, p. 212; Netanel, *Copyright: What Everyone Needs to Know*, *supra* note 643, at 48–49, 166–67 (explaining that many countries, especially former European colonies and Japan, have followed the European authors' rights model. The UK, Australia and Canada have characteristics of both the US and continental European systems. Furthermore, developing countries tend to have relatively weak copyright protection and enforcement for philosophical reasons on ownership, sometimes to gain cheap access to works from other countries and, sometimes, because local pirating industries can also be a source of profit. Furthermore, while the US expressly avoided adopting moral rights with its ascension to the Berne Convention, the domestic laws were made at least minimally compliant by removing the formalities for copyright and through other means of protection for authors' works, namely laws against unfair competition, defamation and those protecting privacy).

to such laws.[703] This approach gives authors stronger property interests in their works, but, in contrast to the goals of real property, exclusion is not the goal. Rather, a limited monopoly is the means by which works can be shared and authors can receive compensation.[704] Supporting the assertion that the US does not have a natural rights basis for copyright is the fact that there have always been term limits and there were once formal notice and mandatory deposit requirements, while up until 1891 foreigners could not receive copyright protection.[705] Before the US began protecting foreign works, it was a "pirate nation" itself.[706] Eventually, the US developed a strong domestic regime, which would protect foreign works as well as moving further in the direction of the authors' rights tradition.[707]

C. The Means and Ends of US Copyright

The US Constitution grants Congress the authority to protect authors' works. The Constitution states: "the Congress shall have the power... to promote the Progress of Science and useful Arts, by securing for limited Times to Authors and Inventors the exclusive Right to their respective Writings and Discoveries."[708] Since the Constitution's drafting, "Writings and Discoveries" have been protected by the *means* of federal copyright and patent law, respectively. While the Copyright Clause expressly enumerates Congress' power to legislate in pursuance of "Progress," its text gives little direction as to what the *ends* of copyright protection ought to be.[709] Although, rewards for authorship are less of a priority than the over-

---

703 Netanel, *Copyright: What Everyone Needs to Know*, *supra* note 643, at 94.

704 Kemp, *supra* note 31, at 828.

705 Netanel, *Copyright: What Everyone Needs to Know*, *supra* note 643, at 95.

706 Lessig, Lawrence. *The Future of Ideas: the Fate of the Commons in a Connected World*. Random House, 2003, p. 106.

707 Netanel, *Copyright: What Everyone Needs to Know*, *supra* note 643, at 96.

708 U.S. Const. art. I, § 8, cl. 8; *see also* Nimmer & Nimmer, *Nimmer on Copyright*, *supra* note 71, at vol. 1, § 1. 09 (suggesting that there may also be a basis for federal copyright protection under the Commerce Clause, art. I, § 8, cl. 3, perhaps for works that commercially affect interstate commerce, but that are not necessarily helpful for the "Progress of Science").

709 Lessig, Lawrence. *Free Culture: the Nature and Future of Creativity*. Penguin, 2004, p. 131 (referring to art. I, § 8, cl. 8. as the "Progress Clause," while others have also referred to it as the "Intellectual Property Clause" or "Copyright and Patent Clause").

all public benefit.[710] Advances in technology and the many accompanying competing interests are to be weighed by Congress when determining an appropriate copyright policy and in enacting legislation. In cases of ambiguity, the courts are left to carefully determine the meaning of constitutional provisions or legislative enactments.[711] The Supreme Court has also played a role in determining the means and ends of the Copyright Clause.

In *Golan v. Holder*, the Supreme Court looked into the aims of the Copyright Clause.[712] First looking at the part, "to promote the Progress of Science and useful Arts," the Court states, somewhat counterintuitively, "Congress' copyright authority is tied to the Progress of Science" and "its patent authority, to the progress of the useful Arts."[713] The Court recognized that the ends of copyright, the "Progress of Science," is furthered through the creation and dissemination of knowledge.[714] Not every copyright provision need "operate to induce new works," but the Copyright Clause generally empowers Congress to create IP regimes that, in its judgment, are well-suited to carry out the Clause's ends.[715] The ends, i.e. the progress of science, are not satisfied merely with the *creation* of new works.[716] Rather, the Court cited evidence that "*dissemination*—as opposed to *creation*—was viewed as an appropriate means to promote science."[717] This is why the federal copyright regime, at least until 1976, incentivized dissemination, not just creation, by granting protection only once works were published.[718]

Although the drafters of the US Constitution left relatively little contemporary record of their rationale in creating the Constitution's Copyright Clause, the Federalist Papers, the arguments made by the drafters in favor of the Constitution's ratification, do provide a source of direct insight. James Madison stated the following in Federalist Paper No. 43: "... [t]he copyright of authors has been solemnly adjudged, in Great Britain, to be a right of common law.... The public good fully coincides... with the

710 Nimmer & Nimmer, *Nimmer on Copyright*, *supra* note 71, at vol. 1, § 1. 03.
711 Sony Corp. of America v. Universal City Studios, Inc., 464 U.S. 417, 430–33 (1984).
712 Golan v. Holder, 565 U.S. 302, 324–27 (2012).
713 *Ibid.* at 302, 324.
714 *Ibid.* at 302, 324–25.
715 *Ibid.* at 302, 325.
716 *Ibid.*
717 *Ibid.* at 302, 326.
718 *Ibid.*

claims of individuals."[719] This is often interpreted to mean that it was the drafters' intention to promote a progressive society with published creative works, beneficial to both author and society as a whole.[720] Furthermore, Madison's "public good" is thought to be a result of incentives to publish, whereas the opposite would occur if authors were afforded no protection for their works, and, thus, held them privately.[721] Finally, it should be noted that "the Progress of Science" may be used interchangeably with the terms the progress of *knowledge* or of *learning*.[722]

Throughout the development of copyright in the US, one can see significant and continuous growth in the scope and duration of these rights. The Copyright Act of 1790, signed into law by President Washington, was the US' first copyright statute; it also substantially resembled the British Statute of Anne.[723] Its scope was limited to only maps, charts and books. Authors were required to first register their works with federal courts and provide notice before publishing. Once the works were registered and published, they received a fourteen-year term of protection that could be renewed only once at the end of the first term.[724] Only around five percent of copyrightable works were registered during this era, and far fewer were renewed.[725] This "two-part copyright regime," requiring an initial registration and later renewal, was designed to promote the flow of works into the public domain.[726]

The American system can be described as utilitarian, seeking primarily to encourage the dissemination of knowledge; protection for authors' economic interests is only afforded as a means of promoting authorship and publication.[727] In other words, authors deriving profits from their works is only a means of promoting publication, not the end in and of

719 Madison, James. "The Federalist Papers: No. 43." *The Avalon Project*, 2008, avalon.law.yale.edu/18th_century/fed43.asp.

720 Kosturakis, Irene. "Intellectual Property 101." *Texas Journal of Business Law*, vol. 46, no. 1, 2014, p. 39.

721 *Ibid.*

722 Loren, *supra* note 651, at 939.

723 Copyright Act of 1790, 1 Stat. 124 (1790).

724 *Ibid.*

725 Lessig, *Free Culture*, *supra* note 709, at 133–34.

726 *Ibid.* at 135 (recognizing that the subsequent removal of registration and renewal has effectively resulted in a tripling of the copyright terms, from an average of 32.2 years in 1973 to ninety-five years today).

727 McSherry, *supra* note 15, at 93 (noting, though, that when authorship is not so easily identifiable, perhaps in cases of employer / employee situations, courts in the US are more likely to inquire further into authors' contributions).

itself. While some suggest, along the lines of John Locke's writing, that a natural right arises when authors take crude ideas and transform them into original works, copyright law in the US has, instead, traditionally been oriented toward the *public benefit tradition*.[728] The public benefit tradition has the goal of "enlarging the public domain."[729] Copyright rights in the US also deviate from the natural rights theory in that they are almost fully alienable and assignable.[730] Although, with its ratification of the Berne Convention in the early 1990's, the US had to conform its domestic statutes to the stronger international regime of authors' rights while simultaneously using the Convention as a new mechanism to protect its massive copyright industries abroad.[731] This has had the effect of American copyright taking on significant amounts of characteristics that are typical within the authors' rights tradition.[732]

With the Copyright Clause's purpose in mind, copyright serves a *production function*, encouraging authorship and dissemination of creative works, a *structural function*, providing a means of financial support, and an *expressive function*, using the heightened regard for constitutional provisions to support the principles of free expression.[733] These three functions will be at the center of this dissertation's assessment as to copyright's contributions toward the progress of science. While there are other functions

---

728 Netanel, *Copyright: What Everyone Needs to Know*, *supra* note 643, at 95; *see* Locke, John. "Second Treatise on Government, Chapter V of Property" *John Locke – Second Treatise on Government*, 1690, http://libertyonline.hypermall.com/Locke/second/second-frame.html, p. 27 (stating:

... the grass my horse has bit, the turfs my servant has cut, and the ore I have digged in any place, where I have a right to them in common with others, become my property without the assignation or consent of anybody. The labour that was mine, removing them out of that common state they were in, hath fixed my property in them.).

729 Baldwin, *supra* note 689, at 72.

730 *Ibid.* (mentioning that copyright holders, who are not the authors, enjoy almost every right that authors would except for, in the past, when term-renewal was standard and in the narrow remaining instance where renewal is still possible).

731 *Ibid.* at 384–85; *but see* Peifer, Karl-Nikolaus. "The Return of the Commons – Copyright History as a Common Source." In *Privilege and Property, Essays on the History of Copyright*, edited by Ronan Deazley, Martin Kretschmer, and Lionel Bently, Open Book Publishers, 2010, p. 348 (describing the reverse-effect that Anglo-American copyright law has had on continental European law following the implementation of the TRIPS Agreement, WIPO treaties and others that have exercised a "property-based" influence on the European systems).

732 Dallon, *supra* note 646, at 366.

733 Netanel, *Copyright's Paradox*, *supra* note 645, at 81.

for copyright law in other traditions, promoting the public welfare by means of creating incentives for publication is the central goal within the US, UK and generally within the common law tradition.[734] Even the word "copyright," the terminology used in common law countries, "has through time become associated with the work and disassociated from the author."[735] Following statutory amendments over the last decades in the US, copyright protection has expanded far beyond *copying*, now encompassing many other uses and means of access.

The first expansion of the scope, in 1802, gave protection to etchings and engravings and the term of protection was stretched to twenty-eight years.[736] With new emerging media forms and means of distribution, copyright followed this general tendency to become broader in scope and longer in duration over the many decades, culminating in the Copyright Act of 1976 and its amendments; this is the modern regime. Registration and renewal requirements were effectively extinguished by 1992, removing all procedure and making copyright automatic.[737] Essentially all creative works fixed into a tangible medium today are automatically copyright protected regardless of the medium and the authors' intentions.[738] While the original copyright laws just prohibited *copying*, the modern regime has been broadened to also prohibit the creation of *derivative works* such as translations and adaptations.[739] The growth in copyright protection may nowadays exceed the bounds of what is necessary to incentivize authorship and dissemination of creative works.

As mentioned in the Part I, public goods are both non-rivalrous and non-excludable. Part I noted that higher education itself is not a public good, despite contributing indirectly to some public goods. Is knowledge, i.e. the content of our copyrightable academic works, a public good? In

---

734 Peifer, *supra* note 731, at 355 (describing, within the continental European context, how the "authenticity function" serves to protect both authors and the public from plagiarism).

735 Keyes, *supra* note 702.

736 2 Stat. 171 (1802); 4 Stat. 36 (1831).

737 Lessig, *Free Culture*, *supra* note 709, at 136–37.

738 Baldwin, *supra* note 689, at 4–7 (mentioning that the growth in scope and applicability of intellectual property protection has also run opposite to the declining protections for real property; where copyrighted materials go untaxed, protection is automatically granted and the growing number of protected media continuously receive longer terms of protection, claims to real property are conversely limited by titles, taxes, and a growing body of regulations and zoning codes).

739 Lessig, *Free Culture*, *supra* note 709, at 136.

terms of its rivalrous nature, one's "consumption" of knowledge in no way impedes other peoples' access to it or affects its scarcity. Much to the contrary, once a creative work is released, it likely that it will be copied and shared with other potential users. Relatedly, creative works are "imperfectly excludable," because their intangible nature makes accessing, copying, sharing and otherwise controlling them significantly more difficult than other forms of personal and real property.[740] Because of its non-rivalrous and non-excludable nature, knowledge can be considered a public good.[741] Of course, some types of creative works require substantial amounts of resources for their creation, so economic free-riding may result in underproduction of goods that cannot be restricted.[742]

Copyright laws grant authors the exclusive right to their works, so that they can exploit them to recover the monetary and time investments that they contributed; this is copyright's *production function*. In order to prevent free-riding, copyright creates an "artificial scarcity," therefore making works more excludable than they would be otherwise.[743] To introduce another economic term; when laws or market conditions allow for producers to charge excessive rates for their products or services, there will be "deadweight loss," i.e. consumers who wish to buy access, but are excluded because of price.[744] Copyright is a delicate balance where, for every right granted to authors, public uses of the work are more restricted.[745] In order to strike an ideal balance of interests, the law should allocate authors "just enough to motivate the creation of original works—while reserving the remaining rights and powers to the public."[746] Is deadweight loss justifiable within a copyright regime? In order to be justified, the privileges and rewards for authorship must actually, not nominally, act to incentivize new "creative works that would not otherwise be available without copyright protection."[747]

Copyright's *structural function* is the next consideration. In some instances, copyright can create a market for authors to sell access to their works, thereby supporting their efforts.[748] In the earliest cases, sovereigns

740 Netanel, *Copyright's Paradox*, *supra* note 645, at 84.

741 Marginson, *supra* note 525, at 5.

742 Netanel, *Copyright's Paradox*, *supra* note 645, at 85.

743 *Ibid.* at 117.

744 *Ibid.* at 123.

745 Bell & Parchomovsky, *Dual-Grant Theory*, *supra* note 642, at 1056.

746 *Ibid.*

747 Netanel, *Copyright: What Everyone Needs to Know*, *supra* note 643, at 90.

748 Netanel, *Copyright's Paradox*, *supra* note 645, at 89.

or churches might have patronized the arts. The role of these patrons, being the primary donors, was reduced in the eighteenth century when improved literacy created demand for all types of works. This demand for works created a market in which some authors could live off their work, also freeing them from patrons' influences and encouraging social critique. While this means of independence was realized in the early days of the US, technological advances beginning in the late nineteenth century catapulted small cottage industries into the era of mass media, which was dominated by the "copyright industries."[749] Despite copyright creating a market for some industries to thrive, other means of sustenance remain. One of the leading experts on copyright law notes:

> ... a robust system of free expression requires interplay among a wide variety of speakers, including commercial mass media, government-subsidized noncommercial media, independent studios and record labels, cottage-industry publishers, political and nonprofit associations, universities, professional and semiprofessional authors, street corner pamphleteers, and peer discussants, creators, bloggers, video-makers, and reporters online. To one extent or another, each of these speakers offsets, complements, and checks the abuses of power, gross inaccuracies, and failings of the rest.... Certainly, our system of expression must include considerable space for decentralized, peer expression on the Internet. But that is not to say that we should aspire, even as a liberal democratic ideal, to an egalitarian expressive universe composed entirely of yeoman speakers or any other single type of speaker.[750]

The third major function of copyright is the *expressive function*, where the US Constitution's Copyright Clause provides symbolic, cultural support for free expression, far beyond that which would be expected from a statute or any other source of law. Not only does copyright aid in stocking the marketplace of ideas, but, moreover, constitutional provisions enjoy a heightened regard for their overarching principles that tie into their system's legal culture.[751] Thus, a constitutional provision attaches a sense of

---

749 *Ibid.* at 90, 92 (noting that the largest of the copyright industries are publishers, film studios, record labels and other media conglomerates); *see also* Lessig, *Free Culture*, *supra* note 709, at 162–63 (describing the wholesale monopolies of the early 2000's that completely dominated music, radio, film and print publishing).

750 Netanel, *Copyright's Paradox*, *supra* note 645, at 104.

751 May, James R., and Erin Daly. *Global Environmental Constitutionalism*. Cambridge University Press, 2015, pp. 32–35 (noting that, due to constitutional

identity to a citizenry that is free to discuss politics, to entertain, create art, inquire into the sciences and express a broad array of viewpoints. It is also in the context of copyright's expressive function that the laymen's view is especially relevant; today, most people would first associate copyright protection with the major copyright industries and their works in music, film, television and entertainment.[752] It may only occur as an afterthought that most academic research and scholarly works are also subject to the limitations of copyright. These perceptions are unsurprising considering that the benefits of scientific research are not so obviously linked to the publications that may have produced them, whereas the enjoyment derived from a song or film, for example, can be instantaneously traced back to the work itself. These types of works are the positive outcomes of the copyright system, but copyright also acts as a restriction on speech, so it is not the only constitutional provision at play. Because of the balance between the Copyright Clause and the First Amendment and their related interests, copyright's expressive function is often at odds with its production and structural functions.

D. Copyright Explained

Far from just protecting the "writings" that are mentioned in the Constitution, modern copyright law covers areas spanning from software, literature, music, lyrics, movies, dramatic works, soundtracks, pantomimes, choreography, photography, graphic works, sculpture, sound recordings, to architectural works.[753] This category of protected works is obviously very broad and encompasses nearly every conceivable medium. Federal law requires that, in order for a work to be protected by copyright, it must

---

provisions being "entrenched," amendments require substantial collaboration, well-beyond what is needed for statutes. Courts can only strike down unconstitutional laws, not the constitutional provisions themselves. Constitutional provisions define what laws may be created as well as their scope. Finally, nations' values are engrained in their constitutions, which act to define the limits of public discourse and to encourage positive behavior); *see also* Tarr, G. Alan., et al. *Federalism, Subnational Constitutions, and Minority Rights*. Praeger, 2004, pp. 174, 178–85.

752 Netanel, *Copyright: What Everyone Needs to Know*, *supra* note 643, at 85.

753 17 U.S.C. § 102 (a) (2012).

be an original work of authorship fixed in any tangible medium.[754] The originality requirement sets forth that protected works be original to the author, but this does not necessarily require novelty.[755] In other words, originality is the *sine qua non* of copyright.[756]

Once copyright protection is in effect, it affords the copyright owner five exclusive rights: the right to reproduce the work, create derivative works, distribute it to the public, perform the work publicly and to display the work publicly.[757] Infringements on copyrighted materials can result in a broad array of remedies including injunctions, impoundment, actual damages, statutory damages, punitive damages, attorney's fees and even incarceration in cases of willful infringement.[758] The rights afforded to authors have continuously grown stronger, especially in light of newer technologies and the laws protecting against the circumvention of the technical controls. When Congress enacted the modern Copyright Act, it also made the criminal penalties substantially more severe.[759] Congress granted original jurisdiction to the federal district courts to hear cases related to copyright infringement.[760]

As to its originality, a work must be created independently by an author and possess at least a minimal degree of creativity. Minimal creativity has been deemed to set a very low standard, thus, even a slight amount of creativity will suffice to pass the threshold. While the term "originality"

754 17 U.S.C. § 102 (2012) (elaborating further that this medium of expression may be either now known or later developed, where something may be "perceived, reproduced, or otherwise communicated, either directly or with the aid of a machine or device.").

755 Feist v. Rural Tel. Serv., 499 U.S. 340, 345–6 (1991) (citing to Sheldon v. Metro-Goldwyn Pictures Corp., 81 F.2d 49, 54 (2d Cir. 1936)) (elaborating that a work may be original while still closely resembling other works, but it cannot be the result of copying. To further illustrate, if two poets both wrote identical poems independently, neither work would be novel, but both would be original and copyrightable).

756 Harper & Row v. Nation Enterprises, 471 U.S. 539, 547–49 (1985).

757 17 U.S.C. § 106 (1) – (5); *see also* 17 U.S.C. § 106 (6) (allowing, additionally, the right to perform sound recordings publicly through digital audio transmission; this has been regarded more as a subset of the § 106 (4) right to perform the work publicly).

758 17 U.S.C. §§ 501–506.

759 Benkler, Yochai. *The Wealth of Networks: How Social Production Transforms Markets and Freedom*. Yale University Press, 2007, pp. 440–42.

760 Note, though, that state courts may still have jurisdiction over cases peripheral to copyright, such as those involving the enforcement of copyright licenses; these cases are, instead, contractual matters; 28 U.S.C. § 1338 (2011).

is not in the Copyright Clause, the Supreme Court first found it to be a constitutional prerequisite in the late nineteenth century. In *The Trade-Mark Cases*[761] and *Burrow-Giles Lithographic Co. v. Sarony*,[762] the Court made this requirement explicit. *The Trade-Mark Cases*, focusing mainly on the scope of "writings," explained, "originality requires independent creation plus a modicum of creativity."[763] Further, in *Burow-Giles*, the Court sought to define "author" in its constitutional sense and, thus, stated that it should be understood as "he to whom anything owes its origin; originator; maker."[764] Originality was once again emphasized, limiting copyright protection to authors' original intellectual conceptions.[765] This constitutional originality requirement has, subsequent to its common law creation, also been codified.[766]

Original works must also be distinguished from facts. Because facts do not originate with somebody's authorship, nobody may claim originality over facts.[767] In distinguishing, one should contrast creation and discovery: if somebody were to discover or uncover the existence of a fact, this is by no means creation or authorship.[768] The discoverer of a fact, thus, acts more as the fact's recorder.[769] Because the factual elements of science,

---

761 100 U.S. 82 (1879).

762 111 U.S. 53 (1884).

763 100 U.S. 82, 94 (1879) (allowing also for a liberal understanding of the word "writings" to include engraving, prints, etc. so long as these "fruits of intellectual labor" are original and "embodied in the form of books, prints, engravings, and the like).

764 111 U.S. 53, 58 (1884).

765 *Ibid.* at 53, 58–59 (1884) (stressing requirement that author who is accusing another of infringement show "the existence of those facts of originality, of intellectual production, of thought, and conception).

766 17 U.S.C. § 102 (a) (2012).

767 Feist v. Rural Tel. Serv., 499 U.S. 340, 346 (1991).

768 *Ibid.*

769 Compilations of facts may actually possess the requisite originality to garner copyright protection. An author, when compiling facts, selects facts for inclusion, arranges them in a particular order, and may arrange it also in a reader-friendly manner; this selection and arrangement can evince a sufficient minimal degree of creativity. For example, a directory consists of facts, i.e. names, telephone numbers, addresses, none of which would individually constitute a written expression. However, if it can be shown that the directory has some sort of original selection or arrangement, the directory, as a whole, could meet the constitutional minimum for copyright protection. As a limitation, even though a work may be copyrighted, that does not afford copyright protection to every element of the work. These factual statements should, thus, remain distinguished from an author or compiler's original contributions. Ginsburg,

history, biographies, and current events are regarded as fact, they are not capable of being copyrighted and are, therefore, part of the public domain.[770] This will be discussed in detail in terms of the *idea / expression dichotomy*, which is an exception to copyright protection in addition to being a safeguard for constitutionally protected free speech.

Fixation, being at the core of copyright, enables and facilitates the progress of science, knowledge and learning.[771] The requirement that a work be "fixed in a tangible medium" has been subject to reevaluation virtually every time that a new type of technology is developed and implemented.[772] Despite complicating factors with newer fixed-forms, they are still treated the same as any other fixed media with regard to copyright law. That also means that rigid copyright protection is applied to digital, highly distributable formats. The modern US Copyright Act, adopted in 1976, was primarily focused on photocopying, but this has, of course, since evolved to include means of fixation relating to the Internet, computers and servers.[773] Fundamentally, in order to consider that a work is in a tangible medium, the medium shall be permanent and stable enough for the work to be "perceived, reproduced, or otherwise communicated for a period of more than transitory duration."[774] The requirement that a work be embodied in a medium capable of being perceived or reproduced is known as the *embodiment requirement*, and the requirement that it remains fixed for more than a transitory duration is termed the *duration require-*

Jane C. "Creation and Commercial Value: Copyright Protection of Works of Information." *Columbia Law Review*, vol. 90, no. 7, 1990, p. 1868; Feist v. Rural Tel. Serv., 499 U.S. 340, 346 (1991) (explaining, as an example, that census-takers copy the figures from the world around them, as opposed to actually creating the data).

770 Miller v. Universal City Studios, Inc., 650 F.2 d 1365, 1369 (5th Cir. 1981).

771 Loren, *supra* note 651, at 963.

772 17 U.S.C. § 101 (2012).

773 *See generally* Crews, Kenneth D. *Copyright, Fair Use, and the Challenge for Universities: Promoting the Progress of Higher Education*. University of Chicago Press, 1993, p. 38.

774 Network LP v. CSC Holdings, Inc., 536 F.3 d 121, 127 (2 d Cir. 2008).

ment.[775] Fixation is considered to have occurred at the moment in which the original work was put into a tangible medium.[776]

I. Various Exceptions to Copyright

The first major exception to copyright law is the *idea / expression dichotomy*.[777] The Copyright Act expressly states that "[i]n no case does copyright protection for an original work of authorship extend to any idea, procedure, process, system, method of operation, concept, principle, or discovery, regardless of the form in which it is described, explained, illustrated, or embodied in such work."[778] In other words, copyright protects the embodiment or expression of ideas, but not the ideas themselves. The idea / expression dichotomy strikes a balance between the First Amend-

---

775 *Embodiment* and *duration* are particularly affected by new adaptations of technology. The Second Circuit was faced with determining whether the streaming of data could constitute a "copy." More specifically, the court looked at *embodiment* and fixation within a medium, and additionally inquired as to "what constitutes a period of more than transitory *duration*." Here, the defendant was a cable television provider seeking to provide a Digital Video Recorder (DVR) service. The defendant sought to provide a "Remote Storage DVR System" (RS-DVR). This service was designed to remotely stream recorded cable programing held on the defendant's central hard drives to the defendant's customers. Data sent from defendant's servers would first be taken into the RS-DVR system's "ingest" and "BMR" buffers that would, respectively, reformat and transmit the content to other components of the RS-DVR system. If a customer wished to view a program, the content could be taken from the ingest buffer and then copied onto hard storage disks. Because of this, the court found that the ingest buffer was sufficiently permanent and stabile, allowing the work "to be perceived [or] reproduced," and that the BMR buffer's communication roles satisfied the *embodiment* requirement. Every second of the work's entirety, passing through the buffer one second at a time, means that the work was embodied in the buffer. Although, data in a buffer is rapidly and automatically overwritten directly after it's processing. Whether something is embodied from more than a "transitory" period is highly fact-specific; here, data being embodied in buffers for 1.2 seconds was determined to be only transitory, thus, failing the *duration requirement*. 17 U.S.C. § 101 (2012); Network LP v. CSC Holdings, Inc., 536 F.3 d 121, 123–24, 127, 129–30 (2 d Cir. 2008).

776 Montgomery v. Noga, 168 F.3 d 1282, 1288 (11th Cir. 1999) (explaining that, while these are necessary to create a copyright, there are additional statutory protections available through registering the copyright).

777 Elsevier Inc. v. Sci-Hub, No. 1:15-CV-04282-RWS, 5 (S.D.N.Y. 2015).

778 17 U.S.C. § 102 (b) (2012).

ment's freedom to discuss facts and the restrictions on authors' expressions through copyright law.[779] Because of this distinction, any idea or fact originating from a copyrighted work is immediately free to be exploited by the public upon its publication. Authors will only be able to claim copyright protection for their expression of the ideas or facts.[780]

The Supreme Court has also described the role of limited copyright duration as a mechanism for balancing the public interest against the limited copyright monopoly.[781] Generally, a copyright, upon publication, will vest in the author for the entirety of his or her life plus seventy years following his or her death.[782] The duration of copyright is different in the case of anonymous works, works made under pseudonym and works made for hire. In such instances, "the copyright endures for a term of ninety-five years from the year of its first publication, or a term of 120 years from the year of its creation, whichever expires first...."[783] Once the term expires, the works enter into the public domain. While knowledge is always a public good in the economic sense, the premise of a limited private monopoly over it is that, the monopoly promotes authorship and dissemination of creative works for a "limited time."[784] Although, under normal circumstances, access issues are exacerbated by the terms of copyright length; protection could easily exceed a century if authors live anywhere near the range of the average life expectancy.[785]

The public domain is the conceptual freedom to copy, distribute, sell, mix and transform materials into new creative works.[786] The wide-ranging debate as to exactly what type of law copyright is, is naturally carried over to the debate regarding the public domain, i.e. the area where copyright

---

779 Eldred v. Ashcroft, 537 U.S. 186, 219 (2003).

780 Golan v. Holder, 565 U.S. 302, 328–29 (2012).

781 Sony Corp. of America v. Universal City Studios, Inc., 464 U.S. 417, 431 (1984).

782 17 U.S.C. § 302 (a) (2011) (amending previous terms of duration, which still should be taken into consideration if a work was created prior to January 1, 1978); *see also* Darnton, *supra* note 543, at 7 (explaining that the term of copyright duration was originally shorter until the 1998 Sonny Bono Term Extension Act, otherwise known as the Mikey Mouse Protection Act, came into effect; this legislation was the result of lobbyists' efforts, namely Disney, whose older characters like Mikey Mouse were falling into the public domain).

783 17 U.S.C. § 302 (2011) (c).

784 Boyle, James. *The Public Domain: Enclosing the Commons of the Mind*. Yale University Press, 2009, pp. 21–25.

785 Baldwin, *supra* note 689, at 3.

786 Liu, Joseph P. "The New Public Domain." *University of Illinois Law Review*, vol. 1, no. 4, 2013, pp. 1395–97.

ceases to apply.[787] Works in the public domain were often previously subject to copyright protection, but no longer are. They could be originating from government documents that were never subject to copyright and, of course, basic facts and observations, which are not protected by copyright.[788] Because they are in the public domain, Shakespeare and Beethoven's works, for example, are free to be adapted and performed just as the writings of Newton are available without copyright restriction.[789] The public domain relaxes copyright's *originality* requirement for subsequent works, otherwise authors could still be plagued with determining whether works really are in the public domain.[790]

Finally, there may be a common law *teacher exception* nestled in under the *work made for hire* rules. In employment situations, the "employer or other person for whom the work was prepared is considered the author."[791] In this context, it is presumed that employers are the authors unless there is a written document between the parties to disclaim an employer's rights.[792] The statutory *work made for hire* rule does not define "employee." Rather, the Supreme Court has indicated that courts should inquire into the extent of employer control over the creation of a work, skill required for the work, materials used, location, relationship between the parties, type of compensation and regularity of the work.[793] Clarity is limited as to what materials created by professors fall within the scope of their employment, and which automatically become university property.

Most universities tend to reserve the rights to works that were made with "substantial" university resources or when specific works are commissioned. Some institutions claim wholesale ownership of faculty works, while a few have no clear policies.[794] Even policies presuming faculty ownership can be legally inadequate, because, in order to transfer these

---

787 Nimmer & Nimmer, *Nimmer on Copyright*, *supra* note 71, at vol. 3, § 9A.01; Boyle, *supra* note 784, at 38–39.

788 Ochoa, Tyler T. "Origins and Meanings of the Public Domain." *University of Dayton Law Review*, vol. 28, no. 2, 2002, pp. 217–19.

789 Note that, despite the works being hundreds of years old, moral rights still might apply in most European jurisdictions.

790 McSherry, *supra* note 15, at 30–31, 192; (citing to Litman, Jessica. "The Public Domain." *Emory Law Journal*, vol. 39, no. 4, 1990, p. 1012) (suggesting that "a public domain allows authors and jurists to avoid the harsh light of a genuine search for provenance or originality.").

791 17 U.S.C § 201 (b) (2002).

792 *Ibid.*

793 Community for Creative Non-Violence v. Reid, 490 U.S. 730 (1989).

794 Rooksby, *Branding of the American Mind*, *supra* note 510, at 184.

rights, there must be a signed agreement transferring works from the university to a professor. Otherwise, the presumption under copyright law is that the university owns the rights.[795] Students' works could also be presumed to be works made for hire. Unclear campus policies leave students questioning whether they own their works; this is all despite the fact that they pay tuition fees and are not employed by the universities. Usage of campus facilities can be enough to couch student creative works in under the *work made for hire*, while many campus policies state that the university owns students' works or that they perhaps retain royalty-free licenses.[796] Students' works in class assignments, covering nearly all courses and projects, are likely to be subject to the work made for hire rules, divesting their IP rights and, instead, giving such rights to the universities or even third parties.[797] Universities have been particularly interested to hold the rights to students' works where faculty and students are active in developing potentially lucrative Internet-based materials and software.[798]

The teacher exception was created by the courts to further professors' rights when the 1909 Copyright Act was still in effect.[799] Treating professors' works as *sui generis*, the courts wished to distinguish them from those of authors involved in industry and entertainment.[800] The 1909 Copyright Act, although vesting works made for hire with the employers, did not have an explicit requirement requiring a written document in order for there to be a transfer of rights. The courts took this as an opportunity to create the teacher exception, permitting oral or implied contracts as the basis for the transfer of copyright.[801] Since the 1976 Copyright Act expressly requires that there be a writing, many scholars argue that the statute has superseded the teacher exception.[802] Despite this, some courts, albeit rarely and inconsistently, continue to apply the teacher exception.[803] The disparity of viewpoints among scholars and courts on this matter leaves only the presumption that "the exception can no longer simply be

795 17 U.S.C. § 204 (2011).

796 Rooksby, *Branding of the American Mind*, *supra* note 510, at 179, 85.

797 *Ibid.* at 188.

798 McSherry, *supra* note 15, at 101–02.

799 *See* Sherrill v. Grieves, 57 Wash. L. Rep. 286 (D.C. 1929) (using the teacher exception for the first time).

800 Priest, Eric. "Copyright and the Harvard Open Access Mandate." *Northwestern Journal of Technology and Intellectual Property*, vol. 10, no. 7, 2012, p. 403.

801 Sherrill v. Grieves, 57 Wash. L. Rep. 286 (D.C. 1929).

802 Priest, *supra* note 800, at 404.

803 *Ibid.* at. 404–08.

assumed."[804] Because the legal defaults often fall short in making clear who owns works, university policies play a substantial role in delineating ownership. As will be discussed below, campus copyright policies must also be carefully crafted to promote innovation while still protecting copyrighted works.[805]

Further exceptions to the ownership rights afforded by the Copyright Act include the following: fair use (§ 107) (*see* discussion on fair use below), library copying (§ 108), the first-sale doctrine (§ 109 (a)), exceptions for public displays (§ 109 (c)), displays and performances in face-to-face teaching and in distance learning (§ 110 (1-2)), computer software (§ 117), architectural works (§ 120) as well as special formats for persons who are blind or have other disabilities (§ 121). In order to avoid liability, users can either try to conform their uses to the specific requirements within these exceptions, seek the author's permission, rearrange one's work to not interfere with the copyright, find alternative materials or rely on fair use.[806] It is important to note here that the expansion in scope and duration of copyright has been matched neither by protections in the idea / expression dichotomy nor growth in societal safeguards such as fair use.[807] The earliest copyright laws in the US narrowly regulated a thin sliver of published works, allowed for fair usage of these works and left the majority of content unregulated; today, it is presumed that nearly all works are regulated by copyright.[808]

While copyright laws are often strict in their application, the common law evolved the doctrine of "fair use" as an affirmative, equitable defense for protecting numerous socially beneficial uses of copyrighted materials.[809] Fair use has never been precisely defined and is exceptional in that it opens the door to a broad array of factual interpretations.[810] Fair use touches directly on the most fundamental balance of copyright law, the

---

804 McSherry, *supra* note 15, at 107.

805 Crews, Kenneth D. *Copyright Law for Librarians and Educators: Creative Strategies and Practical Solutions*. ALA Editions, 2006, p. 26.

806 *Ibid.* at 36.

807 Netanel, *Copyright's Paradox*, *supra* note 645, at 60.

808 Lessig, *Free Culture*, *supra* note 709, at 145.

809 *See, e.g.*, Emerson v. Davies, 8 F. Cas. 615, 619 (C.C.Mass. 1845); Campbell v. Acuff-Rose Music, Inc., 510 U.S. 569, 590 (1994); Harper & Row v. Nation Enterprises, 471 U.S. 539, 561 (1985) (stating that the defense requires a case-by-case analysis).

810 Sites, Brian. "Fair Use and the New Transformative." *Columbia Journal of Law and the Arts*, vol. 39, no. 4, 2016, p. 513 (referring to fair use as a "doctrinal piñata").

balance between compensating authors for their works and promoting the public benefit through the ability of subsequent authors to build upon the works of their predecessors.[811] Fair use, though, is not a wholesale privilege and can only be raised as a defense after a party has ventured to make (possibly fair) usage of a copyrighted work, thereby exposing themselves to legal liability and the associated costs. It should be noted, further, that fair use, being an affirmative defense, puts the burden of proof on the party asserting it; this means that the burden is on content users.[812] This puts quite the burden on those accessing and using copyrighted works, especially because there is no list indicating if works are still protected or who holds the copyright as would be the case for cars or houses.[813] Once somebody is sued for copyright infringement and raises fair use as a defense, its elements are to be considered individually and in light of the others.

If fair use were to be described in economic terms, as copyright often is, one might refer to it as a feature of copyright law addressing inefficiencies, allocating uses directly to the public as well as ensuring productive and allocative efficiency.[814] The courts have broad discretion over their application of the open-ended fair use defense, thereby allowing courts to make policy adjustments in relation to rapidly changing technologies and means of communication.[815] Fair use is to be considered in light of the underlying constitutional interests related to copyright and free expression. Its roots are in the common law and, in an attempt by Congress to reaffirm its role, it was later written into the Copyright Act. Most importantly, in the context of this dissertation, fair use represents one of the most common crossroads between universities and copyright.

---

811 *Ibid.* at 516.

812 Campbell v. Acuff-Rose Music, Inc., 510 U.S. 569, 590 (1994); *but see* Netanel, *Copyright: What Everyone Needs to Know*, *supra* note 643, at 40 (explaining that there are both "exceptions," where users may use works without permission and without paying, and "limitations," where users may use works without permission but with paying, to copyright; for example, the author categorizes fair use as an exception and licensing fees set by the Copyright Office as being limitations).

813 Lessig, *Free Culture*, *supra* note 709, at 222; *but see* "Public Catalog." *Web-Voyage*, United States Copyright Office, 2020, cocatalog.loc.gov/cgi-bin/Pwebrecon.cgi?DB=local&PAGE=First (providing a search function only for registered copyrighted works).

814 Bell & Parchomovsky, *Dual-Grant Theory*, *supra* note 642, at 1052.

815 Elkin-Koren, *supra* note 26, at 1, 4.

The history of copyright protection in the West "is strongly tied to the principle of access to [knowledge and] education."[816] Fair use, originally referred to as "fair abridgment," is rooted in the English common law and was first contemplated following the enactment of the Statute of Anne of 1710.[817] The English courts held that "in some instances fair abridgements would not infringe on author's rights."[818] The English jurist Lord Ellenborough stated, "while I shall think myself bound to secure every man in the enjoyment of his copyright, one must not put manacles upon science."[819] When the First Congress of the US adopted its copyright statute, the courts were left to develop the doctrine because the statute was silent on fair use.[820] The famed American jurist, Justice Joseph Story elaborated on his understanding of fair use in an 1845 court opinion:

> In truth, in literature, in science and in art, there are, and can be, few, if any, things, which, in an abstract sense, are strictly new and original throughout. Every book in literature, science and art, borrows, and must necessarily borrow, and use much which was well known and used before. No man creates a new language for himself, at least if he be a wise man, in writing a book. He contents himself with the use of language already known and used and understood by others. No man writes exclusively from his own thoughts, unaided and uninstructed by the thoughts of others. The thoughts of every man are, more or less, a combination of what other men have thought and expressed, although they may be modified, exalted, or improved by his own genius or reflection. If no book could be the subject of copyright which was not new and original in the elements of which it is composed, there could be no ground for any copyright in modern times, and we should be obliged to ascend very high, even in antiquity, to find a work entitled to such eminence.... What are all modern law books, but new combinations and arrangements of old materials, in which the skill and judgment of the author in the selection and exposition and accurate use of those materials, constitute the basis of his reputation, as well as of his copyright?[821]

---

816 Bannerman, Sara. *International Copyright and Access to Knowledge*. Cambridge University Press, 2016, p. 55.

817 An Act for the Encouragement of Learning 1710, 8 Anne, ch. 19 (Gr. Brit.).

818 Campbell v. Acuff-Rose Music, Inc., 510 U.S. 569, 575 (1994).

819 Carey v. Kearsley (1803) (UK) 170 Eng. Rep. 679, 681; 4 Esp. 168, 170.

820 Campbell v. Acuff-Rose Music, Inc., 510 U.S. 569, 576 (1994).

821 Emerson v. Davies, 8 F. Cas. 615, 619 (C.C. Mass. 1845).

It was Justice Story who first formulated the fair use doctrine in the 1841 decision *Folsom v. Marsh*.[822] This doctrine remained solely in the common law until it was codified in the Copyright Act of 1976.[823] Section 107 of the Copyright Act states in relevant part:

> ... the fair use of a copyrighted work, including such use by reproduction in copies or phono records or by any other means specified by that section, for purposes such as criticism, comment, news reporting, teaching (including multiple copies for classroom use), scholarship, or research, is not an infringement of copyright. In determining whether the use made of a work in any particular case is a fair use the factors to be considered shall include–
> (1) the purpose and character of the use, including whether such use is of a commercial nature or is for nonprofit educational purposes;
> (2) the nature of the copyrighted work;
> (3) the amount and substantiality of the portion used in relation to the copyrighted work as a whole; and
> (4) the effect of the use upon the potential market for or value of the copyrighted work....

Fair use has never been precisely defined. Rather, this codification was a mere acknowledgement of the common law's "equitable rule of reason."[824] The listed criteria are a means for balancing the equities of any particular case, but are together and individually "in no case definitive or determinative."[825] Because of the fair use doctrine's highly factual nature, each case shall be decided on its own facts.[826] The four criteria for determining fair use codified in Section 107 were developed by the courts and Congress' codification of them was with the expectation that they be analyzed today in the same manner as they were under the common law.[827] Although these four factors are codified, the courts are not precluded from considering others.[828] When holistically weighing all of the available factors,

822 Sites, *supra* note 810, at 516 (citing to Folsom v. Marsh, 9 F. Cas. 342, 345 (C.C.D. Mass. 1841)).

823 17 U.S.C. § 107 (2011).

824 H.R. Rep. No. 94–1476, at 65 (1976); *see also* Authors Guild v. Google Inc., 804 F.3d 202, 213 (2d Cir. 2015) (indicating that, in codifying fair use, Congress had no intention to change, narrow or expand fair use policy in any way).

825 H.R. Rep. No. 94–1476, at 65 (1976).

826 *Ibid.*

827 *Ibid.*

828 Campbell v. Acuff-Rose Music, Inc., 510 U.S. 569, 577 (1994).

courts' focus should be to consider them all together "in light of the purposes of copyright."[829]

The usage of works by nonprofit universities is clearly contemplated by fair use, but this, even under the common law and the statutory wording, was always limited and, now, barely carries any weight in a fair use analysis.[830] In striking a reasonable balance, courts still stringently hold nonprofit universities to the constraints of copyright, but, in using their discretion, judges can allow for narrow uses that will not remove the incentives for authorship and publication.[831] The most commonly recognized justifications for copying are in cases of comment or criticism.[832] Furthermore, the numerous noncommercial uses such as criticism and parody,[833] scholarship, research, news reporting and teaching are traditionally come under the fair use doctrine.[834] The "scholarship" element, for example, is included under the doctrine because of the expectation that academics will build upon the work of their predecessors. Although nonprofit or commercial purpose is considered in the fair use analysis, the fact that one of these activities is undertaken by a nonprofit entity is by no means dispositive of a fair use.[835]

The first criteria, regarding the "purpose and character" of the use was included in the Copyright Act as Congress' acknowledgement that the

---

829 *Ibid.* at 578.

830 Crews, *Copyright, Fair Use and the Challenge*, *supra* note 773, at 23.

831 *Ibid.*

832 Authors Guild v. Google Inc., 804 F.3 d 202, 215 (2 d Cir. 2015).

833 Criticism and parody should be distinguished from infringement in that, regardless of how disparaging they may be, there is not a legally protected derivative market for criticism and, perhaps, parody. The determination as to whether there would be a derivative market for such a derivative usage, lies in the question of whether it is the type of market for which an author would grant licenses for his work. It is highly unlikely that an author would issue a license for a derivative work that would highly critical of his original work. Although, a parody might have elements that are protectable in a derivative market; these would be the aspects of the work which exceed mere criticism. Campbell v. Acuff-Rose Music, Inc., 510 U.S. 569, 592–93 (1994); *cf.* Benny v. Loew's, Inc., 239 F.2 d 532, 536 (9th Cir. 1956) (holding Jack Benny's parody of an original work to be an infringement due to excessive copying).

834 17 U.S.C. § 107 (2011).

835 Marcus v. Rowley, 695 F.2 d. 1171, 1175-76 (9th Cir. 1983) (denying fair use defense for a teacher, despite the use being related to nonprofit, educational activities); *but see* Triangle Publications, Inc. v. Knight-Ridder Newspapers, Inc. 626 F.2 d 1171, 1175 (5th Cir. 1980) (holding, conversely, that commercial purposes are also not an automatic bar to a fair use defense).

courts should inquire into the originality of a work in addition to balancing its commercial and / or nonprofit nature.[836] A major consideration under the first criteria is the determination of whether a subsequent work is "transformative."[837] This goes back to Justice Story's discussion of whether a work is merely superseding a previous work or if it is a new work that adds original material, has a different purpose or character, or alters the previous work to create a new expression, meaning, or message.[838] A work must not necessarily be transformative to fall within the fair use defense, but the more transformative a work is, the more likely it is to conform to the creative goal of copyright law.[839] The more transformative that a work is, the less likely that it will be in competition with previous works, thus alleviating any potential financial harm that a prior author may endure.[840] In other words, when a work is highly transformative, it will be less likely that the other factors such as "commercialism" will weigh heavily against it in the fair use balance.[841]

Following the question of whether a work is transformative, courts must weigh whether the uses are for commercial or nonprofit purposes. Whether a use is commercial or nonprofit affords no strict presumption as to whether a use is fair; courts are to focus primarily on transformation, competition in derivative markets and avoid any bright-line approaches.[842] The Supreme Court found there should be no presumption because "nearly all of the illustrative uses listed in the preamble paragraph of § 107, including news reporting, comment, criticism, teaching, scholarship, and research.... are generally conducted for profit in [the US]."[843] Thus, follow-

---

836 17 U.S.C. § 107 (1) (2011); H.R. Rep. No. 94–1476, at 65 (1976).

837 Sites, *supra* note 810, at 518.

838 Authors Guild v. Google, Inc., 804 F.3 d 202, 214 (2 d Cir. 2015) (citing to Folsom v. Marsh, 9 F. Cas. 342, 348 (C.C.D. Mass. 1841)); *see* Sites, *supra* note 810, at 519–20 (explaining that courts should ask whether a second work transforms the content, the purpose or both, of a work; some courts have come to use terms such as "content transformativeness" and "purpose transformativeness.").

839 Campbell v. Acuff-Rose Music, Inc., 510 U.S. 569, 578–79 (1994).

840 Cambridge Univ. Press v. Patton, 769 F.3 d 1232, 1262 (11th Cir. 2014).

841 Campbell v. Acuff-Rose Music, Inc., 510 U.S. 569, 578–79 (1994).

842 The Court in *Sony* acknowledged in its *dictum* a presumption in cases where the court finds a commercial, profit-making purpose, that there is a presumption of no fair use. Contrarily, when a work could be categorized as nonprofit or noncommercial, there was to be a presumption of fair use. Sony Corp. of America v. Universal City Studios, Inc., 464 U.S. 417, 449 (1984) (partially overruled by Campbell v. Acuff-Rose Music, Inc., 510 U.S. 569, 584–86 (1994)).

843 *Ibid.* at 539, 592 (Brennan, J., dissenting).

ing *Campbell*, nonprofits using copyrighted materials for educational purposes will enjoy no special presumption against findings of infringement, just as there will be no presumption against commercial entities in cases where they argue fair use.[844] An entity's nonprofit or commercial nature has no determinative or conclusive role in deciding fair use, but shall be weighed along with all of the other fair use factors.[845] The Supreme Court's interpretation of the fair use doctrine in recent decades has moved away from the analysis of the resulting public benefit of transformative uses and more in favor of analyzing copyright holders' economic interests and incentives.[846]

Section 107's second criterion, the copyrighted works' nature, recognizes that not all works are equal in proximity to the core purpose of copyright protection.[847] The analysis of the copied works' nature can result in works, which are more proximately related to the core purposes of copyright, having more difficulty in showing fair use.[848] The first question under these criteria for courts is whether a work has been published.[849] If the work remains unpublished, there is a narrower allowance for fair use; this is based on the premise that authors ought to be able to determine "when, where and in what form to publish a work."[850] Although somewhat restricting fair usage, this rule does serve to generally promote publication. The courts must then question whether the work is creative or factual. Creative works will receive more extensive copyright protection, whereas there is more of an interest in disseminating factual works.[851] In

---

844 Although the Court does not state this, it seems that an underlying reason for this presumption to be abandoned was that was connected to some of the extensive nonprofit involvement in some of the commercial activities that were discussed in Part I. *Ibid.* at 584.

845 *Ibid.* at 585.

846 Bezanson, Randall P., and Joseph M. Miller. "Scholarship and Fair Use." *Columbia Journal of Law & the Arts*, vol. 33, no. 4, 2010, p. 439.

847 Campbell v. Acuff-Rose Music, Inc., 510 U.S. 569, 586–87 (1994).

848 *Ibid.* at 586–87 (1994) (citing to Stewart v. Abend, 495 U.S. 207, 237–38, (1990)) (analyzing a fictional short story in contrast to factual works); Harper & Row v. Nation Enterprises, 471 U.S. 539, 563-64 (1985) (contrasting the level of protection accorded to published and unpublished materials); Sony Corp. of America v. Universal City Studios, Inc., 464 U.S. 417, 455 (1984) (contrasting "original" motion pictures with factual news broadcasts); Feist v. Rural Tel. Serv., 499 U.S. 340, 348-51 (1991) (contrasting creative works with pure compilations of fact).

849 Harper & Row v. Nation Enterprises, 471 U.S. 539, 564 (1985).

850 *Ibid.*

851 *Ibid.*

other words, the defense of fair use is more likely to be effective for factual works, rather than for fictional ones.[852] Although there is a tendency for courts to favor facts over fiction in fair use analyses, this factor has rarely played an important role in fair use disputes.[853]

The third criteria, "the amount and substantiality of the portion used in relation to the copyrighted work as a whole," requires the courts to analyze the purpose of the copying and to determine if it is reasonable in that context.[854] This third criteria initially requires an analysis of the first criteria to determine the purpose and character of the copying; the scope of permissible copying is dependent on its purpose and character.[855] The case law is not especially clear on what amount of a derivative work may be copied once its purpose and character have been analyzed.[856] Some cases, such as *Sony v. United City Studios*, allowed for the entirety of a work to be copied because the material had already been previously made free for viewers.[857] On the other hand, the Court found in another case, *Harper & Row Publishers v. Nation Enterprises*, that segments from President Ford's memoirs, which were quoted in an unauthorized publication, were a copyright infringement.[858] Going back to their "purpose and character," the Court found that the segments constituted the heart of the unpublished memoirs. This core segment of the text would, of course, act to supplant the original work in potential commercial markets.[859] The third factor is also closely related to the fourth factor; the more content that is copied, and with increasing importance, the more likely it is to displace the market for the original and diminish sales of the copyrighted work.[860]

Finally, the fourth criteria, "the effect of the use upon the potential market for or value of the copyrighted work," requires an analysis of both the actual market harm caused by the alleged infringer as well as the effect on potential markets if conduct, such as the defendant's, were to

852 Bezanson & Miller, *supra* note 846, at 441 (citing Stewart v. Abend, 495 U.S. 207. 237 (1990)).

853 Authors Guild v. Google Inc., 804 F.3 d 202, 220 (2 d Cir. 2015).

854 Campbell v. Acuff-Rose Music, Inc., 510 U.S. 569, 586 (1994).

855 *Ibid.* at 587.

856 Bezanson & Miller, *supra* note 846, at 441.

857 Sony Corp. of America v. Universal City Studios, Inc., 464 U.S. 417, 449-50 (1984).

858 Harper & Row v. Nation Enterprises, 471 U.S. 539, 600 (1985).

859 *Ibid.*

860 Authors Guild v. Google Inc., 804 F.3 d 202, 221 (2 d Cir. 2015).

continue without restriction.[861] The defendant has the burden of showing that his "fair use" of a work subsists in a market different from that of the original work.[862] The plaintiff's burden is to show that a widespread use of the copied work could affect potential derivative markets.[863] When a subsequent use supplants any primary or derivative market for a copyrighted work, it will likely be an infringement.[864] The fourth factor comes back to the level of transformation in the subsequent work; when a work is copied from another, for commercial use, it acts as a market replacement and makes it more likely that there will be a market harm.[865] In contrast, if the subsequent work is transformative, it would be more difficult to show market harm, because the work would act as less of a market substitute.[866] The Supreme Court designated this criteria as the most important element in the fair use analysis.[867]

Despite the fourth element of fair use still requiring inquiry into the purpose of the use, i.e. whether the use is academic or commercial, the analysis is very-much geared toward seeking out commercial markets, even when they may not exist. The fact that this analysis has pushed into the realm of protecting *potential* markets demonstrates the influence of commerciality over copyright and fair use, undoubtedly being a result of the copyright industry's influence. Perhaps an explanation for this could be that the entertainment industry is highly litigious because of their deeper pockets and large portfolios.[868] Due to this, the sheer number of cases including their commercial interests has accordingly influenced courts' analysis of fair use more in the direction of commerciality and further away from academic needs and uses.[869] As will be discussed below, the mismatching of economic incentives with various types of works is tied to this focus on commerciality, which tends to conflate all copyrightable works.[870]

---

861 Campbell v. Acuff-Rose Music, Inc., 510 U.S. 569, 590 (1994).

862 *Ibid.* at 591.

863 Sony Corp. of America v. Universal City Studios, Inc., 464 U.S. 417, 451 (1984).

864 Harper & Row v. Nation Enterprises, 471 U.S. 539, 568 (1985).

865 Sony Corp. of America v. Universal City Studios, Inc., 464 U.S. 417, 451 (1984).

866 Campbell v. Acuff-Rose Music, Inc., 510 U.S. 569, 591 (1994).

867 Harper & Row v. Nation Enterprises, 471 U.S. 539, 566 (1985).

868 While this explanation is quite realistic, other explanations focus on the narrative of copyright industry lobbying.

869 Crews, *Copyright, Fair Use and the Challenge*, *supra* note 773, at 44.

870 This comes back to my adoption of the terms "academic works" and "works made for entertainment." The commerciality analysis tends to find commercial uses within both of these categories, despite the fact that academic works are

II. International Law and Copyright in the US

Due to the territorial nature of copyright jurisdiction, i.e. copyright being enforced by the nation and laws of *where* the violation occurs, US law remains supreme with regard to copyright infringements occurring within the US and ancillary to its jurisdiction. This does not mean that international law has not played a role in shaping US law; in 1989, the US adopted the Berne Convention for the Protection of Literary and Artistic works. Ascension to the Berne Convention was only possible following some amendments to the US Copyright Act.[871] The largest change required to US law was to eliminate the "formalities" of copyright protection; copyright notice, the inclusion of the "©" symbol or "all rights reserved" language, was the most notable formality to be eliminated.[872] Another formality that was eliminated was the requirement that foreign copyrighted works be registered with the federal Copyright Office.[873] Thus, the adaptations that the US made to conform to the international standards under the Berne Convention essentially served to eliminate its domestic technical prerequisites to copyright.[874] The begrudging acceptance of the Berne Convention in the US was driven by the copyright industries and the fact that the US had become a major content exporter, thus requiring a means to compel other countries to enforce copyrights.[875]

---

more closely bound to the Copyright Clause's purposes. I like to compare the finding of commercial uses within academic works to that of the "false positive" in medical testing, i.e. where a test improperly indicates the existence of a condition. It is my contention that, while the commerciality analysis serves the means for copyright when there is a profit motive, it is not well suited for instances of there being no profit motive. The false positive occurs in copyright when a court uses the commerciality test wholesale and identifies commercial markets for academic works that simply do not exist, or if they exist they are likely not facilitating the creation and dissemination of academic works.

871 "Berne Notification No. 121 Berne Convention for the Protection of Literary and Artistic Works." *Treaty/BerneE/121: [Berne Convention] Accession by the United States of America*, 17 Nov. 1988, www.wipo.int/treaties/en/notifications/berne/treaty_berne_121.html.

872 Samuels, Edward B. *The Illustrated Story of Copyright*. Thomas Dunne Books/St. Martins Griffin, 2000, pp. 208-09 (noting that while notice is no longer required, it is still encouraged; this may act as a preventative measure to stop unintentional infringements).

873 *Ibid.* (mentioning that registration with the Copyright Office is still possible, but no longer mandatory).

874 *Ibid.*

875 Baldwin, *supra* note 689, at 11.

The Berne Convention, in addition to protecting "literary" and "artistic" works, sets out to protect "scientific" knowledge as well; this is understood to include "knowledge in the sciences, social sciences and humanities."[876] While the access to scientific knowledge, under the Berne Convention, has diminished over time, this transformation is telling of the direct relationship between copyright policy and access to knowledge. The original Berne Convention of 1886 liberally allowed for the republication of scientific knowledge in newspapers or periodical articles, unless authors or publishers made a positive declaration otherwise. By default, this put scientific knowledge into the public domain.[877] This regime also had language allowing member states to enact legislation permitting extracts of copyrighted works "for use in publications destined for... scientific purposes."[878] Following substantial lobbying from a number of press and writers' associations and the medical publishing industry, the 1908 version of the Berne Convention narrowed its scope to only permit republication of newspaper articles.[879] Because scientific articles were considered to be periodicals, not newspapers, this had the effect of removing scientific articles from the public domain and setting copyright protection for scientific works as the new default.[880] By the time the 1952 iteration of the Berne Convention was signed, it was essentially settled that scientific works would receive the same treatment as literary and artistic works.[881] The 1972 version of the Berne Convention, in contrast to the former regime permitting the use of textual excerpts, allowed for a much more limited use of quotation "by way of illustration."[882] The Berne Convention has continuously evolved over time toward the direction of categorizing scientific, medical and other academic works with other generally copyrightable materials; this has had the largest effect on those without institutional access to specialized databases.[883]

---

876 Bannerman, *supra* note 816, at 34.

877 Berne Convention for the Protection of Literary and Artistic Works, Article 7, Sep. 9, 1886.

878 *Ibid.* at Article 8, Sep. 9.

879 Berne Convention for the Protection of Literary and Artistic Works, Article 9, Nov. 13, 1908.

880 Bannerman, *supra* note 816, at 39.

881 *Ibid.* at 40.

882 Berne Convention for the Protection of Literary and Artistic Works, Article 10(2), July 24, 1971.

883 Bannerman, *supra* note 816, at 51.

As a response to the difficulties of enforcing IP rights in a number of countries, the US, along with 162 other countries, signed The Agreement on Trade-Related Aspects of Intellectual Property Rights (hereinafter, TRIPs).[884] The TRIPs agreement was particularly wide reaching due to being tied to World Trade Organization membership. This served as both a means to compel membership and as a forum for dispute resolution. TRIPs also incorporated many elements of the Berne convention, including the fifty-year term of copyright duration following an author's death.[885] TRIPs was adopted into law in the US through the 1994 enactment of 17 U.S.C. § 104 (a). Another notable treaty affecting copyright in the US is the World Intellectual Property Organization Copyright Treaty (hereinafter, WCT).[886] Adopted in 1996, the WCT, among other things, included computer programs in the definition of "literary works" for the purposes of copyright.[887] The WCT was incorporated into US copyright law via the Digital Millennium Copyright Act of 1998 (hereinafter, DMCA).[888] Comparable to the DMCA is the European Union's *sui generis* protection of databases that was also adopted in 1996; this expansion of protection does not require that the databases satisfy copyright's fundamental originality requirement.[889] While the US has substantially longer copyright duration terms, international agreements such as these still set lengthy mandatory minimum duration terms.

III. Alternatives to Copyright

Copyright restrictions can pose substantial, and sometimes even insurmountable, hurdles for those seeking access to creative works. The copyright laws automatically apply to creative works as soon as they are fixed into a tangible medium, thus creating a rather stringent default standard. The hurdles to access are substantial in cases where knowledge consumers

---

884 Agreement on Trade-Related Aspects of Intellectual Property Rights (TRIPs), Apr. 15, 1994.

885 *See* Berne Convention for the Protection of Literary and Artistic Works, Article 7, Sep. 28, 1979; Agreement on Trade-Related Aspects of Intellectual Property Rights (TRIPs), Article 12, 14, Apr. 15, 1994.

886 WIPO Copyright Treaty (WCT), Dec. 20, 1996.

887 *Ibid.*

888 *See* 17 U.S.C. §§ 101, 104, 108,112, 114, 117, 701, 512, 1201–1205, 1301–1332.

889 Directive 96/9/EC of the European Parliament and of the Council of 11 March 1996 on the Legal Protection of Databases.

can be forced to pay monopolistic prices or face high transaction costs in their attempts to contact authors and receive permission. Because of these difficulties, several legal, illegal and technical alternatives to stringent copyright protection have arisen. Such alternative approaches are a result of initiatives by the federal government, universities, other nonprofits, individual authors and pirating enterprises.

1. Open Access

Open access initiatives, which promote the free and open distribution of materials online, have been so effective in their attempts to make academic works available that they have been compared with the original Gutenberg revolution.[890] It was the printing press that originally bridged the educational boundaries between the universities and the public at large.[891] Open access, similarly, opens the door for the public to access first-class works. "Open access" is defined as "... the free availability of peer-reviewed literature on the public Internet, permitting any user to read, download, copy, distribute, print, search, or link to the full texts of the articles."[892] Many open journals are sharing their results with the public in a way that promotes the circulation of their knowledge through unrestricted online access.[893] Another major benefit of open access is that the printing and distribution costs of past eras can be bypassed.[894] Open access journals cover essentially every discipline and are published all around the world.

Open access, as a concept of democratizing knowledge, is reminiscent of the first informal societies created to share members' common interests, inevitably leading to a greater flow of knowledge and ideas.[895] It should be noted, though, that open access does not exactly mean "free access;" there are still hardware, software and networking costs that must be carried by at least one of involved the parties.[896] The publication of just one open

---

890 Willinsky, *supra* note 36, at 5.

891 *Ibid.* at 192.

892 Hagemann, Melissa. "Overview of Open Access." *Budapest Open Access Initiative / Overview of Open Access*, 16 Jan. 2003, www.budapestopenaccessinitiative.org/pdf/Melissa_Hagemann.pdf/view.

893 Willinsky, *supra* note 36, at 5.

894 Denicola, Robert C. "Copyright and Open Access: Reconsidering University Ownership of Faculty Research." *Nebraska Law Review*, vol. 85, 2006, p. 357.

895 Willinsky, *supra* note 36, at 30.

896 *Ibid.* at xii.

access article may still have around $3,000 to $4,000 in associated editorial costs.[897] While scholarly journals have been quite successful in terms of digitalization, sometimes in the context of open access, scholarly books have not experienced the same phenomenon.[898] Naturally, the largest for-profit publishers have been resistant to open access initiatives, but private professional societies and individual authors have also been slow to venture into open access publishing.[899]

In an attempt to make federally funded research open access to the public, Congress required, as of 2008, that any publications funded by the National Institutions of Health be open access within a year of publication; funding is made dependent on this requirement.[900] A few other open access mandates by federal funding authorities were made subsequently. Most recently, the Department of Education similarly required that research funded by its grants be made openly accessible within a year.[901] These open access mandates, although certainly helpful toward increasing access to materials, are limited in scope and, at their core, patchwork approaches to improve a copyright system that is in need of comprehensive reform.

Universities have pushed for stronger open access policies, requiring faculty members to make their articles open access within a year of publication.[902] One means of overcoming stringent commercial publishing contractual terms is for the universities to assume all of the faculty members' copyrights and then to make all publications automatically available in their own open access databases, following a limited embargo-period.[903] Such approaches are helpful, allowing faculty to still commercially publish with non-exclusive licenses and, further, to provide faculty the ability to tailor the uses of their works with open licenses that clearly spell out what uses are permitted and what is retained by the author. For works that are under more restrictive licensing with publishers, authors may still be able to make their pre-publication copies available in open access

---

897 Denicola, *supra* note 894, at 357–58 (noting that higher submission rates at more prestigious journals lead to greater costs).

898 *Ibid.* at 15.

899 Denicola, *supra* note 894, at 356–57 (noting that many private professional societies finance their research through the sale of jounals).

900 Consolidated Appropriations Act, 2008, 218 Stat. 110–161 (2008).

901 Open Licensing Requirement for Competitive Grant Programs, 2 CFR Part 3474, RIN 1894-AA07 (2017).

902 Netanel, *Copyright: What Everyone Needs to Know*, *supra* note 643, at 202.

903 *Ibid.*

repositories. Private, nonprofit universities and nonprofits in general, are at the forefront of promoting open access journals and assisting authors in licensing their works for open access.

2. Creative Commons Licenses

The Creative Commons (hereinafter, CC), a nonprofit organization, provides finely tuned licenses according to authors' wishes and requirements in most countries around the world.[904] The CC's goal is to increase access to content via open licensing, allowing "legal use, sharing, repurposing, and remixing."[905] When publishing a work with the CC legal tools, authors are free to select licensing conditions that may require attribution for using their works, restrict uses of derivative works, limit commercial uses or prohibit unpermitted derivative works.[906] Over 1.4 billion CC licensed works have made their way onto platforms such as Flickr, Wikipedia, YouTube, Internet Archive and MITOpenCourseware, just to name a few.[907] An interview with CC's legal counsel disclosed that their greatest momentum is in the area of academic publishing, but photographers have also been very open to CC licensing.[908] It should be noted that the CC is not providing non-copyrighted materials, but is rather acting to encourage individuals to share and reuse copyrighted knowledge well-within the parameters of copyright law. Remaining within the parameters of copyright requires licenses such as those available through the CC. These license types, along with the CC's mission statement, highly encourage authors to provide the greatest amounts of access to others.

---

904 Telephone interview with Sarah Pearson, Senior Counsel Creative Commons (Nov. 14, 2018).

905 "Use & Remix." *Creative Commons*, creativecommons.org/use-remix/.

906 "CC Licenses and Examples." *Creative Commons*, creativecommons.org/share-your-work/licensing-types-examples/.

907 "Share Your Work." *Creative Commons*, creativecommons.org/share-your-work/.

908 Telephone interview with Sarah Pearson, Senior Counsel Creative Commons (Nov. 14, 2018).

3. Pirating

Some other types of platforms have been created online, providing free, unrestrained and illegal access to academic journals and books.[909] Whereas CC provides open access with licensing limitations, platforms like Russia-based Sci-Hub and Library Genesis make millions of papers, articles and books available for free and without restriction. The mass-copying required to provide access to these materials is generally in contravention of US copyright laws. To put these platforms' impact into context, Sci-Hub makes over 64.5 million papers available. This is estimated to be about two-thirds of all published research.[910] Although it is not entirely clear how Sci-Hub acquired all of its academic papers, it is commonly believed that it acquired login credentials from academics to access databases and automated data mining behind numerous for-profit paywalls.[911]

4. Technical Barriers

Finally, technical barriers to access—paywalls, password protected databases and hard-to-copy formats—have played a major role in how copyrighted material is accessed. The major copyright industries for entertainment are all moving the bulk of their content onto streaming platforms.[912] Netflix, HBO Now, Hulu, Disney Plus and Amazon Prime Video are the current leaders in film streaming; a user could subscribe to all of these for a mere fifty dollars per month, granting them access to thousands of titles.[913] Similarly, hundreds of thousands of audiobooks are available to be instant-

909 These databases are operating illegally not only due to their accumulation of non-licensed copyrighted materials, but also due to their means of acquiring the materials. It is likely that they circumvented some technological measure that was originally meant to protect the content in another, "legal" database; if this is the case, then a DMCA claim could be raised parallel to a claim of copyright infringement.

910 Graber-Stiehl, Ian. "Meet the Pirate Queen Making Academic Papers Free Online." *The Verge*, 8 Feb. 2018, www.theverge.com/2018/2/8/16985666/alexandra-elbakyan-sci-hub-open-access-science-papers-lawsuit.

911 *Ibid.*

912 Telephone interview with Paul S. McGrath Esq., Business and Legal Affairs Coordinator, Skydance Media (Feb. 26, 2019).

913 Honorof, Marshall. "Best Streaming Video Services 2019." *Tom's Guide*, Tom's Guide, 9 Sept. 2019, https://www.tomsguide.com/us/best-streaming-video-services,review-2625.html.

ly streamed by a few platforms, charging between ten to fifteen dollars per month.[914] This is not to mention the millions of songs made available by music streaming platforms. Academic publishing, as discussed in more detail below, was similarly put behind paywalls. Unfortunately, though, the lower transactional costs promised by technology did not translate into increased access and lower prices. Much to the contrary, articles exclusively behind paywalls have never been more expensive than they are today. Not only are most of these works subject to copyright (once they are accessed), but they are also likely to be difficult to access in the first place.

E. Assessment of Copyright Law

I. Access—Rings of Regulation

Like the discussion concerning higher education in Part I, *access* is also an essential factor for copyright. Copyright law, for better or worse, creates an artificial scarcity through copyright holders' ability to exclude others from reproducing works, creating derivatives, distributing works, performing and displaying them. The level of access to any particular work is dependent on related technologies, the sources' trustworthiness and the mass of existing knowledge.[915] Less apparent, though, are the concentric rings of rules and regulation that have been formed within and outside of the Copyright Act, impeding access to copyrighted knowledge. At the center of the copyright protection scheme lies the corpus of congressionally made copyright law. Moving outward, the codification of the fair use defense may have tapered the flexibility of fair use, thus possibly watering-down the defense for those using copyrighted materials. The resulting congressionally adopted guidelines and interpretations for fair use effectively added another layer of regulation. Out of a desire to avoid liability and uncertainty, university administrators have created campus policies of their own, adding the outermost regulatory ring.

914 Parker, Jacob. "The Best Audiobook Sites 2020: Easy Listening Anywhere." *TechRadar*, 3 Feb. 2020, www.techradar.com/best/the-best-audio-book-sites#4-kobo-audiobooks.

915 Mokyr, *Gifts of Athena*, *supra* note 12, at 8.

1. The Core of Copyright Protection

Distinguishable from but related to the Copyright Act of 1976, the DMCA, enacted in 1998, prohibits the circumvention of technology meant to protect copyrighted materials.[916] It was primarily an attempt to address the piracy of digital works and how easily and quickly they could be copied and disseminated.[917] Congress took further steps to modernize the law, especially with relation to universities and the Internet. The Technology, Education and Copyright Harmonization Act (hereinafter, TEACH Act), enacted in 2002, was an attempt to strike a balance between academic usage of copyrighted materials and fair use in the context of online distance learning.[918] The TEACH Act sets forth various full and limited uses for digital recordings, and, in doing so, requires that institutions create clear compliance policies and that institutions provide information to faculty and students regarding copyright restrictions.[919] In terms of technical restrictions, the institutions should seek to limit access to copyrighted materials used in distance education by means of passwords and restricted access and by making materials available for only limited periods of time.[920] There is not much of an expectation that once materials are made available to students they will not be copied, so the TEACH Act provides a means for institutions to shield themselves from liability by deterring unlawful copying through technological restrictions.[921] Initial implementation of the TEACH Act was modest especially due to its rigor and complexity.[922]

---

916 17 U.S.C. §§ 512, 1201–1205, 1301–1332; 28 U.S.C. § 4001 (1998).

917 Crews, *Copyright Law for Librarians and Educators*, *supra* note 805, at 94; *see also* Lessig, *Future of Ideas*, *supra* note 706, at 187 (describing the DMCA protections using the metaphor of car theft. Copyright law would be comparable to the statutes against car theft. The DMCA, though, would be analogous to some type of law prohibiting car thieves from picking locks or disabling alarm systems).

918 17 U.S.C. §§ 110, 112 (2012).

919 *Ibid.*

920 *Ibid.*

921 Crews, *Copyright Law for Librarians and Educators*, *supra* note 805, at 70.

922 *Ibid.* at 73.

2. The Effects of Fair Use Codification

Beyond the copyright laws themselves, the codification of the common law fair use defense has effectively added another layer of regulation.[923] Despite Congress' express intention not to want to alter the law of fair use by codifying it, fair use became a rigid statute that can only be substantially changed through the gridlocked legislative process. This still allows for minor adaptions by courts and private litigants, but they remain somewhat limited in their ability to make major adaptations for changing circumstances and new technologies.[924] The initial codification of fair use provided neither clarity to the law of fair use nor any specific guidelines for going forward. Codifying fair use is, on the one hand, helpful in ensuring that the defense continues to exist, but haphazard in the sense that it does not provide the same flexibility afforded under the common law and could become meaningless if the courts go on to interpret fair use in a new light.

In response to criticism that the fair use statute was unclear in its meaning, Congress adopted the "Classroom Guidelines" not long after in an attempt to shed light on the relationship between fair use and nonprofit educational institutions.[925] Ideally, these non-binding Guidelines were meant to add a degree of clarity to fair use, far beyond what was included in the statute.[926] The Guidelines, while aiming to set permissible "minimum" uses, effectively set a "maximum standard" with the system of word counting that it put forth.[927] Its system of word limitations, requirements to receive authors' permission and limits on the overall number of copies were not clarified by the unclear considerations of "brevity," "spontaneity" and "cumulative effect" that users were supposed to make.[928] The wording, which was drafted by private lobbies and adopted by Congress, suggests that this was only meant to be a tentative approach.[929] Those familiar with the Guidelines see compliance with them as being an "unrealistic

923 17 U.S.C. § 107 (2011).

924 Crews, *Copyright, Fair Use and the Challenge*, *supra* note 773, at 33.

925 H.R. Rep. No. 94–1476, at 68–70 (1976).

926 Crews, *Copyright, Fair Use and the Challenge*, *supra* note 773, at 35.

927 H.R. Rep. No. 94–1476, at 68–70 (1976).

928 Cambridge Univ. Press v. Patton, 769 F.3 d 1232, 1245 (11th Cir. 2014).

929 *Ibid.*

nuisance" and their lack of specificity caused concern on many campuses about the potential for unpredictability.[930]

3. Campus Policies

Moving outward through the regulatory rings, universities' reactions to copyright, fair use and the Classroom Guidelines form the next ring. Following a lawsuit where a company was held liable for nearly $2 million in damages for copying educational materials, many universities developed internal copyright policies of their own.[931] Such lawsuits, although predominantly not directed toward universities, created an expectation of enforcement and aided in the usage of the Classroom Guidelines in interpreting the fair use statute. Because of the intensive usage of copyrighted materials, especially by research universities, campus policies based on the Guidelines were used regularly to guide faculty research and teaching and, at the very least, to ward off unwanted litigation. The Guidelines have been integrated into most universities' campus policies.[932]

Some universities' policies are geared more toward protecting the institution from litigation, whereas others are focused on ensuring fair use for core academic purposes. The most restrictive policies have tended to treat the Classroom Guidelines as a "safe-harbor," suggesting that uses beyond the Guidelines are subject to liability.[933] Of these universities, most adopt the Guidelines wholesale, some with a few changes and few with substantial differences. In short, the Classroom Guidelines have become entrenched in university policies.[934] In addition to these original Classroom Guidelines covering photocopying, at least ten renditions have since been made on a broad array of issues.[935] The down side of the cam-

---

930 Crews, *Copyright, Fair Use and the Challenge*, *supra* note 773, at 35; "Copyright in the Classroom." *Copyright in the Classroom | UC Copyright*, copyright.universityofcalifornia.edu/use/teaching.html.

931 *See* Basic Books, Inc. v. Kinko's Graphics Corp., 758 F. Supp. 1522 (S.D.N.Y. 1991).

932 Crews, *Copyright, Fair Use and the Challenge*, *supra* note 773, at 10, 47, 73.

933 *Ibid.* at 51, 63 (indicating that administrators, not faculty, are predominantly responsible for creating campus policies, thus leading to a result that is more conservative towards liability and less centered on academic purposes).

934 *Ibid.* at 74.

935 "Research Guides: Copyright and Fair Use: Copyright in the Classroom." *Copyright in the Classroom – Copyright and Fair Use – Research Guides at Texas A&M University – Central Texas*, tamuct.libguides.com/copyright.

pus policies is that fair use becomes more rigid, but they do provide the positive benefit of predictability in most cases. It should be recognized that none of Congress' guidelines on fair use have the force of law, but they have still nonetheless added rigidity to campus policies, created narrower than necessary interpretations along with numerous misinterpretations.[936]

4. How the Rings of Regulation Affect Access

Each ring of regulation creates additional hurdles to accessing creative works. The DMCA, for example, is extremely broad in scope. First, it does not necessarily require that a copy even be made, the files just must be accessed and, second, even if usage of the material would be covered by the fair use exception, the DMCA affords no such exception.[937] In other words, the DMCA acts more as a restriction on access to materials rather than a limitation on what a user may do with them, regardless of whether the underlying content is even copyrighted! Despite the specific technical restrictions proscribed by the TEACH Act, it still leaves content users ultimately reliant on fair use.[938] It is quite unrealistic that the provisions put forth, while meant to liberalize usage of copyrighted materials, are capable of being understood and followed by individual faculty members. Rather, the TEACH Act's requirements have pushed institutions to centralize their copyright policies and administrations in order to comply.[939] The institutional policy, technology and instructional planning requirements are relatively detailed and demanding, thus making it less likely that individual faculty members would be in a position to conform their activities alone.[940] Finally, overbearing campus copyright policies could hamper research and teaching; administrators should be particularly careful to resist overly-restricting their faculties while still cautiously permitting fair use.

Acquiring access to creative works is a critical step in the information and innovation process. Students are no longer limited to their traditional libraries and online databases, which are traditionally offered by universities. There is now a variety of openly accessible databases of digitized texts. The Digital Humanities, for example, is an evolving area, incorporating

936 Crews, *Copyright, Fair Use and the Challenge*, *supra* note 773, at 63.
937 Netanel, *Copyright's Paradox*, *supra* note 645, at 17.
938 Crews, *Copyright, Fair Use and the Challenge*, *supra* note 773, at 67.
939 *Ibid.* at 68.
940 *Ibid.*

computing and digital technologies into the study of the humanities in order to analyze these issues with digital tools and methods.[941] These collaborations do not only include professors; they liberally allow students and non-academics to participate as well. Such research possibilities relate back to the traditional role of the university and tend to integrate them with newer approaches; education leads to improved human capital and research results in substantially more publications. Restrictive copyright laws can "frustrate" innovation on campuses, thereby impeding overall knowledge outputs. In addition to the laws, campus policies tend to divest faculty and students of their own creative works.[942] Frustrated research and innovation is the result of the many rings of regulation, stifling both individuals and institutions. In order to ascertain whether this is justifiable, a closer look at copyright's specific functions is provided below.

II. The Three Sectors as Gateways to Knowledge

The many different constellations of how copyrighted scholarly works are accessed unsurprisingly come into direct contact with the three major sectors in American society: the governmental sector, for-profit sector as well as the nonprofit sector. The greatest governmental involvement in supporting knowledge networks comes in the form of extensive subsidies granted to libraries, universities as well as other educational organizations. Direct governmental involvement in the dispersion of knowledge is present in the federal government's Library of Congress. Likely being the world's largest collection, the Library of Congress claims to provide access to over a hundred million items.[943] Of course, there is also state-level governmental involvement in the libraries, digital collections and teaching activities by state universities. In terms of scholarly works, a few major publishers that keep most first-class works locked behind paywalls dominate the for-profit sector. Other for-profit ventures include databases and streaming platforms full of second-class works, which can be accessed at the cost of users' data and exposure to advertising. Nonprofits are well represented in

941 *See, e.g.*, Coleman, Nicole, and Stanford University. "Mapping the Republic of Letters." *Mapping the Republic of Letters*, 2013, http://republicofletters.stanford.edu/.

942 Rooksby, *Branding of the American Mind*, *supra* note 510, at 203.

943 "Research and Reference Services: Frequently Asked Questions." *Library of Congress*, www.loc.gov/rr/res-faq.html.

terms of access to scholarly works. Private, nonprofit universities and other organizations are at the center of a vibrant publishing culture as well as being pioneers in the area of open access publishing. Finally, online, illegal pirating initiatives have also made a notable impact on the availability of academic works.

1. The Governmental Sector

Both the federal and state governments make major financial contributors to knowledge creation and dissemination in the US, but there are some serious concerns about their involvement. Government involvement risks mismanagement along with more nefarious attempts at censorship. As an example of mismanagement, one can look to the Library of Congress' attempts in the 1950's to convert old texts, primarily newspapers, to microfilm. Not only was microfilm subject to degradation, impractical and expensive, but billions of pages of irreplaceable content had also been destroyed in this endeavor.[944] Government censorship is also a reality; such attempts sometimes lead to the wholesale destruction of books or other materials.[945] The Ninth Circuit Court of Appeal's 2014 issuance of a secretive injunction, requiring the removal of the inflammatory and distasteful film *Innocence of Muslims*, was a clear example of copyright being wielded to suppress free expression.[946] This decision was later overruled, but the court noted the "unconscionable result" of there being a fifteen-

944 *See generally* Darnton, *supra* note 543, at 109–129.

945 *See e.g.*, McGreal, Chris. "Pentagon Tries to Buy Entire Print Run of US Spy Expose Operation Dark Heart." *The Guardian*, 13 Sept. 2010, www.theguardian.com/world/2010/sep/13/pentagon-afghanistan-spy-book-pulp (detailing the Pentagon's 2010 attempt to censor accounts of combat in Afghanistan outright, and, when that was denied, their attempts to buy and destroy the book to limit its circulation).

946 Nimmer, David. "Innocence of Copyright: An Inquiry into the Public Interest." *Journal of the Copyright Society of the USA*, vol. 63, no. 3, Summer 2016, p. 403 (citing to Garcia v. Google, no. 12-57302 (9th Cir. Feb. 26, 2014) (order) (ordering preliminary injunction for YouTube to remove "an anti-Islamic film, which used a performance that the plaintiff made for a different film")) (overturned); Garcia v. Google, no. 12-57302 (9th Cir. May 18, 2015) (*en banc*) (ruling that not only had the actress failed to demonstrate a copyright interest in the film, but also that "the injunction was unwarranted and incorrect as a matter of law and was a prior restraint that infringed the First Amendment values at stake.").

month-long "unconstitutional injunction" that restrained free expression over issues of public interest.[947]

The US and many western European countries could be fairly accused of allowing Internet service providers to restrict users' access without due process and transparent rules, but it does not seem that this is some general "conspiracy" to silence certain individuals or groups.[948] Past attempts of censorship, i.e. book burnings and prior restraints on publication, are now being permitted or required in the form of online content removal, the deletion of streaming channels as well as outright, lifelong bans on individual users by private companies that run some of the largest forums for political discussion. On the other hand, some countries such as China, Iran, Saudi Arabia and Russia have set up such significant obstacles to user access, limits on content and incursions into users' rights that they are "not free" and users face the fear of political repercussions, legal repercussions, or both.[949] A diverse array of sectors being involved in the provision of knowledge and "independence from government control" both strengthen the public discourse and flow of knowledge.[950] Remembering that free expression and privacy should be paramount to academic research, government libraries, infrastructure and databases are incomplete without the diverse and independent collections of the other sectors.

2. The For-Profit Sector: Paywalls

Tremendous amounts of first-class works are locked behind paywalls. Without payment for the content or subscription for a service, the content behind a paywall is not accessible.[951] Following a surge of journals being founded between the 1950's and 1970's, for-profit publishers started growing in prominence. Today, the for-profit publishers Elsevier, Springer, Taylor & Francis Group and Wiley each have thousands of journals in

947 Garcia v. Google, no. 12-57302 (9th Cir. May 18, 2015) (*en banc*).

948 Lessig, *Future of Ideas*, *supra* note 706, at 115.

949 Shahbaz, Adrian. "The Rise of Digital Authoritarianism." *Freedom on the Net 2018*, Oct. 2018, freedomhouse.org/sites/default/files/FOTN_2018_Final Booklet_11_1_2018.pdf.

950 Darnton, *supra* note 543, at 48.

951 Elkin-Koren, *supra* note 26, at 1, 2 (suggesting that most academic scholars, researchers and students in the US and Europe may not even notice these paywalls due to their institutional subscriptions).

their portfolios.[952] These four publishers alone own a hefty majority of the world's notable academic journals. Due to the strong continental authors' right tradition, the overwhelming majority of the largest publishing houses are, non-coincidentally, European.[953] Their virtual monopoly over academic publishing positioned them to charge monopoly prices and empty university library coffers. Students suffer directly as well; the average student will likely have to pay well over $1,000 just for their course books every year.[954] The for-profit printing monopoly was carried over into the digital realm, where, unlike in the entertainment realm, digitization has only resulted in price increases. Some students avoid buying textbooks altogether and their accompanying digital access codes that grant access to homework and other supplementary materials. Those that do pay for them complain about the extra costs associated with doing simple class assignments.[955]

The acquisition of so many journal titles, while beneficial to the major for-profit publishers, increases prices for those who wish to access the journals. Such acquisitions result in, on average, a twenty percent price increase.[956] This involvement of for-profit publishers has spawned many criticisms. Just to name a few, for-profit publishers are accused of com-

---

952 Marciani, Dante. "Boycott of Elsevier Journals: Can New Ideas Reduce the Cost for Scientific Publications?" *Enago Academy*, 23 May 2018, www.enago.com/academy/boycott-of-elsevier-journals-brings-new-ideas-about-cost-for-scientific-publications/ (publishing more than 2,500, 2,900, 2,400 and 1,500 journals, respectively).

953 Baldwin, *supra* note 689, at 366 (stating:
... that seven of the world's eight largest publishing corporations were European in 2010, while only the smallest one (McGraw Hill) was American.... From the 1980's and on, two of the three publishers (Reed Elsevier, Springer, and Wiley) with a monopoly (forty-two percent) of the 25,000 leading English-language scientific periodicals were European. No other publisher controlled more than three percent of the market.).

954 Nguyen, Nicole A. "Not All Textbooks Are Created Equal: Copyright, Fair Use, and Open Access in the Open College Textbook Act of 2010." *DePaul Journal of Art, Technology and Intellectual Property*, vol. 21, 2010, p. 105; *see also* "Average Estimated Undergraduate Budgets, 2019-20- Research – College Board." *Research*, 1 Nov. 2019, research.collegeboard.org/trends/college-pricing/figures-tables/average-estimated-undergraduate-budgets-sector-2019-20 (suggesting that students should budget atleast $1,200 per year for textbooks and other course materials).

955 Johnson, *The Uncertain Future*, *supra* note 73, at 80-81.

956 Willinsky, *supra* note 36, at 18; *see also* Graber-Stiehl, *supra* note 910 (noting that yearly subscriptions for chemistry journals in 2017 cost $4,773 on average while more generalized scientific journals averaged $1,556 per year).

moditizing academic knowledge, restricting access to those with fewer financial resources (this has proven particularly true in poorer countries), charging excessive fees, privatizing the fruits of publicly funded research, exploiting academics, editors and authors as unpaid reviewers as well as turning inordinately high profits.[957] Generating some of the highest profit margins of any industry, these major publishers do so by essentially selling academics' own works back to them.[958] Journal and database subscriptions, now usually costing universities between $500,000 and $2 million per year, have become so exorbitant that even the top universities in the US have called it unaffordable, while other institutions abroad have been forced to cancel their subscriptions altogether.[959]

A 2006 study demonstrated the disparity in costs for accessing ecology journals from three different sample groups: nonprofit publishers, for-profit publishers and nonprofits in cooperation with for-profits. The nonprofit private societies and university presses charge on average $0.29 per page, the joint undertakings averaged $0.92 per page and for-profit publishers averaged $1.42 per page.[960] The authors of this study emphasized that higher prices are not a seal of higher quality, and, actually, that "[nonprofit] journals tend to be older, more prestigious, and more highly cited than their for-profit counterparts."[961] These pricing tendencies occur not only with regard to ecology, but have been recorded in economics, mathematics, neuroscience, physics and other atmospheric sciences as well.[962] Another study on economic journals in 2001, measuring the frequency of citations thereto, found that, along with being more prestigious, nonprofit journals were substantially more affordable; subscriptions to the six top nonprofit journals cost $180 per year, whereas a subscription to the top five for-profit journals averaged around $1,660 per year.[963]

---

957 Fuchs et al., *supra* note 37, at 428–29 (comparing publishing houses' rates of profit, averaging 18.9 percent in the study, with those of Exxon Mobil at 10.7 percent and Walmart at 3.6 percent).

958 Baldwin, *supra* note 689, at 296.

959 Graber-Stiehl, *supra* note 910 (describing the German University of Konstanz's decision to cancel its subscription to Elsevier journals in 2014); *see also* Denicola, *supra* note 894, at 352 (describing how yearly subscriptions to some individual journals may cost in excess of $20,000).

960 Bergstrom, Carl T. "The Economics of Ecology Journals." *Frontiers in Ecology and the Environment*, vol. 4, no. 9, Nov. 2006, p. 489.

961 *Ibid.*

962 Fuchs et al., *supra* note 37, at 428, 430.

963 Bergstrom, Carl T. "Free Labor for Costly Journals?" *Journal of Economic Perspectives*, vol. 15, no. 3, 2001, p. 183.

One reason the for-profits charge significantly more may be related to the scarcity of information that they create. Not only does their heavy involvement in some areas of publishing give them monopolies over entire areas of content, but they can also exercise absolute control over it with their paywalls. These monopolies are justified on the basis of copyright law and further entrenched by the DMCA's safeguards against technological circumvention. Because suitable substitutes for the content may not be available elsewhere, for-profit publishers tend to request prices far exceeding their costs as well as prices that are significantly higher than some of the high-quality, nonprofit journals. The one area in which for-profit publishers are lagging is in the open publishing of first-class academic works.

In a study observing whether publishers were nonprofit or for-profit, and whether their journals are open or closed access, a randomly selected sample of all journals showed that seventy-one percent of the sample group tended to be published by for-profit organizations, whereas the other twenty-nine percent were nonprofit.[964] While twelve percent of the journals overall were categorized as "open access," this category was highly dominated by nonprofit organizations; nonprofits published eighty-four percent of the open access journals.[965] Conversely, eighty-eight percent of the journals were "closed access" and of those, for-profits played the largest role, publishing seventy-eight percent of them.[966] The authors of this study criticized the for-profit publisher Thomson Reuters, suggesting that their monetization and stronger promotion of closed access journals leads to a marginalization of open access journals in the academic world.[967] Publishers' efforts to restrict access behind paywalls prevents most of their articles from being seen in the realm of open access; a minor exception exists where authors electronically publish pre-peer reviewed articles or

964 Fuchs et al., *supra* note 37, at 428, 430–31 (noting that the authors selected 8,600 journals total from Thomson Reuters' Science Citation Index, Social Scieces Citation Index and the Arts and Humanities Citation Index; of these, their randomly selected sample consisted of 210 journals. This database includes journals only with "high visibility," that is, journals that they promote because of the apparent publishing standards, content, international diversity of authorship and, most importantly, data indicating how often they are cited).

965 *Ibid.* at 428, 31.

966 *Ibid.*

967 *Ibid.* at 428, 32.

they make their work available in an electronic archive in accordance with the publishers' terms.[968]

Whether nonprofit or for-profit, publishers justify their services by conducting peer review, searching for plagiarism, editing, typesetting, adding data, distributing and promoting the journals.[969] Some of the most highly regarded journals protect their prestige, in part, by using external peer reviewers, whereas others, usually open access journals with limited resources, are dependent on their staff for peer review.[970] These services by publishers are not without value, but must be weighed against the publishers' impediments to the access of knowledge. Regardless of whether academic value is in fact added to the final journal publication, the publishers (most often those that are for-profit) will have exclusive license to the authors' works as well as the contributions of the editors that they hire.[971] Although, publishers have not been so effective in assuming copyrights for books. In many cases the publishers will negotiate only the right of first publication; between this and the higher fixed costs associated with book publication, they are able to protect their interests.[972]

The authors of this study left open the possibility that open access journals are "of less quality, attract less interest, and therefore have fewer citations," thus, potentially leaving open access journals generally underrepresented.[973] Nevertheless, even if this were the case, it would be indicative of a "vicious cycle of reinforcing reputation for journals published in for-profit journals," meaning that the closed access journals, receiving preferential database indexing, will accumulate more citations and greater perceived reputation over time, perpetuating the structural favoritism toward closed access journals. Another reason that open access journals may be slower to gain traction is because they are also less selective in their choice of what to publish; fewer authors make submissions to these journals.[974] This reputation element also plays a major role in the selection of journal subscriptions in the university libraries; faculty members are driven to enhance their academic prestige, so they naturally desire to publish

968 Willinsky, *supra* note 36, at 42.
969 Graber-Stiehl, *supra* note 910.
970 Denicola, *supra* note 894, at 360–61.
971 Willinsky, *supra* note 36, at 44–45.
972 *Ibid*. at 47.
973 Fuchs et al., *supra* note 37, at 428, 432.
974 Denicola, *supra* note 894, at 360.

with and have access to the most exclusive journals, leaving their librarian colleagues to make the tough budgeting decisions.[975]

Closed access publishing, and its constantly increasing subscription costs, should be viewed in in light of its inputs; most of the publications are written and edited by university professors who receive no compensation.[976] The profits, rather, go to the for-profit publishers and their shareholders. Furthermore, these works will likely be subject to the most stringent copyright protection and the greatest technological hurdles to access. For-profit publishers currently maintain *status quo* with their self-perpetuating system. On the other hand, open access journals and articles are increasing in quantity.[977] There is reason to believe that open access journals are increasing in article citations, but they are still currently not competitive with the closed access journals in terms of *citation impact* because of their lower visibility and lower journal rankings.[978]

3. The For-Profit Sector: Free Access

Numerous for-profit Internet-based platforms provide "free access" to knowledge.[979] A growing number of free access sources provide users with access to quality information and permission to use it; the majority of this content would qualify as second-class works.[980] Upon a simple online search, a user could access free information from websites such as YouTube, Google Books, Google Scholar or millions of other websites.[981] Furthermore, some platforms, namely Google, have begun assembling massive digitized book collections that provide unparalleled search capabilities. As mentioned above, these platforms tend to make content avail-

---

975 Darnton, *supra* note 543, at 71.

976 Netanel, *Copyright: What Everyone Needs to Know*, *supra* note 643, at 201.

977 Dorta-González, Pablo, et al. "Reconsidering the Gold Open Access Citation Advantage Postulate in a Multidisciplinary Context: an Analysis of the Subject Categories in the Web of Science Database 2009-2014." *Scientometrics*, vol. 112, no. 2, 2017, p. 876.

978 *Ibid.*

979 I refer to these sources as "free access" because, especially with regard to peer review, they do not fit strictly into the category of "open access.".

980 *See e.g.*, "Directory of Open Access Journals." *Directory of Open Access Journals*, 2020, doaj.org/about.

981 *But see* Elkin-Koren, *supra* note 26, at 1, 3 (noting in the case of "free content" that it is not entirely free because users may be paying with their own personal data, which is subject to any number of uses included targeted advertising).

able for "free" through advertising and the exploitation of users' data. Users' data and online habits are tracked, packaged and sold off just like any other commodity; users who believe that they are the *consumers*, may be surprised to learn that they have been transformed into a *product* as well. The collection and exploitation of data by online platforms—mostly by for-profits, but also by some nonprofits—raises a whole set privacy issues but is generally justified by the trade-off between user data and access to the platforms' services. Regardless of the platform-type, whether the provider is for-profit or nonprofit makes a tremendous difference in how accessible the materials are to users.

Many organizations within all sectors are spearheading the effort to digitize vast swaths of our collective patrimony; while the technology makes their efforts constantly more feasible, copyright remains as an obstacle.[982] Of the works that have already been digitized, the overwhelming majority are already in the public domain.[983] Digital archivists still face the rigors and expenses of copyright licensing, but many works are also orphaned, i.e. their authors are either unknown or just not capable of being found. One suggestion has been to remove copyright protection from orphaned works.[984] This, of course, leads into the debate of whether to give some type of privilege to government agencies or nonprofit organizations, which could advance their efforts to digitize. Regardless of the entity form, all digitization efforts until now have been restricted because of lingering copyrights.[985] Digitizing materials is not only a means of providing more content, but also a way to add value to the content; accessibility will be increased, new ways of analyzing massive amounts of data will be facilitated and, finally, old works could be brought back into prominence.[986] As was seen in the case of Google digitizing millions of books, efforts to digitize can expose organizations to massive legal costs and potential liability.

Google tested the boundaries of fair use in its mass-digitization project. Following its digitization of millions of books, the Authors Guild sued for various copyright infringements.[987] Plaintiffs claimed that Google, through its Library Project and its Google Books project, infringed their copyrights by digitizing copies of tens of millions of books from major

982 Netanel, *Copyright's Paradox*, *supra* note 645, at 202.
983 *Ibid.*
984 *Ibid.*
985 *Ibid.* at 203.
986 Netanel, *Copyright: What Everyone Needs to Know*, *supra* note 643, at 157.
987 Authors Guild v. Google Inc., 804 F.3 d 202, 206 (2 d Cir. 2015); Authors Guild v. Google Inc., 136 S.Ct. 1658 (2016) (denying certiorari).

libraries without the permission of rights holders.[988] With these digital copies, Google made a publicly available search function that allows users to conduct no-cost searches within the texts. Users would only be able to see portions of the texts, displaying a maximum of five "snippets" of text containing their search terms.[989] Additionally, Google made the copies, in their entirety, available to participating libraries. In return, the libraries were required to agree that they would not use the digital copies in violation of the copyright laws.[990] The Second Circuit Court of Appeals determined that the fair use defense applied to the alleged copyright infringements.

In its fair use analysis, the court began by restating the goal of copyright: "[t]he ultimate goal of copyright is to expand public knowledge and understanding.... Thus, while authors are undoubtedly important intended beneficiaries of copyright, the ultimate, primary intended beneficiary is the public, whose access to knowledge copyright seeks to advance by providing rewards for authorship."[991] The court put the greatest emphasis on the fourth factor for fair use, i.e. the effect on potential markets, while also concluding, under the first factor, that Google's search function was "highly transformative."[992] Google's presentation of the texts differed substantially in purpose, character, expression, meaning and message from the originals.[993] Citing precedent regarding nonprofit or commercial purpose, the court also decided that there was "no reason in this case why Google's overall profit motivation should prevail as a reason for denying fair use over its highly convincing transformative purpose."[994] This determination was supported by the argument that the "most universally accepted forms of fair use, such as news reporting and commentary, quotation in historical or analytic books, reviews of books, and performances, as well as parody,

988 Authors Guild v. Google Inc., 804 F.3 d 202, 207 (2 d Cir. 2015).

989 *Ibid.* at 207.

990 *Ibid.*

991 *Ibid.* at 212.

992 *Ibid.* at 216, 223–25 (noting that Google's snippets provided access to no more than sixteen percent of any book; this became especially relevant for the fourth factor, in that it did not negatively affect copyright holders' potential revenues).

993 *Ibid.* at 217.

994 *Ibid.* at 219 (noting that Google neither placed advertisements on these search functions nor charged users any fees. Plaintiff's argument that this "free" service contributes to Google's "dominance of the world-wide Internet search market" went unaddressed in the court's decision).

are all normally done commercially for profit."[995] In this case, Google was allowed to proceed with its project, but the boundaries of fair use remain unclear.

As was alluded to above, for-profits have data and privacy issues, especially in cases where they make content available for "free." Instances, in which their content is freely accessible, i.e. not behind a paywall, usually come at the cost of users trading personal data in exchange for access. Not only will users' search histories be traced and stored, but also this information is likely to be sold to third parties for other marketing or advertising purposes. For those for-profit providers without paywalls like Google, there is also a serious concern that they can monopolize access, regardless of whether the materials are copyright protected or in the public domain, and then go on to bundle and sell access to the materials back to the public.[996] Public collections are subject to being acquired by eager entrepreneurs who which to commoditize public materials as nothing other than assets.[997] Finally, another major issue is longevity. For-profit business will continue in their endeavors only if they remain profitable. Once the profits are diminished, the for-profit entrepreneurs will be forced either to change their business models or to go out of business entirely. As inconceivable as it may be, today's giants such as Google could also fall prey to superior competition and changing markets; in fact, it would be exceptional for this not to happen.

4. The Nonprofit Sector

The nonprofit sector provides a workable and rather good alternative to the governmental and for-profit sectors for the creation and distribution of knowledge. Many of the most pressing issues with today's massive for-profit publishers are addressed by the nonprofit and, frankly, pirating efforts to promote open access. Some pirates are fueled by the ideology that all knowledge ought to be brought into the public domain, but those in academia, are mostly outraged by the major publishers' rent-seeking,

995 *Ibid.* (stating, in dictum, "[j]ust as there is no reason for presuming that a commercial use is not a fair use, which would defeat the most widely accepted and logically justified areas of fair use, there is likewise no reason to presume categorically that a nonprofit educational purpose should qualify as a fair use.").

996 Darnton, *supra* note 543, at 14, 47 (describing this scenario as being a "public access license").

997 *Ibid.* at 11.

taking advantage of both public knowledge and university resources.[998] Universities, while still restricting students' and professors' ownership rights and generating most of the content found behind paywalls, paradoxically, are the leaders in open access publishing, at least to the extent that is permissible within the regulatory rings.[999] Many professors are now beginning to publish articles and even some textbooks openly. One could see this, for example, at New York University Law School where IP professors have made their copyright law course book openly available.[1000] This particular book is now in use at universities around the world, along with some of the most prestigious universities in the US.[1001] Nonprofits also have aspects that are not entirely optimal; access to nonprofit services can be exclusive and expensive. Like the Library of Congress' microfilm mismanagement, Yale University alone is rumored to have eliminated half of its American history collection during such an undertaking.[1002]

Since universities in the US now invest more than ever before into scholarship and research, a tremendous amount of resources is allocated to supporting faculty and providing them with the proper facilities and equipment. Some of the largest private collections of books and journals can be found throughout the numerous nonprofit university and library collections.[1003] As a rule, most university libraries in the US have institutional subscriptions to research databases. With a subscription, a university receives a limited license to access vast amounts of knowledge.[1004] Not only is access to the databases restricted to paying users or institutional members, but also the works themselves are often restricted beyond the scope of copyright protection, as was discussed above. This is especially problematic with regard to users' rights in instances where publishers do not own the copyrights to works, and, furthermore, many of the works may not even be subject to copyright protection. Part I demonstrated

---

998 Baldwin, *supra* note 689, at 388.

999 *See generally* Crews, *Copyright, Fair Use and the Challenge*, *supra* note 773, at 11.

1000 "This Information Wants to Be Free: Casebooks by NYU Law IP Professors Are Available at No Charge." *NYU School of Law*, 5 Sept. 2019, www.law.nyu.edu/news/ideas/Fromer-Sprigman-Beebe-copyright-trademark-casebooks.

1001 Fromer, Jeanne C., and Christopher Jon Sprigman. "Copyright Law: Cases and Materials." *Copyright Law: Cases and Materials*, www.copyrightbook.org/about.

1002 Darnton, *supra* note 543, at 115, 17 (reporting that libraries in the US destroyed some 975,000 books in their efforts to covert to microfilm).

1003 *Ibid.* (distinguishing the variety in American collections from their European counterparts, which generally tend to be publically held).

1004 Bannerman, *supra* note 816, at 46.

that universities have, in their quest to become accessible, instead become prohibitively costly to attend. The rest of the citizenry unfortunately does not share their unparalleled level of access to academic works.

IP laws and policies also affect university insiders. Divesting faculty and students of their copyright ownership, or allowing for uncertainty as to ownership, is particularly reprehensible when students are paying tuition fees. However, more generally, creativity, innovation and entrepreneurship can be stifled in an environment where knowledge creation and dissemination should be the focus, not licenses and restrictions. Knowledge dissemination can best be aided by "new copyright rules and norms that champion openness, the rights of individuals, and creative freedom over institutional claims to and restrictions of rights."[1005] Academia's tendency to press ownership claims over IP tends to interfere with a culture of openness and decelerate innovation.[1006] While various for-profit undertakings and universities have forged the pathways for knowledge over the last centuries, technology has enabled an unprecedented, "powerful grassroots consumer movement [to spring] up on behalf of the public domain."[1007]

5. The Pirates

The largest movements pushing for a greater public domain are led by online pirating organizations. In 2015, publisher Elsevier, owner of over 2,500 journal titles, sued Russia-based Sci-Hub for its extensive reproduction and distribution of Elsevier copyrighted material for a preliminary injunction and damages.[1008] Elsevier documented that between 2,000 and 8,500 of its articles were being pirated by the defendants daily; access to the individual articles ranged between $19.95 and $41.95 each.[1009] Because, even by the defendant's admission, the articles were "willfully" taken, reproduced and distributed, the requested statutory damages ranged from $750 to $150,000 for each work.[1010] Sci-Hub's founder, Alexandra Elbakyan, did not appear before the court, but, rather, remained in Russia

1005 Rooksby, *Branding of the American Mind*, *supra* note 510, at 205.
1006 *Ibid.*
1007 Baldwin, *supra* note 689, at 297.
1008 Elsevier Inc. v. Sci-Hub, No. 1:15-CV-04282-RWS, 2 (S.D.N.Y. 2015).
1009 *Ibid.* at 3.
1010 *See* 17 U.S.C. § 504(c) (2011).

and cited the "public interest" as her defense to the initial preliminary injunction.[1011]

In a letter to the judge, focusing on the public interest, Elbakyan wrote that Sci-Hub provided access to journals that would otherwise not have been accessible in developing counties. Further, she argued that for-profit publishers, such as Elsevier, keep the majority of their materials behind paywalls, authors receive no financial benefit in exchange for Elsevier to assume their copyrights and finally, she argued that such publishers "limit distribution of knowledge."[1012] Elsevier, also focusing on the public interest, responded that this reproduction should be enjoined "to protect the delicate ecosystem which supports scientific research worldwide."[1013] From its perspective, Elsevier argued that its profits via journal fees support discovery, contribute toward new journals, help maintain a scientific record, aid in counteracting bad science and that this injunction would serve as a disincentive for pirating.[1014] Furthermore, Elsevier argued that Sci-Hub's free distribution of copyrighted material "disserved the public interest."[1015]

Citing precedent on the "public interest," the court recognized two countervailing public interests in what it called the "owner-user balance;" that is, the rights of users to access creative works weighed against *copyright owners*' rights and incentives for creative efforts.[1016] The court expressed its concern that not observing *copyright owner*'s rights "*can* threaten the store of knowledge to be accessed."[1017] It is crucial to recognize that, in undertaking its owner-user balance, the court never addressed Ms. Elbakyan's point that Elsevier is merely the copyright owner, not the author. In addition, the court simply accepted that lax copyright protections *can* affect the store of knowledge but made no further inquiry into whether her infringement *did* or *would* affect the supply of academic materials. Finally, the court used Elsevier's existence as proof that "publication of scientific research generates substantial economic value."[1018] The court's statement here stops short of inquiring for whom the economic value is generated. Furthermore, the court also stopped its analysis short of most

1011 Elsevier Inc. v. Sci-Hub, No. 1:15-CV-04282-RWS, 4 (S.D.N.Y. 2015).
1012 *Ibid.*
1013 *Ibid.* at 5.
1014 *Ibid.*
1015 *Ibid.*
1016 *Ibid.*
1017 *Ibid.*
1018 *Ibid.*

of the serious considerations brought up in Elbakyan's letter to the judge. This missed opportunity for the court to explore these issues was hardly its own fault though; Elbakyan, who did not appear, also did not hire counsel to plead her case.

In ruling in Elsevier's favor, the court cited the idea / expression dichotomy, fair use doctrine and limited terms of duration as sufficient protections for the public interest.[1019] Following the 2015 issuance of the preliminary injunction and defendants' non-appearance, the court, in 2017, issued a permanent injunction and ordered the payment of $15 million in damages with interest.[1020] Because the defendants remained in Russia, they did not stop their activity, paid no fines and, due to the attention generated from the lawsuit, their website traffic increased exponentially.[1021] It has been estimated that Sci-Hub provides access to about eighty-five percent of all scholarly articles that are ordinarily kept behind paywalls.[1022]

Pirated academic works can be found on an ever-growing number of websites and download torrents. An immense amount of materials are shared peer-to-peer by individuals who may be idealistic about the sharing of information, politically motivated or, even, admirers of authors, who want to promote them by increasing the works' exposure. The logic of doing so would be that exposure and dissemination of a work would add more value to it than withholding it behind a paywall.[1023] Those activists who involve themselves in the hacking and pirating of academic works are likely doing it out of "the democratic and Enlightenment tradition of throwing open humanity's common patrimony to all."[1024]

Movements toward a more expansive public domain, supported by digital technologies, are the newest iteration in the competition between authors' interests and the public's ability to access works. Piracy met mainstream politics in 2006 with Sweden's Pirate Party (*Piratpartiet*) being founded to fight the restrictions on patents and copyright. Their platform, based on the free-flow of knowledge, has recently been expanded to in-

---

1019 *Ibid.*

1020 *Ibid.* at 2.

1021 Graber-Stiehl, *supra* note 910.

1022 Kwon, Diana. "Sci-Hub Loses Domains and Access to Some Web Services." *The Scientist Magazine*, 25 Oct. 2018, www.the-scientist.com/daily-news/sci-hub-loses-domains-and-access-to-some-web-services-30264 (noting that, as a result of the Elsevier and another major lawsuit, Sci-Hub's daily downloads increased from 200,000 per day in 2016 to 600,000 in 2017).

1023 Baldwin, *supra* note 689, at 322.

1024 *Ibid.* at 387.

clude privacy and transparency issues.[1025] The party gained notoriety when police raided the associated Pirate Bay facilities in 2010.[1026] Germany's Pirate Party and similar parties in dozens of other countries were founded not long after Sweden's. These political parties have not turned out to be major political forces but have nonetheless made the world more aware of the legal issues affecting the flow of knowledge.[1027]

III. Production Function Assessment

Copyright's *production function*, i.e. incentives for authors to create and disseminate their works, is the cornerstone of the American copyright system. On one hand, if incentives for authorship are negligible or inadequate, it could reasonably be expected that fewer creative works will be brought to fruition. On the other hand, if the incentives go too far or do not coincide with authors' actual interests, many potential consumers of the copyrighted works may be unnecessarily excluded. Another way in which the public should be benefited by copyright is through the limitations on the rights afforded to copyright holders' monopolies; users should be able to access, use and build upon materials.[1028] Copyright's exclusion of some is a form of deadweight loss, leading to the critical question for this analysis: do the incentives created by copyright *actually* drive the creation of new works that would have otherwise not been created? If the incentives do promote authorship, a certain amount of deadweight loss can be considered justifiable. In order to determine if authorship is promoted, it will be necessary to identify the various types of authors within the realm of copyright while observing their interactions with the incentives for authorship.

Copyright is indispensable in the entertainment industry; most works are created with financial profit in mind and copyright is the basis for licensing and enforcement.[1029] Academic publishing does not follow the same incentive patterns as the entertainment industry. Even if they have a profit motive, academic authors are likely to see little or no profits from

---

1025 "Principprogram." *Piratpartiet*, 2020, piratpartiet.se/principprogram/.

1026 Zetter, Kim. "Pirate Bay Has Been Raided and Taken Down: Here's What We Know." *Wired*, Conde Nast, 3 June 2017, www.wired.com/2014/12/pirate-bay-raided-taken-down/.

1027 Baldwin, *supra* note 689, at 342.

1028 Netanel, *Copyright: What Everyone Needs to Know*, *supra* note 643, at 86.

1029 Telephone interview with Paul S. McGrath Esq., Business and Legal Affairs Coordinator, Skydance Media (Feb. 26, 2019).

their journals or manuscripts due either to their employer-universities restricting their rights or because of the publishers retaining the profits.[1030] For most academics, there is essentially no financial profit-motive to publish. This is most evident in the growing category of open access journals that sometimes charge the authors thousands of dollars to make their works openly available to the public.[1031] The likelihood of any work, let alone an academic one, being a major financial success is the same as being struck by lightning; an author that is cited to a hundred times can already consider him- or herself to be in the top 1.8 percent of authors in terms of citation frequency.[1032]

Rather than being incentivized by profit, academic authors publish for prestige. Prestige within the academic community increases with citations and recognition. These may lead to salary increases, better positions, consultancies as well as highly coveted positions as board members and editors of reputable journals.[1033] The overwhelming majority of academic authors have little objection to their works being circulated openly, just as long as there is some attribution for their contributions.[1034] Considering the numerous incentives that come into play in incentivizing authorship and publication, while generally trying to promote progress and learning, the Supreme Court acknowledged the "difficult balance between the interests of authors" and "society's competing interest in the free flow of ideas, information, and commerce."[1035]

This delicate balance between competing interests is materialized in the rules of copyright law and its exceptions, namely fair use. In an attempt to describe copyright and its interaction with fair use, many turn to the field of economics, and namely the "market failure" theory.[1036] This ap-

---

1030 Willinsky, *supra* note 36, at 6.

1031 *Ibid.* at 5.

1032 Beaulieu, Luc, and Parminder Basran. "How Many Citations Are Actually a Lot of Citations?" *Ruminating...*, 28 Dec. 2018, https://lucbeaulieu.com/2015/11/19/how-many-citations-are-actually-a-lot-of-citations/ (stating that around forty-four percent of all manuscripts are never cited to and only the top twenty-four percent of publications receive ten or more citations).

1033 Willinsky, *supra* note 36, at 21.

1034 Denicola, *supra* note 894, at 356.

1035 Sony Corp. of America v. Universal City Studios, Inc., 464 U.S. 417, 463 (1984).

1036 *See generally* Gordon, Wendy J. "Fair Use as Market Failure: A Structural and Economic Analysis of the Betamax Case and Its Predecessors." *Columbia Law Review*, vol. 82, 1982, p. 1600; *see also* Posner, Richard A. *Economic Analysis of Law*. 7th ed., Wolters Kluwer Law & Business, 2007.

proach incorporates the free market theory of Adam Smith, saying that an efficiently functioning market system, based on voluntary transfers between individuals, will "create a socially desirable pattern of resource allocation."[1037] Maximization of value, i.e. perfect market conditions, can only be realized when the following preconditions are present: the costs and benefits of a transaction must be "internal" to those participating, consumers must have "perfect knowledge" as to the available products as well as those offered by competitors and, finally, there must be no "transaction costs," the costs associated with obtaining information, costs of negotiation and costs of enforcing rights.[1038]

No system has all the preconditions for value maximization. Some reasons for this include government created monopolies, government subsidies, a lack of information between parties and potentially high transaction costs. Thus, all systems are on a spectrum where they can be viewed as being either relatively more or less desirable for resource allocation. Applying this to copyright, market failure occurs when the costs of a transaction between two negotiating parties exceed the potential social benefits of the transaction. Fair use is, thus, according to this theory, used as a mechanism to force a nonconsensual transfer of rights from one party to another.[1039] In other words, when a market failure occurs, i.e. when the costs for voluntary transactions are prohibitive, fair use should allow for a small, limited use.[1040] This theory has become the most dominant in scholarly attempts to describe the relationship between copyright and fair use as well as being fundamental to legislative policy and judicial decisions.[1041]

1. The Production Function and the Different Types of Works

In addition to the free market theory being applied to traditional consumer goods and services, its application also provides a good rough approximation for resource allocation relating to copyright.[1042] The copyrighted materials' types—entertainment or academic—are determinative as

1037 Smith, *Wealth of Nations*, *supra* note 323; Gordon, *supra* note 1036, at 1605.

1038 *Ibid.* at 1607–08.

1039 *Ibid.* at 1615.

1040 Bell & Parchomovsky, *Dual-Grant Theory*, *supra* note 642, at 1053.

1041 *Ibid.*

1042 Under the market theory, the allocation of resources occurs as an aggregate result of all market participants' actions, limitations and decisions. This in conto how these resources are allocated. Copyrighted materials for entertainment are generally produced by identifiable private parties, the alternatives and prices are somewhat standard and, especially in the era of music and video streaming, the transaction costs are limited. While there are certainly inefficiencies, this results in an ideal market where copyrighted entertainment can be produced and consumed in a near-optimal manner. Contrary to copyrighted works for entertainment, copyrighted academic materials are not disseminated nearly as efficiently.

Academic works, observed through the lens of the free market theory, tend heavily towards market failure due to their non-desirable resource allocation. Legal "authorship" may be unclear when professors are creating works within universities that likely own the rights to their works. Furthermore, their research may be subsidized by federal grants that precondition their funding on open access publishing requirements. The "consumers," other academics or outside researchers, may not be involved in the procurement of the works, often done via library or employer licensing, and may not have direct knowledge of the actual costs associated with procurement. Their knowledge is also limited in terms of what product they may be receiving; most researchers have experienced reading through, at one point or another, misleading and uninformative article abstracts prior to accessing the works. Finally, the "transaction costs" are astronomically high in the area of academic research. Academic materials simply are too expensive for individual access and licenses for institutional access to databases, arguably the most efficient means of negotiation, continually become more expensive.[1043]

Creative works that are fixed into digital files without technical restrictions are unparalleled in their ability to be copied, shared and distributed. At virtually no cost, one can save and share digital files without degrading their technical quality.[1044] This aspect of technology has substantially low-

---

trast to command models, where a centralized authority makes all allocative decisions.

1043 Netanel, *Copyright's Paradox*, *supra* note 645, at 76.

1044 Digital media are still not immune from the problems that have affected traditional print media. Digitally stored bits can degrade, documents can be lost in cyberspace, hardware and software become obsolete at ever-increasing rates and works that are currently being "born digital" will never have a hard-copy backup in case they ever encounter any of these issues. Furthermore, as long as digital works are available, they can be continuously edited; this raises serious questions of whether content is the same from one day to the next. These concerns with digital media, though, do not discount its promise of preserving

ered the transaction costs in the realm of copyrighted works in entertainment—recall the affordable bundle of video streaming platforms—whereas the costs for academic materials are exorbitant; the market failure theory would suggest that this is a greater reason to apply fair use.[1045] Individual negotiation for access to academic materials has become so unaffordable that it is untenable. Furthermore, potential litigation costs, i.e. transaction costs, likely dwarf any investment made for a given academic work. The artificial scarcity created by copyright creates a "societal deadweight loss" in that reduced access leads to higher, monopoly-like prices, inevitably leading to the exclusion of willing consumers.[1046] If, theoretically, copyright did not exist and there were a free and competitive market for creative works, copies of most works would likely be distributed at substantially lower prices, also eliminating the need for derivative authors to purchase licenses in order to use the original works for their own creations. With copyright, though, works are priced in excess of their competitive, market prices; deadweight loss, an unfortunate result of copyright law, is the outcome.[1047]

Deadweight loss is also unevenly dispersed among the different types of creative works. The many avenues over the Internet have diversified consumers' options. Even pirating websites, albeit illegal, have provided further access to content. For those looking for entertainment, cheap or free access creates very little deadweight loss. On the other hand, access to scholarly books and journals, especially the most current ones, can be astronomically expensive for both individuals and institutions alike.[1048] Take the treatise *Nimmer on Copyright* for example, which is widely regarded as being the most authoritative source on copyright law.[1049] An individual looking to acquire a copy would likely not wish to pay the $6,000 price (plus $3,940 per year for the annual updates), thus the potential buyer becomes the deadweight loss in this scenario.[1050] Institutions in the US

---

and making works available everywhere and to everyone. Darnton, *supra* note 543, at 37; Lessig, *Free Culture*, *supra* note 709, at 109, 226.

1045 Bell & Parchomovsky, *Dual-Grant Theory*, *supra* note 642, at 1054.

1046 Netanel, *Copyright's Paradox*, *supra* note 645, at 123.

1047 Netanel, *Copyright: What Everyone Needs to Know*, *supra* note 643, at 87.

1048 *Ibid.* at 88.

1049 Bartow, Ann. "The Hegemony of the Copyright Treatise." *University of Cincinnati Law Review*, vol. 73, 2004, p. 587.

1050 Accessing *Nimmer on Copyright* was a learning experience for me. The print version of the treatise at the University of Cologne was last updated in the 1960's, years before the Copyright Act of 1976 came into force. Even on a

would be more likely to be able to afford such treatises, but, as they start to accumulate larger collections, library costs become unsustainable. A side effect of these costs is the accompanying pressure on administrators to raise tuition fees. A further example of deadweight loss regarding academic materials is also apparent at the many institutions in developing countries that cannot afford the most expensive subscriptions.

2. The Production Function and Academic Works

Returning to the question of whether deadweight loss is justifiable, it should first be noted that the entertainment realm of copyright has relatively little deadweight loss, whereas the academic realm has a great deal of deadweight loss. For the entertainment industry, this does not necessarily mean that the copyright regime caused the materials to be accessible at reasonable prices, but, rather, that it has provided a means of protecting authors' works without acting as a significant hindrance to access.[1051] In contrast, many individuals and institutions are unable to access academic works because of the costs; this monopoly pricing is the product of publishers' ability to put the copyrighted materials behind DMCA-protected

---

research trip to Duquesne University School of Law, I was not able to find a current version of the treatise in print. Both universities have it available electronically, but one must be enrolled at one of the universities in order to access it. The lesson here being that the digitization of academic works is acting to remove (current) books from the shelves and replacing them with highly restricted and expensive paywalled databases. Fair use was developed with the understanding that people would generally be able to pull a book off of the shelf and *only* their usage of it need be scrutinized. Now, fair use continues to exist as a defense, but the books are no longer on the shelves and they can only be accessed digitally in the ivory tower, beyond a paywall. Nimmer, David. "Nimmer on Copyright." *LexisNexis Store*, Matthew Bender Elite Products, https://store.lexisnexis.com/products/nimmer-on-copyright-sku usSku10441.

1051 I suspect that there are other factors at play, such as market competition, which tend to drive access costs down. Although this and many other aspects of copyrighted works made for entertainment are beyond the scope of this dissertation, they are very-much deserving of further study. Nimmer, David. "Access Denied." *Utah Law Review*, no. 3, 2007, p. 783 (noting that since one of the incentives of copyright is to bring unpublished works into the public realm, the automatic application of copyright protection to unpublished works upon fixation, regardless of whether they are ever shared, seriously calls this system of incentives into question).

paywalls. There is little- to no financial incentive for authors in academia, so the significant detriment to society, i.e. deadweight loss, is hardly justifiable; copyright's production function falls short in this regard. As a practical result, this should mean that constitutional safeguards such as the idea / expression dichotomy or fair use then become relevant, providing a means of access for those who have been left out. Whether these safeguards provide an adequate degree of access is discussed in greater detail below in the assessment of the expressive function.

IV. Structural Function Assessment

Copyright's structural function is what allows authors to support themselves with their works. Copyright does, indeed, create a market of its own for authors to sell access to their works, but even in the absence of copyright protection, some works would still be marketable.[1052] The structural function, similar to the production function, is a balance, meant to promote authorship, which sometimes results in deadweight loss. For this reason, the structural function will similarly be analyzed by asking the same question that was posed above: do the incentives created by copyright *actually* drive the creation of new works that would have otherwise not been created? In the context of the structural function, the means of support for authors will be closely observed, while considering whether the incentives remain necessary to promote authorship. Deadweight loss can be justified only when authorship continues to be promoted by the copyright system, thus requiring that potential market-alternatives for copyright be taken into consideration. The story of copyright's structural function has also been one of influence over the content, quality and quantity of works being created.[1053]

1052 Lessig, *Free Culture*, *supra* note 709, at 64 (making a convincing argument that even when copies are pirated and sold cheaply in poorer countries, they do not actually displace sales in the US; if people in poorer countries only had the option of paying full price, they would simply not buy a copy. There is no lost profit when a pirated copy is bought in these instances. This is a clear case of a market, albeit illegal, functioning without copyright enforcement).

1053 *See generally* McLuhan, Marshall, and Quentin Fiore. *The Medium Is the Massage*. Random House, 1967, p. 50 (describing the evolving media landscape and how "...the printed book added much to the new cult of individualism. The private, fixed point of view became possible and literacy conferred the power of detachment, non-involvement.").

Considering early patronage systems, the precursors to copyright and modern copyright, this section will consider how technology and networking have provided other, workable structures for authorship. Clergy, university professors and scattered book collections, which are some of the earlier sources of knowledge, saw enormous changes with the invention of the printing press, expanding transportation networks, telegraph, radio, television and, now, again with the modern, digital revolution.[1054] Modern access to knowledge includes an abundance of options including printed and electronic materials, but to put this into perspective, it is essential first to look at the precise role played by the printing press in the dispersion of knowledge. This section will discuss how early systems of patronage were replaced by the marketplace for works created by copyright monopolies. More importantly, looking at the platforms that have come to provide alternatives to the marketplace created by copyright, this section will look at the modern issues regarding authorship and dissemination of works.

1. Structure in the Print Era

The invention of the printing press in the mid-fifteenth century marked the transition from Europe's Middle Ages to the Renaissance.[1055] Many mathematical, scientific and other works sharing "extremely valuable knowledge" from the Classical period had been either forgotten or neglected by medieval scholars.[1056] With the help of the printing press, Renaissance academics were empowered to correct texts, make proper translations and to comment on ancient works, which would have otherwise remained unknown. This reinvigoration of Classical works directly and substantively affected the scientific research of the Renaissance, enabling both academics and amateurs to work from a foundation of information and knowledge.[1057] Support for academics in this era commonly came in the form of direct papal or royal patronage and indirectly through university professorships.

This new-found access to information brought about by the printing press not only improved the form and content of mathematics and the sciences, but changed the "composition of the world of learning" entire-

1054 Baldwin, *supra* note 689, at 54.
1055 Drake, *supra* note 40, at 43–44.
1056 *Ibid.*
1057 *Ibid.*

ly.[1058] Prior to the printing press, academics typically had both access to important manuscripts in their fields, as well as a general awareness of significant works through their communities.[1059] It is also worth noting that oral university lectures and disputations were the norm during the Middle Ages, and later, with the spread of printed books, the written word became dominant.[1060] In contrast, amateurs outside of the universities would neither have had access to such manuscripts, nor reliable information regarding them prior to the invention of the printing press.[1061] The term *amateur*, in this context, is referring to those who were educated and had some talent in the fields in which they occupied themselves, while not being part of academia.

Once the printing press was invented and printed materials became widely available, the greatest leaps in innovation and improvements in access to knowledge occurred outside the universities.[1062] During the Middle Ages, the study of physical sciences, for example, was monopolized by the universities. Following the spread of the printed book, the door was opened for amateurs to educate themselves and to make their independent contributions to the sciences.[1063] State and religious patrons, who granted numerous privileges but also played strong regulatory roles, supported these universities.[1064] Because the universities began losing control over the flow of knowledge, and, thus, authority over the content, amateurs and independent scientific societies became more relevant than ever before. Despite this, universities retained their grasp on professional licensing, acting as a gatekeeper to the admission to many professions.[1065]

1058 *Ibid.* at 43, 45.

1059 *Ibid.* at 43, 48.

1060 Rüegg, Walter. "The Rise of Humanism." *A History of the University in Europe: Volume I, Universities in The Middle Ages*, edited by Hilde De Ridder-Symoens, Cambridge University Press, 1992, pp. 442, 467.

1061 Drake, *supra* note 40, at 43, 46, 48 (noting that, by 1500, books were widely available and relatively inexpensive throughout Europe).

1062 *Ibid.* at 43, 48.

1063 *Ibid.* (listing a number of prominent medieval writers on the sciences who were almost certainly all university professors, some of which even wrote materials for university lectures. Moreover, as a contrast, listing the leading thinkers of the sixteenth century in the physical sciences, and noting that the majority of them never taught at a university).

1064 De Ridder-Symoens, *Management and Resources*, *in* VOLUME II, UNIVERSITIES IN EARLY MODERN EUROPE, *supra* note 149, at 165–67 (describing many instances of European sovereigns meddling in university affairs).

1065 McSherry, *supra* note 15, at 52.

Printing houses also played a substantial role in encouraging amateurs and their research. Directly following the invention of the printing press in the late fifteenth and early sixteenth centuries, a great number of printers failed due to their commercially unviable, usually humanist, printed collections.[1066] The majority of early printers were commercial ventures, which, while facing the risk of losing their large capital investments, were incentivized to publish novel theories.[1067] Of these initial printers, the most successful outside of the universities were those selling to major commercial centers such as Venice, Antwerp or Paris.[1068] There were also printers who set up their operations in university towns and acquired monopolies to print all of the academic materials. The monopolies came at the cost of prioritizing university printing, doing so at pre-established fixed prices and subjecting themselves to local laws.[1069] There was also a third, minor category of printing presses; some institutions, such as the University of Oxford, in 1636, and the University of Cambridge, in 1698, established their own presses that only remained in existence due to their legal monopolies to print certain books.[1070]

The sixteenth century universities at the beginning of the Scientific Revolution were especially conservative organizations, focused on preserving the status quo. Their primary role was to "preserve learning, examine it critically, and impart it," while research or the creation of new knowledge was not an objective.[1071] In fact, there was little expectation that there would have been any real innovation within the universities of that era.[1072] Universities were actually somewhat hostile to the modern methods that where developing outside of their walls.[1073] The private printers, on the other hand, began by printing many classical texts, but then, in the search for new markets, began publishing numerous, novel texts by amateur authors.[1074] This tendency put the development of the sciences

1066 De Ridder-Symoens, *Management and Resources*, *in* Volume II, Universities in Early Modern Europe, *supra* note 149, at 155, 202.

1067 Drake, *supra* note 40, at 43, 47.

1068 Baldwin, *supra* note 689, at 55.

1069 De Ridder-Symoens, *Management and Resources*, *in* Volume II, Universities in Early Modern Europe, *supra* note 149, at 155, 202.

1070 *Ibid.* at 155, 204.

1071 Drake, *supra* note 40, at 43, 47.

1072 Porter, *Scientific Revolution and Universities*, *in* Volume II, Universities in Early Modern Europe, *supra* note 192, at 531, 533.

1073 Frijhoff, *Patterns*, *in* Volume II, Universities of Early Modern Europe, *supra* note 21, at 43, 45.

1074 Drake, *supra* note 40, at 43, 47.

onto two parallel paths where university professors' and outside amateurs' manuscripts could be published, commented upon and reconsidered in later research.[1075] Although both of these pathways were noticeably different in how they approached research, they did occasionally intersect; many of the independent amateurs, who drafted original works, translated classical mathematics or wrote scientific commentaries were typically university-educated and just did not remain at the universities to be professors.[1076]

There are a few other notable observations regarding the interrelationship between the printed word, the universities and the scientific world as a whole during the Scientific Revolution. The sixteenth and seventeenth centuries were a time of immense advances in the sciences, breaking with the methods of Antiquity. Classical, Aristotelian approaches used metaphysics, morals and theology as the means of attempting to understand nature.[1077] The Scientific Revolution generally set these Aristotelian approaches aside for its modern advances in astronomy, matter theory, theories of motion, inertia and gravity, mechanics, kinetics as well as the quantitative and "mathematical approach to nature."[1078] Printing helped, in part, to "kill off" reliance on Classical theories; the mass dissemination of printed information contributed towards "a climate of scientific controversy, criticism and competition."[1079]

Despite not playing a major research role, universities still contributed to the Scientific Revolution. A great majority of scientific contributors of that era attended university (studying the Classical curricula), many were on university payrolls (despite making their best intellectual achievements aside from their university work), students had access to some of the greatest minds and, finally, universities facilitated access to libraries, natural collections, telescopes and anatomical theaters.[1080] The greatest scientists of the Scientific Revolution, beneficiaries of readily available printed materials, were generally not university educated in their new, expanding fields. These fields simply did not yet exist as areas of substantive study. For those that were university educated, their foundation in Aristotelian

1075 *Ibid.*; *see also* Kostylo, *supra* note 540, at 22 (noting the growing interest in research coming from the "material world of craftsmanship and mechanical inventions).

1076 Drake, *supra* note 40, at 43, 52.

1077 Porter, *Scientific Revolution and Universities*, *in* VOLUME II, UNIVERSITIES IN EARLY MODERN EUROPE, *supra* note 192, at 531, 36, 50.

1078 *Ibid.* at 531, 49.

1079 *Ibid.* at 531, 40.

1080 *Ibid.* at 531, 542–47.

dogma often provided a competent basis upon which they would criticize theories and improve upon them.[1081]

Amateur scientists forging new territory in the sciences, which were still amenable to the traditional university curricula—metaphysics, classical geometry and mathematics—began receiving a warmer reception from academia. However, those amateurs engaging in the newer "more applied, descriptive, empirical or field sciences," such as chemistry, navigation, agriculture, geography and navigation, experienced a much slower adoption of their fields by the universities. If any of these newer fields were to be adopted, the universities tended to provide mere training without the development of academic study and the deeper analysis of new theories.[1082] Many academics within the universities expressed growing interest in mechanics and their writings brought academic theory in their disciplines closer to artisans' practices.[1083] With the rise of experimental sciences, many of the era's innovators actually received their educations through apprenticeships.[1084] A growing body of intellectual discussion among numerous scientific societies also acted as a bridge of information between study in universities and integration in society.[1085]

With a growing mass of knowledge accumulating in the numerous, new fields, the growing number of published works began finding their way into books and journals. Prior to the nineteenth century, there were few scientific journals in circulation, but they would go on to increase greatly in number.[1086] Another new phenomenon of the eighteenth century was the emergence of substantial book collections that numbered in the thou-

---

1081 *Ibid.* at 531, 550–53.

1082 *Ibid.* at 531, 551–53.

1083 Kostylo, *supra* note 540, at 44 (describing the transformation of trades and crafts into academic disciplines in that it "helped to separate the notion of invention from the immanent specific machine and resulted in a new definition of the author's work as a product of the mind.").

1084 Porter, *Scientific Revolution and Universities*, *in* VOLUME II, UNIVERSITIES IN EARLY MODERN EUROPE, *supra* note 192, at 531, 54, 58 (noting a major exception to this phenomenon, education in medicine always remained within the universities without any serious competition; it is thought that the students coveted the prestige associated with a university education, they were nonetheless required to have a university degree for licensure and they were provided a safe environment where they could legally dissect cadavers).

1085 *Ibid.* at 531, 55.

1086 Marciani, *supra* note 952 (explaining that the journals of the nineteenth century were predominately published by private clubs, which were supported primarily by their members).

sands.[1087] Sovereigns funded most of these collections, but some private donors were also known to have made an impact.[1088] Few institutions were able to keep up with the growing demand for access to books; "[o]nly rich colleges like those in Oxford, Cambridge, Louvain and Paris could afford to systematically acquire books."[1089]

The first fledgling American universities were substantially influenced by colonial legislatures, but this had a rather insubstantial effect due to them not engaging in research.[1090] This, though, was the point at which they began being founded more frequently as private institutions, laying the foundation for what would become a massive network of independent institutions that would transform into publishing powerhouses.[1091] While the eighteenth century was ending, American printing entrepreneurs had their own independent printing houses.[1092] Although the options for publishing were expanding around the time of the American Revolution, a culture of openness, lively public debate and protections for individual expression were lagging. A majority of all authors at this time found it wise to write under pseudonyms; this includes nearly all of the US' Founding Fathers in their letters, journals and pamphlets.[1093] Booming demand for books and intensive capital investment into private publishing would eventually turn US cities such as New York, Philadelphia, Boston, Baltimore and Richmond into some of the largest publishing hubs of the nineteenth century.[1094]

1087 De Ridder-Symoens, *Management and Resources*, *in* VOLUME II, UNIVERSITIES IN EARLY MODERN EUROPE, *supra* note 149, at 155, 196.

1088 *Ibid.* (noting the 1602 donation of books and manuscripts by Thomas Bodley to the public library at Oxford).

1089 *Ibid.* at 155, 197.

1090 Roberts et. al, *Exporting Models*, *in* VOLUME II, UNIVERSITIES IN EARLY MODERN EUROPE, *supra* note 165, at 272.

1091 *Ibid.* at 381.

1092 Smith, Steven Carl. An Empire of Print: the New York Publishing Trade in the Early American Republic. The Pennsylvania State University Press, 2017, pp. 2–3.

1093 Rounce, Adam. "Authorship in the Eighteenth Century." *Oxford Handbooks Online*, Mar. 2015, p. 2, doi:10.1093/oxfordhb/9780199935338.013.38.

1094 Smith, *supra* note 1092, at 2–5.

2. Structure in the Digital Era

Twentieth century media, in the form of film, television, digital recordings and books, came to be the building blocks of the major copyright industries. These industries were especially dominant because of strong copyright laws, the lack of alternative media outlets and the lack of black market, high-quality copies. Photocopies and VCR recordings were simply no replacement for industry-made works. Digital technologies and works in digital format have revolutionized the ability to make high quality, nearly identical copies of works and to share them as well.[1095] Unlicensed copying and illegal pirating are only two factors that have been detrimental to the major copyright industries, but digitization has struck these industries' infrastructure for finance, marketing and distribution particularly hard as well.[1096] These modern realities have polarized the traditional copyright industries against all of the newest Internet alternatives and forced the copyright goliaths in some instances, to adapt their infrastructures to keep monetizing their content while also adopting entirely new formats.[1097] Digital media have come to affect not only the major copyright industries, but traditional libraries as well.

In a recent trend, many libraries, both public and institutional, are being purged of their book collections; some have already compared them with ancient "ruins."[1098] While the traditional campus library was home to a broad range of books, journals, letters, recordings, etc., new technologies and funding limitations are shrinking the role of the traditional library. With increasing journal prices, librarians working on limited budgets frequently reduce their purchases of monographs. Monographs in the humanities and social sciences are usually the first to fall victim.[1099] This is especially troubling for those seeking to promote the arts and humanities, because experts in these fields tend to prefer to publish monographs, as opposed to articles.[1100] What books remain is within the librarians' discretion. They usually retain books that are newer and in popular demand. Recall, though, that publishing has not decreased, the works are just being more frequently adapted for digital formats.

1095 Netanel, *Copyright: What Everyone Needs to Know*, *supra* note 643, at 59.
1096 *Ibid.* at 75–76.
1097 *Ibid.* at 79.
1098 Cole, *Toward a More Perfect University*, *supra* note 142, at 201.
1099 Darnton, *supra* note 543, at 70 (describing the decrease in publication output by university presses due to the decreased demand for monographs).
1100 Brint, *Two Cheers for Higher Education*, *supra* note 75, at 45.

Further, not all materials that are disposed of will be digitized. The digitalization of library materials requires the appropriate copyright permissions, technical wherewithal, financial means and initiative by the librarians. Librarians are still hesitant, in many cases, to digitize collections that may still be subject to copyright, opting, rather, to go first for collections that are considered "low-risk."[1101] Accessing academic works still requires a multi-faceted approach, incorporating the use of both printed and digital works, but the shrinking of libraries pushes a stronger dependence on digital collections. With some collections now being only digitally available and with there being fewer paper-options, the largest for-profit publishers are seizing the opportunity to monetize their collections to the furthest extent possible.

3. Universities as a Structural Alternative to Copyright

One professor points out that American universities "employ ten times as many people as the motion picture and recording industries" and that this is an indication that we are now "[living] in a new age of patronage."[1102] Today's universities account for the greatest percentage of peer-reviewed publications by far. The extensive amount of peer-reviewed journals, somewhere between 24,000 to 28,000 worldwide, and the estimated 200,000 non-peer-reviewed journals (numbers that have been doubling nearly every decade), host millions of works on every conceivable topic in hundreds of disciplines.[1103] University research is booming in terms of the publication of academic content, but the marketplace for the content creates an inordinate amount of deadweight loss. Beyond for-profit publishers, the digital revolution was also embraced by many educational organizations, including private universities, many of which made efforts to contribute to the public domain with open access initiatives.[1104] These open access initiatives are only starting to gain traction, though, while the majority of university research output remains behind for-profit paywalls.

1101 Rooksby, *Branding of the American Mind*, *supra* note 510, at 200.

1102 Baldwin, *supra* note 689, at 408.

1103 Brint, *Two Cheers for Higher Education*, *supra* note 75, at 45 (listing the following disciplines with the greatest to least amounts of publishing: engineering, computer science, chemistry, mathematics, physics, social sciences, arts and humanities).

1104 Baldwin, *supra* note 689, at 292.

Patronage for faculty research first comes in the form of extensive government support for universities. This is materialized through massive government research grants, the many subsidies provided by the federal and state governments, privileges such as tax-exemption and massive university budgets supported by federally subsidized student loans. The support for faculty research output by expending massive amounts of public resources has resulted in a booming knowledge-sector, but this resource-intensive approach is not supported by the copyright law's system of incentives. Universities have provided the "structure" for the faculty output of first-class works, while copyright has primarily been used *ex post* by the largest for-profit publishers to monetize faculty research. In other words, direct university and government support for research supplants copyright law' *ex ante* incentives, leaving only copyright's *ex post* restrictions behind.

An interesting dynamic is now coming about with the relationship between universities and the Internet wherein MOOCs, open online databases and search engines provide alternatives to brick-and-mortar universities. On the plus side for universities, MOOCs draw in entirely new demographics of students and, in some instances, can replace the need for expensive physical facilities. Depending on students' level of "maturity," online courses can also offer a challenging curriculum.[1105] While they are promising, online courses are not currently regarded as being able to "replicate the range of skill-building opportunities of face-to-face instruction."[1106] Beyond universities' online course offerings, the massive amount of knowledge available online brings universities' role as gatekeepers to *education* into question. Critical programs focusing on the humanities are yet to have been replaced. Otherwise, universities are losing their gatekeeper function in terms of providing factual knowledge and professional training. MOOCs may not be a replacement for critical-thinking based courses, but they may provide an excellent alternative for other job training programs.[1107] Despite this, universities still currently maintain their gatekeeper-function as institutions of *certification* and *research* (*see* Part I). Using the Internet as an alternative structure for accessing knowledge has other limitations when it comes to copyright and DMCA restrictions on the content.

1105 Brint, *Two Cheers for Higher Education*, *supra* note 75, at 380 (mentioning, though, that online students will not be challenged with the same face-to-face encounters and unlikely to establish relationships through their studies).

1106 *Ibid.* at 353.

1107 Kirp, *supra* note 260, at 224.

4. Alternative For-profit Structures

Beyond procuring the growing mass of hard-to-access first-class works, some for-profit undertakings have provided valuable access to a trove of second-class works. Online audio and video streaming, which is freely accessible, has truly democratized access to knowledge by breaking down barriers to entry. Audiences are no longer passive consumers of information, but, rather, now active participants in most discussions. Geography, which was once the greatest limitation on rural inhabitants who wished to access knowledge, is no longer a limitation if viewers can access the Internet. Political boundaries can be circumvented by the usage of VPNs. Finally, finance, traditionally being one of the greatest barriers to entry, is no longer prohibitive for most people. At no cost, one can go onto YouTube to watch political debates live, access in-depth videos on world history, listen to multi-hour podcasts on virtually every topic, educate oneself on basic philosophical principles, learn how to repair anything, entertain oneself with late-night comedy or watch sports highlights. If viewers wish to engage in any of these areas of discussion, they can post their own comments or videos at no cost.

These audio and video streaming formats facilitate long-form discussion, allowing for the injection of nuance into serious discussions, which would have previously only been available within books. "Scholars, bloggers, archivists and activists" have all found a home on the Internet and its innovative means of access; this is clearly in contrast to older uni-directional media that streamed only from the direction of major media outlets toward passive media consumers.[1108] Many contributors are financed through either advertising revenue from the platforms or external crowdfunding support through websites such as GoFundMe or Patreon. Just as is the case with universities, sources of funding for online contributors are crucial. Wikipedia, the epitome of open access platforms, is built almost entirely from private crowd sourcing, but many of these contributors may not have access to the top, first-class works.[1109] Moreover, these platforms may have less quality control over their content, especially in cases where authorship remains anonymous. Although, false reporting, poor research, low standards and bogus peer review are not unique to any particular for-

1108 Netanel, *Copyright's Paradox*, *supra* note 645, at 9.

1109 Note that, although Wikipedia is a nonprofit organization, it and its authors face structural issues similar to comparative for-profits.

mat. Those who are accessing works, regardless of whether they are first- or second-class, should approach all content on all platforms cautiously.[1110]

Many audio and video streaming platforms are accustomed to routinely removing copyrighted content because of the DMCA. The DMCA created a safe-harbor provision for Internet service providers and other neutral platforms that, upon notification of there being copyright-infringing material on their platforms, promptly remove the content.[1111] This so-called "notice and takedown" procedure allows Internet users to notify the Internet service providers of a copyright infringement, leading to the service provider removing the content and related hyperlinks.[1112] The Internet service provider must notify the user whose content was removed of the takedown.[1113] Users may protest the takedown by sending a counter-notice, possibly leading to the content being restored.[1114] There are billions of notice and takedowns per year, leading the largest Internet service providers to rely on their algorithm-based, automated systems, whereas smaller service providers still use manual, human review.[1115] Despite the massive amount of notice and takedowns, it appears that the system is hardly abused; rather, "a lot of flagged material is blatantly infringing."[1116] Although the system is removing facially infringing content, little consideration is given as to whether the "infringements" constitute fair, permissible uses.

1110 *See e.g.*, Wilson, Helen. "Retracted Article: Human Reactions to Rape Culture and Queer Performativity at Urban Dog Parks in Portland, Oregon." *Gender, Place & Culture*, 22 May 2018, pp. 1–20., doi:https://doi.org/10.1080/0966369X.2018.1475346 (being retracted from the peer-reviewed Journal of Gender, Place & Culture, a subsidiary of Taylor and Francis, once its authors admitted that the submission was a hoax); *see also* Schuessler, Jennifer. "Hoaxers Slip Breastaurants and Dog-Park Sex into Journals." *The New York Times*, The New York Times, 5 Oct. 2018, www.nytimes.com/2018/10/04/arts/academic-journals-hoax.html (detailing the multiple, fantastical article submissions that were published by a number of journals, including some with peer-review); "List of Predatory Journals." *List of Predatory Journals | Stop Predatory Journals*, predatoryjournals.com/journals/ (listing hundreds of "predatory journals" that partake in various behaviors that "cheapen intellectual work" or are otherwise exploitative and misleading).

1111 17 U.S.C. § 512 (c) (2011).

1112 *Ibid.*

1113 *Ibid.*

1114 *Ibid.*

1115 Netanel, *Copyright: What Everyone Needs to Know*, *supra* note 643, at 59.

1116 *Ibid.*

Notice and takedown allows a quick and efficient means for copyright holders to remove content from the Internet, while shielding Internet service providers from potential liability.[1117] This approach has roused dissatisfaction on numerous fronts; copyright holders complain that the takedowns do not do enough to prevent the material from being reposted, Internet service providers are concerned about the tremendous responsibility to filter content and Internet activists complain that dragnet tactics result in the removal of non-infringing content. The greatest complaints are that there should be more transparency and increased reliance on human review.[1118] YouTube's automated Content ID content removal system has become the most prominent over the last decade. Content ID adds an alternative to simple content removal by providing copyright holders the option to monetize the copyrighted materials that were used.[1119] As mentioned above, it does not seem that the notice and takedown system has necessarily been abused, but it does not account for fair use.[1120] The lack of consideration for fair use means that the incorporation of copyrighted content for, perhaps, commentary or parody, could lead to the removal of the content, despite its permissibility. Formal legal process, where plaintiffs have the burden of proof and defendants can affirmatively prove fair use, is set-aside on major platforms like YouTube. Instead, copyright owners complain, content is taken down and few users file counter-notices because they either lack the wherewithal or see little urgency due to there being no formal legal proceeding.[1121]

Considering that an extensive amount of content on the Internet is not behind a paywall, authors must find a way to finance their efforts. The newer content-marketplaces have problems of their own. In instances of contributors being dependent on advertising revenue, they are especially susceptible to "deplatforming." Where a *takedown* involves the removal of content, *deplatforming* entails the removal of the speaker or their means of expressing themselves. Content and accounts can be automatically deplatformed by algorithms that detect the usage of copyrighted materials or by purposeful removal (often when controversial issues are involved), re-

1117 *Ibid.* at 60.

1118 *Ibid.* at 59.

1119 "What Is Fair Use?" *YouTube*, YouTube, https://www.youtube.com/about/copyright/fair-use/#yt-copyright-protection.

1120 *Ibid.*

1121 Netanel, *Copyright: What Everyone Needs to Know*, *supra* note 643, at 59.

gardless of whether such usage is fair and without due process.[1122] Deplatforming can lead to contributors' channels being removed and advertising revenue being withheld. Most streaming and social media websites have been extremely non-transparent regarding their policies and procedures for content removal and deplatforming. Independently-wealthy individuals with so called "f— you money," i.e. a financial basis whereupon these speakers need not fear repercussions from outside financers, organizations or employers, are less-threatened by deplatforming, although removal from Twitter or YouTube could still devastate their ability to participate in public discussions.[1123] For those who are not independently wealthy, crowd funding serves as a decent alternative to support their audio / visual works in particular areas. These creators, though, are still dependent on donors' willingness to donate.

The commercial justifications for copyright law, i.e. infrastructure and capital investment, have been substantially undermined by digital technology.[1124] With the Internet allowing essentially everybody to participate in the public forum, the major media conglomerates are trying to come to terms with this, while still protecting their large copyright portfolios. The large copyright industries, for the most part, have cemented their positions by putting their content onto streaming platforms, but the largest publishers of academic books and journals have been slow to adapt. These publishers are still heavily reliant on the limited-monopoly afforded by copyright, despite not authoring the majority of the works that they make available.[1125] With the Internet lowering the costs of advertising and distribution, opening up other means of finance and putting content behind new technological barriers, it has provided alternative structures for au-

---

1122 Brannon, Valerie C. "Free Speech and the Regulation of Social Media Content." *Congressional Research Service, Free Speech and the Regulation of Social Media Content*, 27 Mar. 2019. https://fas.org/sgp/crs/misc/R45650.pdf.

1123 *See e.g.*, Knight First Amendment Inst. at Columbia Univ. v. Trump, 302 F. Supp. 3d 541 (S.D.N.Y. 2018), *aff'd*, 928 F.3d 226 (2d Cir. 2019) (ruling that President Donald Trump's Twitter handle @realDonaldTrump was a public forum for First Amendment purposes and that the deletion of critical posts was an instance of unconstitutional viewpoint discrimination).

1124 Netanel, *Copyright's Paradox*, *supra* note 645, at 75.

1125 While it is hard to justify highly restrictive copyright protection for academic materials in the digital era, such restrictions might have had a better basis in the print era. Since one of copyright law's functions is to provide a market structure, the limited monopolies that it affords were an incentive, at least for publishers, to invest substantial capital into editing, printing operations, advertising and distribution networks.

thors to support themselves with their works.[1126] Although, it is questionable whether the public trust should be placed in for-profit platforms that treat copyright purely as a means for increasing revenues, compensating authors and, while only nominally, respecting fair use principles.

This section, looking at copyright's structural function, demonstrated how particular media forms relate to content creation and how authors can support themselves financially in the digital age. Copyright is just as relevant as ever before, but fair use has been left far behind. Newer media forms have cultivated a broad culture of creativity, simultaneously providing an alternative structure to the one created by copyright. Copyright law originally provided a structure meant to remove dependence on government funding or philanthropy from wealthy patrons.[1127] It would be misleading to suggest, though, that the federal government has no patronage role; it provides massive funding for communications infrastructure, grants to artists and authors, supports universities and creates laws and policies that shield expression.[1128] The largest for-profit publishers have dominated the academic market, while contributing relatively little in terms of authorship or additional content. Other for-profit undertakings marketed at the public have, indeed, provided great access to many sources, but at the price of users' data about their online habits, time spent watching advertisements and small subscription fees. Nonprofit open access publications are at the forefront of providing an alternative structure for academic authorship. These open access publications are entirely in line with nonprofit university missions, while also serving the public benefit in terms of knowledge dissemination.

Considering that universities are the engines fueling the greatest amount of first-class research output in the US, *without there being a profit motive for professors*, the substantial deadweight loss created by locking their research behind paywalls is entirely unjustifiable. The other sources of educational content, i.e. online open or free access projects (both for-profit and nonprofit), have less-apparent deadweight loss in the sense that consumers are not locked out, but authors on these platforms are not necessarily ensured access to the first-class research materials. So, while this is not deadweight loss *per se*, consumers on open platforms are still indirectly affected by the for-profit publishers' paywalls. Despite the structural difficulties in making first-class academic works available to users

1126 *Ibid.* at 86–89.
1127 *Ibid.* at 5.
1128 *Ibid.* at 36.

and there being little financial incentive, authorship continues to boom. Thus, the limited monopoly created by copyright laws in the instance of academic publishing does not drive authorship, leaving the societal deadweight loss unjustified. In the case of academic publishing, the costs between parties exceed the social benefits of the transactions, resulting in a market failure. Keeping this market failure and the issues arising from the other content-marketplaces in mind, i.e. free speech implications, deplatforming and the public benefit, the adequacy of fair use and the other constitutional safeguards are considered next in terms of copyright's expressive function.

V. Expressive Function Assessment

Copyright's *expressive function* highlights the principles of free expression and symbolic support thereof, arising out of both the US Constitution's Copyright Clause and the First Amendment.[1129] There is extensive Supreme Court jurisprudence on speech-related issues; such cases often concern the interplay of First Amendment protection with speech relating to politics, journalism, scholarly debate, artistic expression, entertainment, documentaries, commercial advertising and even with speech-based crimes.[1130] As one can see, "speech" comes in many forms and copyrighted materials are inevitably used in purveying many of these forms. However, the freedom of speech is not just limited to "speaking," rather, it goes further to encompass the "dissemination of information, access to infor-

---

1129 There is a normative nexus between constitutional provisions and the nation's values that is not paralleled with other sources of law, such as statutes. Americans have a strong tendency to identify with constitutional provisions, sometimes even expressing pseudo-religiously that we "believe" in certain rights. Although the Copyright Clause is unmistakably present in the Constitution, it does not have the same cultural appeal that some other provisions enjoy. Perhaps it is no coincidence that in virtually every discussion with current students, recent graduates and even professors (from multiple countries including the US and Germany), they unabashedly admit to downloading unauthorized copies of course books from pirating websites or other torrents. *Ibid.* at 81; May & Daly, *supra* note 751, at 32–35.

1130 Some examples of criminal or tortious speech include fraud, criminal conspiracy, threats of violence and defamatory statements.

mation and knowledge."[1131] Copyright tends to burden speech outright by limiting expression, limiting access to works, allowing monopoly pricing and enabling copyright conglomerates to accumulate massive content portfolios that substantially burden individual users.[1132] The constitutional interests in free speech, which are key to the fair use defense, should act as a counterbalance. This section will inquire into the relationship between the Copyright Clause and the First Amendment's freedoms.[1133]

Since this section looks carefully at copyright's constitutional nature, it is first worthwhile to note the cultural norms relating to copyright. The entertainment industry's campaigns in the early 2000's, shaming video and music pirating as "theft," were never paralleled in academic publishing. Today's "born-digital generation" generally views strong authors' rights—along with various other burdens such as paywalls, upload filters, regulations, etc.—as a nuisance, an impediment to the free flow of information as well as a hurdle to accessing our common heritage.[1134] Considering that the digitization of our collective patrimony has now lead to every instance of *accessing* academic works being an instance of *copying*, millions of Americans and many more foreigners are exposed to major criminal and civil liability. Once copyright's system of incentives fails to serve the public benefit and users' activities become increasingly subject to scrutiny and liability, the natural result is for them to "move away from use and respect for the law."[1135] This raises the serious question of whether these drastic measures are "really necessary in order to achieve the proper ends that copyright law serves."[1136]

Massive potential legal costs burden individuals in their usage of digitized academic works, even when it could be considered fair use.[1137] With paywalls and other technological licensing mechanisms, e.g. mass-market

---

1131 Nimmer & Nimmer, *Nimmer on Copyright*, *supra* note 71, at vol. 5, §§ 19E.01–02 (reminding that fair use is for "such quintessential free speech activities as criticism, commentary, news reporting and teaching.").

1132 Netanel, *Copyright's Paradox*, *supra* note 645, at 109.

1133 Nimmer & Nimmer, *Nimmer on Copyright*, *supra* note 71, at vol. 5, § 19E.01 (noting that focus on this relationship is a relatively recent trend, whereas courts of the past tended to, in many ways, explain it away, resolve it separately or deny its existence).

1134 Baldwin, *supra* note 689, at 385.

1135 Kemp, *supra* note 31, at 834.

1136 Lessig, *Free Culture*, *supra* note 709, at 202, 207 (estimating that some forty to sixty million Americans access content electronically in a way that could subject them to criminal or civil liability, including music and video).

1137 *See generally* Crews, *Copyright, Fair Use and the Challenge*, *supra* note 773, at 35.

licenses or terms of use on websites, transaction costs are reduced, but, simultaneously, so is the allowance for fair use.[1138] The degree of control that mass-market licenses exert over content is unprecedented. If somebody buys a book in print from a brick-and-mortar bookstore, copyright's *first sale doctrine* allows for him or her to read their copy of the book an unlimited number of times and to resell it as he or she pleases. On the other hand, the licenses on e-books or other digital texts may permit only a limited number of views as well as forbidding resale.[1139] These technical or contractual controls override many of the common law and statutory permissions.[1140] In this way, technical and contractual controls have extended restrictions onto works that would have never been conceivable under the law, while using the law as a springboard to do so. The burdens imposed by copyright are not just limited to those found in the statute, but the potential litigation costs, overbearing protection of copyrighted materials, the forfeiture of rights via mass-market licensing and users' uncertainty as to the extent of permissible fair use or other exceptions must be considered as well.[1141]

Eldred v. Ashcroft, decided by the Supreme Court in 2003, touched on the scope of the Copyright Clause as well as the counterbalance between copyright and First Amendment, free speech principles.[1142] The Petitioners in *Eldred* brought their claims following Congress' addition of twenty years to the term of copyright protection.[1143] Petitioners' claim was that the twenty-year extension was unconstitutional, because it exceeded a "limited" term of protection and that it ran afoul with First Amendment principles for works that had already been published or were otherwise in existence.[1144] In denying petitioners' arguments, the Court first stated that, a twenty-year extension to copyright protection is in accordance with

1138 Netanel, *Copyright's Paradox*, *supra* note 645, at 65.

1139 *Ibid.* at 70 (noting that mass-market licenses tend to treat fair use and other exceptions to copyright merely as waivable contractual rights); Baldwin, *supra* note 689, at 152.

1140 Lessig, *Free Culture*, *supra* note 709, at 152.

1141 Netanel, *Copyright's Paradox*, *supra* note 645, at 115.

1142 Eldred v. Ashcroft, 537 U.S. 186 (2003).

1143 The extension was a product of the 1998 Sonny Bono Term Extension Act, which extended terms from life-of-the-author plus fifty years to life-of-the-author plus seventy years.

1144 *Ibid.*

the Constitution's allowance for Congress to create "limited" terms.[1145] Under this internal analysis of the Copyright Clause, the Court essentially deferred to Congress' discretion over such matters.[1146] *Eldred's* legacy, though, will likely be tied closer to its second issue; the external relationship between copyright and free speech.[1147]

Justice Ginsburg's opinion, writing for the majority, stated that "copyright's limited monopolies are compatible with free speech principles," supporting this with the fact that both constitutional provisions—the First Amendment and Copyright Clause—were adopted so proximately in time to each other.[1148] Furthermore, the Court recognized that copyright does positively support free speech as an engine of creation, expression and publication.[1149] Although, the Court qualified its ruling based on the sufficiency of copyright's "built-in First Amendment accommodations," namely, the *idea / expression dichotomy* and *fair use*.[1150] Fair use, according to the Court, is a sufficient safeguard because of its numerous allowances for "scholarship and comment."[1151] Finally, the Court expressly rejected the lower court's proposition that copyright is "categorically immune from challenges under the First Amendment."[1152] This ruling was supported by the subsequent case *Golan v. Holder*, in which the Court declined to apply First Amendment scrutiny to a particular copyright law, but, nonetheless, reaffirmed that the safeguards of fair use and the idea / expression dichotomy may not be diminished.[1153]

1145 The Court did not inquire into the extent of what "limited" means. This could conceivably leave the door open to Congress extending terms to life-of-the-author plus 100 or even more years. *Ibid.*

1146 *Ibid.*

1147 Nimmer & Nimmer, *Nimmer on Copyright*, *supra* note 71, at vol. 5, § 19E.05 (explaining that the implications of *Eldred* are particularly relevant between digital technologies and the fair use defense. *Eldred* is suggestive that there could be a substantive expansion of the First Amendment in cases where the safeguards actually fail to protect free speech).

1148 Eldred v. Ashcroft, 537 U.S. 186, 190 (2003); *but see* Abrams & Ochoa, *supra* note 660, at § 1: 21 (arguing that this logic is somewhat questionable, though, because the First Amendment is an amendment to the text of the original Constitution, which contained the Copyright Clause. Thus, as a matter of interpretation, it should be more relevant that one was ratified after the other, and not that they were both ratified proximately in time).

1149 Eldred v. Ashcroft, 537 U.S. 186 (2003).

1150 *Ibid.*

1151 *Ibid.* at 190.

1152 *Ibid.* at 221 (citing to Eldred v. Reno, 239 F.3 d 372, 375 (D.C. Cir. 2001)).

1153 Golan v. Holder, 565 U.S. 302, 327–33 (2012).

The *Eldred* Court hardly could have foreseen the shrinking physical libraries, dependence on electronic databases, changing Internet technology and, more specifically, the usage of content filtering systems that would come to be used by the largest Internet service providers. YouTube's Content ID system and its algorithm-based filters are exceptional in their ability to identify copyrighted material and remove it from certain platforms. Such systems, though, make no distinction for fair use when content may be used for commentary, education or other permissible uses.[1154] *Eldred* was premised on fair use and the idea / expression dichotomy being sufficient protections, "permitting free communication of facts while still protecting an author's expression."[1155] Thus, a weakening of these protections for free speech could allow copyright to "impermissibly burden freedom of speech."[1156] Unfortunately, for those seeking materials online, the idea / expression dichotomy, free speech and the public domain are hardly an option for navigating prohibitively expensive paywalls or finding content that has been taken down. These constitutional safeguards are of very little help to people who are unable to access materials. Considering these hurdles to access, it is problematic that *Eldred* did not set forth any test for determining the *sufficiency* or *adequacy* of the constitutional safeguards.

Regardless of whether it be litigated on the First Amendment, the Copyright Clause or on other constitutional grounds,[1157] substantial Supreme

---

1154 Netanel, *Copyright: What Everyone Needs to Know*, *supra* note 643, at 139.

1155 Eldred v. Ashcroft, 537 U.S. 186, 219 (2003); Netanel, *Copyright: What Everyone Needs to Know*, *supra* note 643, at 45 (referring to this balance of interests between the Copyright Clause and First Amendment as the "definitional balance test").

1156 *Ibid.*

1157 Going further afield, Rosenfield, also looking at fair use through the constitutional rights lens, argues that there is a "right of *reasonable* access" buried in the First Amendment's protection of free expression and generally in the Ninth Amendment's retention of unremunerated rights. Noting that both the common law and statutory embodiment of fair use act to counterbalance copyright restrictions with the public benefit, he insists that a right to reasonable access is a precursor to the freedom of expression. He defines the freedom of the press as not being "limited to the owner of a physical press" nor to those specific readers, but, rather, it being a universal right of all American citizens, equating the "right to know" with the "right to print." The necessity of a free press arises, thus, from the need and "right of every American to be informed." While it is not impossible that the Court may eventually look further into the Ninth Amendment, it is unlikely. The Ninth Amendment has fallen into obscurity and, when discussed, is generally treated as a limitation on the overreach of federal powers, not a grant of specific, individual substantive rights.

Court involvement in the area of users' rights under copyright would be a means of strengthening access to the public domain. Other areas of law, such as defamation, have been "constitutionalized" by elevating them and their defenses from common law principles to fundamental constitutional rights.[1158] More simply, the Supreme Court's "legitimating function," through extensive involvement with particular issues, labels the issues with an extra level of importance, while binding them closer to the Constitution.[1159] The Supreme Court's past jurisprudence on copyright issues has had the tendency to focus narrowly on individual issues within copyright, to side step the more comprehensive countervailing constitutional factors or to avoid these factors entirely.[1160] For example, the *Eldred* Court rightfully said that fair use and the idea / expression dichotomy are mechanisms that protect the flow of information, but made no further inquiry into the adequacy of these constitutional safeguards.[1161]

In ruling that the First Amendment's safeguards are "generally adequate" to support free expression, the *Eldred* Court stated that, "the First Amendment securely protects the freedom to make or decline to make one's own speech; it bears less heavily when speakers assert the right to make other people's speeches." Rosenfield, Harry N. "The American Constitution, Free Inquiry, and the Law." *Fair Use and Free Inquiry: Copyright Law and the New Media*, edited by John Shelton. Lawrence and Bernard Timberg, Ablex, 1980, pp. 288, 296–97; Lash, Kurt T. *The Lost History of the Ninth Amendment*. Oxford University Press, 2009, pp. 343–50; Eldred v. Ashcroft, 537 U.S. 186, 221 (2003).

1158 *See generally* N.Y. Times Co. v. Sullivan, 376 U.S. 254 (1964).

1159 Spann, Girardeau. "Constitutionalization." *St. Louis University Law Journal*, vol. 49, 2005, p. 719 (noting that this effect has been seen in the areas of desegregation, capital punishment, privacy and many more issues).

1160 *See e.g.*, Eldred v. Ashcroft, 537 U.S. 186, 190 (2003).

1161 Although, the fact that the court suggested the possibility of there being a constitutional balance to copyright laws is suggestive of a general willingness to expand this area of jurisprudence. This may also be one of the areas where political polarization and interpretational differences among justices are not observable; *Eldred* was decided by a majority of seven justices (Ginsburg, Rehnquist, O'Connor, Scalia, Kennedy, Souter and Thomas), all of which had substantially differing views on constitutional interpretation. The justices' political-leanings are not an explanation for the Court's reasoning in *Eldred*. To the contrary, Lawrence Lessig, Eric Eldred's attorney, specifically tailored his arguments to address precedent, which he believed that the conservative-leaning justices would be warm to and the arguments overwhelmingly failed. Reflecting apologetically in his book, Lessig attributes his loss at the Supreme Court to his failure to demonstrate why a weakened public domain is an important issue to the country. Lessig, *Free Culture*, *supra* note 709, at 228–46; Eldred v. Ashcroft, 537 U.S. 186, 190, 217–21 (2003).

The Copyright Clause exists to promote the creation and dissemination of scientific works. While Congress is clearly entitled to make laws in pursuance of this goal, most of these laws interfere with free speech through either removal, outright censorship or monopoly pricing. This balance of interests is represented in the relationship between the first two functions of copyright—the production and structural functions—with copyright's expressive function. Ideally, the production and structural functions should operate to incentivize authorship and to create a market for works, while the expressive function incorporates constitutional provisions for users' access. The analysis of academic publishing's production function showed that the incentives for academic authorship are not justified in light of the extensive deadweight loss that is created. Similarly, under the structural function, the incentives for academic authorship are not justified by market created by copyright; these authors support themselves by other means. *Eldred* made clear that even outcomes like these, despite how restrictive they are on the expressive function, are permissible so long as the constitutional safeguards are sufficient means for alternative access and limited usage. So, are fair use, the idea / expression dichotomy and copyright term limits sufficient to protect expression?

Determining whether the constitutional safeguards are adequate must first begin with a consideration of how accessible academic works are. First-class works that end up behind paywalls are generally inaccessible due to their subscription costs. They are not inaccessible because the for-profit publishers wish to withhold content, but, rather, because they can charge monopoly prices, and they do. Outright technical barriers preclude access to those who cannot pay. Only once institutions, mostly universities, pay millions of dollars in yearly subscription fees, are the materials made available. For those that do not have institutional access, i.e. the overwhelming majority of the population, they cannot make *fair usage* of these academic works. Instead, they will make *no usage* of them. This is, of course, different from during the print era, when the expectation was that journals and books could be freely pulled from the shelf and borrowed. Many of the journals and books are now being thrown away and / or digitized.[1162] Can fair use in its current state possibly be adequate here? It seems that the answer is no.

1162 There is a growing body of research on the usage of e-books and other digitized materials. Beyond the legal, economic and structural issues, some research has focused on the specific utility of works in different formats. There is reason to believe that readers engage with printed materials more thoroughly,

The idea / expression dichotomy offers no additional assistance to users; even though certain first-class works may be within the public domain, they can still be unnecessarily locked behind a paywall. This is a signal, in these instances, that copyright protection is overbearing and, by the logic in *Eldred*, there could be a First Amendment challenge to copyright and DMCA protections that enable private corporations to withhold the bulk of academic works. A constitutional challenge would necessarily focus on users' inability to access the public domain. It could also be shown that scientific and technological innovation have accelerated far beyond the pace of content falling into the public domain and that reduced access to academic materials retards the innovation process.

The wealth of second-class works that are now available on for-profit platforms also bring up serious constitutional issues regarding access and usage. Content, regardless of whether it is copyrighted or in the public domain, is subject to be taken down or deplatformed without any fair use consideration or due process. This is not an instance of market failure in the sense that content is unaffordable, but, rather, that takedowns or deplatforming are wholesale barriers to access. There is no interest balancing when content is removed, rather, just a question of whether there was seemingly a copyright infringement. These cases of no-access have rendered fair use entirely inadequate and the cultural norms regarding reasonable access to academic works have been abandoned.[1163] As a result, the marketplace of ideas is stocked predominately by second-class works. Ironically, in considering how to approach issues like "fake news" in the Internet, Congress' only serious considerations, until this point, have been to restrict online speech and provide Internet service providers the tools to do so. No effort has been made to make the massive amounts of academic works behind paywalls more available.[1164] Requiring Internet service providers to remove content without any constitutional safeguards may very well be a reinvigoration of the old English stationers' monopoly, just in a new form. Outside of the paywalls, a wealth of first-class works are

---

whereas e-materials are more useful for "quick reading." Although, this does not discount the utility of e-materials; they still promise—*ceteris paribus*—to provide an unprecedented amount of content, which may compensate for the decline in "deep reading." Clark, Ann Marie. "A Social Scientist Uses E-Books for Research and in the Classroom." *Academic E-Books Publishers, Librarians, and Users*, edited by Suzanne M. Ward, et al., Purdue University Press, 2016, pp. 202–07.

1163 Lessig, *Free Culture*, *supra* note 709, at 132.

1164 Brannon, *supra* note 1122.

now available through some nonprofit open access initiatives but are still limited in the amount of content that they can make accessible.

F. Copyright Law and the Public Benefit

Part II established the purposes and goals of copyright law as seen through its historical and legal development. First, this part emphasized the importance of technology regarding the creation and dissemination of knowledge. Legal constraints on publication are mostly reactions to newfound means of publication such as printing and modern technologies. Before copyright law existed, several earlier systems enabled sovereigns to control the flow of information and for, in some instances, credit to be attributed to authors. Following reforms in England, the American Revolution and the ratification of the US Constitution, copyright law took its modern form and the US Congress was given a constitutional mandate to create copyright laws to "promote the Progress of Science...."

In order to determine the purposes and goals of copyright law, this part first inquired into the drafters' intentions behind the Constitution's Copyright Clause. Promoting the "Progress of Science" is the underlying goal of Congress' competency to enact copyright laws. Subsequent case law has defined the specific "ends" or goals of these laws to be for both the creation and dissemination of knowledge. The "means" of incentivizing authorship in the US' *public benefit tradition* entails granting authors protections over their works, but only to the extent to which is necessary to promote authorship. Copyright laws granting excessive terms of protection, eliminating formalities and increasing authors' control over subsequent uses of their works may exceed the constitutional mandate given to Congress. In describing how copyright law functions, this part also provided extensive detail on its exceptions, such as fair use, the effect of international law on domestic copyright law as well as several alternatives to copyright law that are available through CC licenses and technological controls.

Part II's analysis first demonstrated that all the rings of regulation have grown significantly in scope and strength, restricting access to copyrighted academic works and making it more expensive and exclusive than ever before. Working with this reality, the governmental, for-profit and nonprofit sectors have all taken different approaches toward making knowledge accessible, but these have resulted in an inadequate patchwork response. In the meanwhile, these approaches have not addressed the fact that most academic works still lie behind for-profit paywalls. Pirating websites now provide the most significant catalyst for change but, in providing access to our collective patrimony, they expose themselves and their users to civil and criminal liability. Furthermore, the pirates' leadership in the digital realm has little foundation in the legal system; their avoidance of court proceedings develops no case law in the favor of the public benefit and disserves the legitimate arguments that they make against copyright's creation of monopolies that enable massive for-profit paywalls.

Part II ended by analyzing the three major functions of copyright law: the production, structural and expressive functions. Analyzing the production function, Part II described the economic incentives for authorship and demonstrated the significant shortcomings of the system regarding academic works. Copyright's structural function has changed over the course of time corresponding with technological advancements. The stringent monopoly created by copyright law to promote the authorship of academic works has been mostly supplanted by universities' support for research. Despite this phenomenon, stringent copyright monopolies remain, and most works created within the universities land in paywalled databases. Copyright's expressive function has also fallen short of its aim of protecting free speech and free debate through fair use. Because of the difficulty in accessing first-class works and the many misaligned incentives discussed above, the US copyright law regime does not benefit the public in relation to academic works.

G. How Can Copyright be Improved Through the Law?

Academia has provided an alternative structure that not only fosters authorship, but which is also a particularly good match for open access publishing. There may be added benefits for universities to proactively promote open access publishing. Current university rankings make great usage of library metrics, calculating in square-footage as well as the sizes of book collections.[1165] Although there is substantial doubt that this metric for access to knowledge was ever particularly helpful, it could be replaced by a metric measuring the extent to which universities make content openly accessible.[1166] A step further would be to account for their procurement

1165 Cole, *Toward a More Perfect University*, *supra* note 142, at 203.

1166 The greatest hindrance to this is, as mentioned in Part II, that many academics are still drawn to publish with for-profit publishers because of the perceived

of rare books or otherwise special collections.[1167] Universities fighting for brand name recognition can improve their overall standing by attaching their insignia to all of the books, articles, journals and treatises that they publish openly. This could promote healthy competition among universities in the area of open publishing, while making more first-class works openly available.

Currently, the open access system that requires authors to pay the costs of publication is a disincentive, but some have suggested shifting the costs of open access publication onto academic institutions or employers.[1168] Within universities, this would create new costs, but a gradual tapering of their commercial databank and other subscriptions could offset these new expenses.[1169] A shift such as this would have the twofold benefit of reduced reliance on expensive databases as well as the promotion of a normalized, expanding sphere of open access publications. An added benefit of institutions becoming more proactive in open access publishing would be the opportunity for them to gain prestige in the publishing realm. Greater recognition for publishing has historically translated into better federal research funding opportunities and there is no reason why this cannot be accomplished through open access publishing.

Open access publishing has the potential to make academic works more accessible, but, in and of itself, open access is still only an approach that is limited to the current parameters of copyright law. Significant changes to the legal system are also necessary. Until copyright laws in the US can be amended, another provisional fix could be for Congress to require universities, perhaps those receiving Pell Grants and federally subsidized student loans, to make all their publications openly accessible within a short time of their initial publications. Recall that, under the work made for hire rules, universities have default ownership of their faculties' works—and probably students' works as well—made using university resources. This would be at best a half-measure, because, rather than changing copyright laws, it would just add another condition for universities to receive federal funding. It seems that the immediate effect of such a measure would be increased open access publishing, but it would not address the general

---

prestige associated with their journals. At the very least, creating competition within open publishing would require a social change, where open publications could be held in higher regard. Further, universities can exercise their rights as copyright holders to require open publishing.

1167 Cole, *Toward a More Perfect University*, *supra* note 142, at 203.

1168 Denicola, *supra* note 894, at 358–59.

1169 *Ibid.*

over-regulation of copyright, it would reduce university independence and further promote the reckless financing schemes in which the government and universities are already engaged.

Another approach would be for universities to relinquish ownership of their faculties' and students' works either voluntarily or as a matter of law. Changes to the default *work made for hire* rules could aid in promoting a vibrant and robust knowledge commons within higher education.[1170] While helpful in the context of the work made for hire rules, it appears that this is just one aspect of the GST analysis of copyright law that brings to light the need for much more comprehensive changes. Changing the work made for hire rules might be a particularly useful approach to incentivize the creation of works with high potential value, i.e. patents or works made for entertainment. Shifting ownership from institutions to individual authors alone, though, does not address copyright's faulty system of incentives, as was discussed above under the production function. If universities were to return their copyrights to the original authors, it would likely result in just another iteration of the current copyright dilemma; authors would continue publishing their works with the largest for-profit journals and, in turn, hand over these rights to the publishers directly. Works made for hire certainly are an area in need of repair, but a fix to these rules should be part of a more comprehensive reform.

Since knowledge is a public good, there should be no first- or second-class distinctions. Such distinctions arise from a general lack of nuanced understanding by legislators and judges who fail to recognize that different types of works are associated with different economic incentives. Treating most copyrighted works as if they follow the same economic incentives as works made for entertainment is one of the most obvious failures to distinguish. Despite currently having different classes of works, all types of works are still clustered together under a one-size-fits-all regime. Constitutional safeguards such as fair use and the idea / expression dichotomy should provide a means to make academic works accessible and useful, but these safeguards have only been diminished as the body of copyright restrictions has continuously grown. Pirating efforts have opened the knowledge floodgates to countries with traditionally poor access to knowledge, but improved access to our collective patrimony should not have to come at the cost of risking massive criminal or civil liability. All academic works should be openly available.

1170 Rooksby, *Branding of the American Mind*, *supra* note 510, at 268.

Of all the licensing variations and pirating schemes described, none of them considers potential substantive changes to core of the Copyright Act. CC open licenses are convenient in the sense that authors can clearly define the parameters of use for their works, but this is dependent on authors' willingness to participate in such a system. Likewise, pirating provides immense access to academic materials, but this comes at the cost of legal liability for those who possess, duplicate and distribute copyrighted works. Considering that access to academic materials is still so restricted, even in light of these patchwork responses, what room is there for substantive changes to copyright law? Suppose that a reduction of the term of copyright duration were to be proposed; in addition to publishers' political lobbying, major legal hurdles remain in the path to any major change of term of copyright duration in the US. Now, the political hurdles are great, but the legal hurdles arising in both domestic and international law are overwhelming.

Treaties, which are signed and ratified by the US, have the effect of becoming the domestic "supreme law of the land."[1171] A few particular treaties, such as the Berne Convention, TRIPs agreement and the WCT, set the minimum standards for the international protection of IP; the minimum term of copyright duration is fifty years.[1172] Although the world reached a near-consensus on IP under these treaties, the digital revolution threw this order into disarray and the US is still bound by them. Even if Congress wished to lower the terms of copyright duration, it would have to do so in compliance with its international obligations. Without substantial changes to the Berne Convention itself, there would be very little room to reduce the terms of copyright duration. Since the Berne Convention is in effect, though, the greatest flexibility permitted for Congress and the courts to promote the free flow of academic materials would be to strengthen fair use. Although, to draw a metaphor, a work-around such as this might very well be the creation of a new monster to combat an old one that is running amok. Fair use is a common law doctrine left vague specifically to afford the flexibility that is required. Any attempts to use fair use wholesale, uniformly and statutorily will likely come with a long list of unintended, undesirable consequences.

1171 U.S. Const., art. VI, cl. 2.

1172 *See* Berne Convention for the Protection of Literary and Artistic Works, Article 7, Sep. 28, 1979; Agreement on Trade-Related Aspects of Intellectual Property Rights (TRIPs), Article 12, 14, Apr. 15, 1994; WIPO Copyright Treaty (WCT), Dec. 20, 1996.

Berne was adopted to help protect the US' major copyright industries abroad but came with a trade-off requiring the removal of formalities in the US and minimum terms of copyright protection. This specifically has limited Congress' ability to make statutes that could make academic works more available to the public. If the US were to withdraw from the Berne Convention, Congress would then be free to significantly shorten, or even eliminate, the terms of copyright protection for academic works in order to expand the public domain. This would be a weakening of copyright restrictions, but likely a necessary one because of the inability of fair use to keep up with copyright's expansion. Furthermore, an opt-in system of activating copyright protection through registration would also be a possibility. Such a system could require authors that wish to exercise copyright protection over their works to, first, file for protection. Further solutions toward removing impediments to digitization include amending the Copyright Act to allow for automatic permission for older works to be digitized and allowing authors to opt-out of the regime by filing a waiver of rights with the Copyright Office.[1173] Other suggestions include the creation of statutory licensing rules, which could free-up noncommercial uses, provide increased access to older works, more uses of orphaned works and put specific time and usage constraints onto digital works.[1174]

Any approach using wholesale distinctions between academic works and works made for entertainment would likely draw objections regarding the ability to define and categorize certain works. My first rebuttal to that is, when we apply fair use, we already allow judges and juries the discretion to distinguish transformative from non-transformative works, commercial from nonprofit uses and, even, creative from factual works! Similarly, the Berne Convention used to make these distinctions before they were gradually lobbied out of existence. People have privately been able to distinguish, leading to separate markets for academic and other works, and plenty of easily identifiable categories—e.g. fiction, history, science—for stocking books on their shelves.[1175] Why could authors, the courts or

1173 Netanel, *Copyright: What Everyone Needs to Know*, *supra* note 643, at 161.

1174 *Ibid.*

1175 There are admittedly grey areas—e.g. documentaries, news reporting and satire —where distinguishing between academic works and works made for entertainment are more complicated. I believe that, in these instances, the best approach is to use an opt-in system, where authors can register their works according to how they believe it should be categorized. Authors that register their works as works made for entertainment can receive more stringent copyright protection, whereas those registering academic works could still receive

the Copyright Office not distinguish between academic works and other types of works? Finally, the authors themselves can define the categories for their works. The current regime puts the burden on defendant users to demonstrate the fair use factors; an opt-in system would shift that responsibility to distinguish to the parties requesting copyright protection. If there were to be an opt-in system with varying terms of protection, allowing substantially stronger and longer protection for works made for entertainment, the entertainment industries would be quick to label their output as entertainment-oriented and register for copyright protection. Even authors of academic works who are optimistic that they will generate a profit would still be free to file for copyright protection, albeit for a shorter period.

protection over a short period before the work enters the public domain. Registering a work as "academic," may also attach an intrinsic importance to a work. Other works, which are not registered, would immediately enter the public domain.

Part III: Summary

Academic works have never been less affordable for all interested parties in the US than they are today and private, nonprofit universities and copyright laws are two major systems directly linked to their creation and dissemination.[1176] This dissertation set out to ask *if* private universities and copyright law benefit the public, and, if so, if it is in accordance with the organization of their legal systems. Additionally, once these systems were described and analyzed, potential suggestions for improvement were made. Despite the massive investment of resources that Americans make into knowledge production and dissemination—through various privileges including tax deductions and subsidies—most individual Americans are excluded from directly accessing our collective patrimony. Although their ability to participate directly is limited, they still do benefit indirectly from the innovations occurring within these knowledge systems. This work referred to the exclusion of willing participants as "deadweight loss" and demonstrated why deadweight loss concerning knowledge, a public good, is unnecessary. Instead of fine-tuning knowledge systems to stoke innovation, a wasteful, resource-intensive approach has been implemented.

Inquiring as to whether private, nonprofit universities benefit the public, Part I began with a historical background to provide context to modern university activities. As American universities evolved to incorporate features of the British and German systems, a new university type arose, the American system, which is characterized by autonomy, private giving and unique structural and pedagogic approaches. The autonomy of any university is directly bound to its sources of funding, therefore making private giving most compatible with the private universities that have, in large part, come to represent the modern American system. Well-intentioned subsidies from the federal government were meant to proliferate this American system, but the disregard for the nonprofit model's underlying premises resulted in numerous negative outcomes for most interest-

1176 The differential between rich and poor access to knowledge correlates with "old forms of inequalities" but should be approached differently than the economic factors relating to material inequality. *See* Drahos, Peter. *A Philosophy of Intellectual Property*. ANU EText, 2016, e-booksdirectory.com/details.php?ebook=11824, pp. 135–37.

ed parties. Yet, despite these shortcomings, private, nonprofit universities continue to benefit the public.

Part I outlined the expectations set by students, perhaps the most apparent of all interested parties, on the professional, mobility and social pathways. Every pathway is integrated into each institution to varying degrees. Private, nonprofit universities offer students on these pathways the greatest opportunities for serious studies, mobility when students overcome stringent admissions standards and the greatest social benefits. The professional pathway is predominant in the most elite universities. The mobility pathway is well represented in universities elsewhere on the spectrum. Private universities disproportionally populate the higher-rankings, while underfunded state institutions, community colleges and for-profit universities generally represent the lowest-rankings. Students attending the lowest-ranked universities are likely to be saddled with the greatest amounts of debt, while receiving fewer of the benefits of higher education. This is not to dismiss community colleges' and for-profit universities' success in providing professional training; they are quite effective at this type of instruction and beneficial for the students who manage to graduate without debt. The social pathway looks substantially different at the most elite universities, as opposed to the middle- and lower-tiers. Socialization at elite universities offers the extra benefits of being surrounded by peers with powerful social networks.

Assessing the various university goals showed that there are some generalizations that can be made about private, nonprofit universities in terms of education, research, certification and social mobility. Regarding education, nonprofits are generally regarded as offering high-quality programs. If universities are offering meaningful higher education, teaching students to inquire, think critically, analyze issues and to communicate effectively, university graduates are presumed to be better qualified to navigate the current information / disinformation landscape. Going back to the distinctions made in Part I, the information for professional training is already readily available online, but a rigorous schooling in the humanities may be the best means for equipping modern citizens to distinguish between news and fake news, between articles and advertisements and between facts and untruths.

History has proven that humanities programs have been part of the formula for longevity, whereas professional training has been subject to abrupt market and technological changes, exposing these institutions to the same risks encountered by for-profit businesses. For-profit businesses are regularly founded, adapt to markets, fail to adapt to markets and go out of business as soon as their model is no longer profitable. Treating private, nonprofit universities similarly risks the institutions' ability to survive over long periods; shuttered universities serve nobody. While there have never been perfectly drawn lines between education in the humanities, professional training or research efforts, the universities that have outlived the rest have had a foundation built on the humanities. Both legal and cultural protections for academic freedom and free speech are essential to maintaining meaningful education in the humanities. Without the bulwark of free discourse, any university discipline can be transformed into a platform for repressive, vogue orthodoxies or ideologies, thus diminishing its educational value.

Publishing academic works is one of the most direct ways in which universities create and disseminate knowledge. However, research is closely bound to a small group of elite private, nonprofit and large state universities. The role of university research is quite misunderstood; research should be thought of as an opportunity for academics to share their expertise through publication, not necessarily through generating patents.[1177] Due to professors' expertise, quality research and peer review, their research is generally highly regarded while also making up most of the first-class works. Once having made significant contributions to the public domain in the nineteenth century, modern universities continue to create, disseminate and expand areas of new knowledge. Certification of quality education and knowledge itself has always been one of the distinct roles and privileges for universities. Especially with newer media forms introducing unprecedented amounts of content, the role of universities as degree-issuing institutions and quality publishers has never been more necessary for informing the public; this public trust "privilege" also encourages institutional longevity.

Social mobility is highly intertwined with all the other factors. Of the different types of students within higher education, students from

1177 Patenting does offer a valuable system of incentives to bring inventions into the public sphere, but it is also a major impediment to publication. Any publications concerning an invention can be treated as a prior work and, if the inventor fails to file for a patent within a year of publishing, he may never receive patent protection. This curb on publishing is only one issue; the major resource investments and choices for applied research are also controversial. Shifting focus away from publishing and more on patenting is antithetical to the nonprofit model. If a university either invests into developing profitable, applied technologies or shifts resources from research entirely, this would be more in line with the for-profit model.

low-income families and minorities are most likely to be on the mobility pathway. The mobility pathway is least represented in the top private universities, partially because most admitted students, those on the professional pathway, enjoy many advantages during secondary education that their peers simply do not. In addition, underrepresentation of the mobility pathway at top, private universities is linked to these high school graduates never even applying to the elite universities. If admitted to private universities, they will almost certainly be the beneficiaries of university grants, scholarships as well as most of the other intangible benefits associated with attending top universities. Unfortunately, students on the mobility pathway are, rather, more likely to be enrolled in institutions suffering from significant underfunding. This underfunding can be tied back to the misunderstandings of and failure to distinguish between the university types, leading to the poor distribution of resources, which could otherwise be used to support these institutions and their students. This failure to properly direct resources is harmful to both private and public nonprofit university types.

The American system is still substantially reliant on the nonprofit model, despite governmental funding agencies having disregarded its fundamental premises. Nonprofits are thought to be better suited for the provision of services that are subject to contract failure, i.e. complex services with multiple interested parties, as opposed to standard goods whose values, prices and parties are more apparent. In the case of the services provided by nonprofits—higher education in this instance—normal market competition is inadequate to incentivize for-profit entities to charge reasonable prices. In such cases of contract failure, nonprofits' non-distribution constraint should work to encourage the delivery of quality services at reasonable costs. Although, the non-distribution constraint, the policing tool for price and quality, has been neutralized primarily through the infusion of student loans. The non-distribution constraint has been further weakened by legal safe-harbors and a culture that has become complacent with debt, excessive tuition fees and university spending.

The law of nonprofits offers little recourse now because of weak enforcement, safe-harbor provisions and lax interpretation of the IRC's tests. Nonetheless, universities should be more stringently scrutinized for their non-exempt, commercial, activities. The greatest issues arise mostly under the commerciality doctrine and operational test. The commerciality doctrine is a tool that courts are obviously hesitant to use. If it were strictly applied to a university substantially engaged in sports-entertainment, for example, that university would lose its tax-exemption. In order to avoid such an extreme outcome, the IRS prefers to apply the UBIT instead, which is applied sparingly. The operational test has similarly been declawed by the safe-harbor, which has encouraged administrative compensation *benchmarking*. This has led to a ratcheting-up of administrative compensation. If not falling within the broad safe-harbor, this compensation could lead to the loss of tax-exemption, but in all practicality the most extreme punishment will be intermediate sanctions for excess benefit. While more scrutiny from attorneys general or the IRS could be encouraged, they are limited in their ability to confront extravagant university expenditures due to the extensive safe-harbors by which universities are protected.

Since the non-distribution constraint has been neutralized, every type of university in the US is currently charging excessive fees to finance their expenses. The value of their services, under any set of circumstances, is difficult to judge because it would ordinarily be left to former students' subjective value judgments on a case-by-case basis. But, since the government has become an intermediary by issuing student loans, former students are even further-removed as interested parties. While former students were never able to enforce their expectations through arm's length contracts, the government's continuous infusion of resources, lacking any serious assessment of costs, quality or the value of services, disables the mechanism by which nonprofits protect both their students and the public as interested parties. The US is pouring an immense amount of resources into these institutions without proper price-control mechanisms. This is no trivial point; the failure to provide affordable access to higher education either excludes many lower-income Americans or requires them to take on crushing debt. Access can be better promoted through adherence to nonprofit norms.

This vortex of rising costs is a result of the failure of nonprofit universities to operate according to their premises, making their incentive structure more like that of for-profit organizations. With the carry-over of for-profit characteristics, a bevy of other negative symptoms arise in the nonprofit system. One negative symptom is the trickle-up effect where middle-tier universities are most influenced by the for-profit university model. This model is dependent on mildly effective, paywalled online courses and increased class sizes, both of which have much more to do with cost cutting and less to do with quality instruction. The neutralized non-distribution constraint, allowing for commercial activities and excessive administrative compensation, also leads to reduced *warm glow*; alumni and other donors are less likely to contribute to private universities and, conversely, more student loans and price increases are encouraged. In other words, if universities are flooded with funding derived from student loans, this will likely offset donations. Outrage by interested parties will be less of a constraint upon the universities. In the age of skyrocketing costs for prospective students, the private universities that have weeded-out student loans and returned to other means of finance are a beacon of light; they are reclaiming the nonprofit model.

After a thorough discussion in Part I, it was determined that the university system generally continues to benefit the public. They benefit the public in accordance with their legal structure, but the structure itself has been neglected. Some private, nonprofit universities remain dependent on charitable giving, but lending has supplanted private charity and even government grants for the rest. When private universities without large endowments begin competing for students who are primarily financed by loans, the self-perpetuating cycle of adding expensive amenities and rising costs has become the norm. This vicious cycle has not only challenged private universities by affecting their autonomy through finance, but public universities as well. The greatest cost increases have occurred at public institutions. Considering the perverse incentives for reckless lending without regard to educational outcomes, for-profit universities and their shareholders have been the largest beneficiaries of the federal finance schemes; their students certainly have not been. One can no longer clearly segment the various types of universities away from each other considering how they are financed. Thus, all interested parties of private, nonprofit universities need to be vigilant to prevent nonprofits from adopting for-profit incentive structures and the tactics. Private, nonprofit institutions are much too valuable to the public to allow them to share the pending fate of their for-profit counterparts.

Part II similarly began with a historical background in its inquiry as to whether copyright law benefits the public. Prior to there being copyright law, authors were funded by various state or religious patrons. The precursors to copyright, such as the stationers' monopoly in England, granted privileges mainly to control the flow of knowledge and information. Once copyright created an alternative means for authors to sustain themselves financially, based neither on patronage nor privilege, authors were free to express themselves to a degree that had previously never been possible. Copyright fueled authorship for many decades in the US but has failed to keep up with technological innovation. Today, all types of Internet-based platforms can exercise nearly complete control over their content with technical and contractual mechanisms, while copyright law only strengthens their stranglehold. On one hand, many of these platforms have made immense amounts of both first- and second-class works available, but, on the other hand, their absolute control over content risks the removal of the copyright's most fundamental constitutional safeguards. With Internet-based platforms, copyright, thus, becomes much more of a mechanism for control and less of an incentive for the free flow of information.

Regarding copyright's production function, Part II demonstrated that authors of academic works are not incentivized by the extensive protections afforded by copyright. Thus, copyright law does not benefit the public regarding academic works. I reached this conclusion primarily because academics are caught in the cycle of producing free content and then buying it back at exorbitant rates; these costs are inevitably passed onto students and the public. Copyright law, in this context, only provides the means for stringent protection, while not incentivizing authorship. If academics' works do have some type of financial marketability, it is less likely that revenues would be derived from copyright proceeds and much more likely, instead, that they would come from patents. This even applies to non-academics; the Wright Brothers made a livelihood from their patents, while their publications on aviation earned them recognition, prominence and prestige.[1178]

The public rights tradition, upon which the US system of copyright law is based, strives for the greatest amount of content creation and dissemination possible. One major limitation on this has been the US' ratification of the Berne Convention, which mixed elements of the European authors' rights tradition into the American system. US copyright law previously afforded a greater degree of flexibility and allowance for fair use for all types of copyrighted materials. Ever since the ascension to the Berne Convention, copyright law in the US has become continuously more restrictive, encompassing and lengthy. Relative to the strengthening of copyright law, fair use and the other constitutional safeguards have been inadequate. This has resulted in most academic works being locked away behind expensive paywalls, which are only accessible by institutions that can afford the exorbitant licensing fees. While the Internet and universities promote content production and provide alternative structures for authors, the antiquated copyright regime is more restrictive than it is supportive for the output of academic works. This has resulted in the public being unnecessarily excluded from our collective patrimony.

In the context of the expressive function, Part II also described copyright and its restrictive relationship with free expression. The Supreme Court

1178 *See generally* McCullough, *supra* note 1, at 252.

made clear that extensive copyright protections are constitutionally permissible if the safeguards are in place to sufficiently protect the free flow of ideas. Unfortunately, the Supreme Court did not provide guidance for determining whether the constitutional safeguards of fair use and the idea / expression dichotomy are adequate in relation to the burdens that copyright puts on free speech. Instances in which Internet service providers have used copyright to hinder free expression—using copyright as a pretense to monetize content or to remove content that they do not like—are reminiscent of the English stationers' printing monopoly centuries ago. Part II also discussed the access issues in all sectors and how the ability to access works is a precondition to having meaningful safeguards such as fair use. It seems that access is the most essential element. When academic works are too expensive to access, readers will not even be able to make fair use of them.

Part II demonstrated the necessity of, first, distinguishing between academic works and works made for entertainment and, second, first- and second-class works. Being able to distinguish these categories allows for a thorough understanding of the purposes of copyright law, leading to appropriate suggestions for improvement. Thus, Part II highlighted the incompatibilities arising under US law from the Berne Convention, from which the US should reconsider its membership. A withdrawal would give Congress the power to reinstate shorter terms of protection, an opt-in system and filing requirements. In the meanwhile, some smaller changes are already possible: shifting burdens of proof onto copyright holders, creating statutory licensing rules, creating special rules for digitizing works, changing work made for hire rules, conditioning grants on open publication, shifting publication costs onto institutions and generally promoting a culture of open publishing within academia.

Private nonprofit universities and copyright have many linkages as systems because they are both open systems with a common goal: the creation and dissemination of academic knowledge. These are both systems operating to produce a public good, so it makes sense that, at least within the scope of this common goal, their economic incentives are similar. There is a point of direct contact between the two systems, where the universities supplant copyright's production and structural functions. Most academic works are produced because of the university structure and not because of the limited monopolies afforded by copyright law. Furthermore, another essential linkage extending from private, nonprofit universities to copyright is derived from the universities' independence to educate and publish without interference. Copyright's expressive function works particularly well within universities specifically because they have unparalleled access to academic works. Although, if their research output continues landing behind for-profit publishers' paywalls, the public will remain locked out; this is a failure within both knowledge systems.

Conclusion

In order to counteract the incompatibilities between theory and practice that arise within legal systems, GST analyses, such as this one, are necessary to bring the systems' inner workings to light, develop a fundamental understanding and to suggest improvements that correspond to their constantly changing environments. This GST analysis explained how the systems operate, their underlying premises and how both have faced the introduction of numerous external chaos-inducing elements. Many external elements of both public and for-profit universities entered the nonprofit university system, stressing the ability for private, nonprofit universities to provide affordable access to their services. Universities, the recipients of massive amounts of public resources, are now the largest interface of general research output. Without a change to the law and their policies, though, the public cannot share in the fruits of university research.

This GST analysis of US copyright law and the effects of the Berne Convention highlighted how an open system can be affected by inputs, or flows, from other systems. The negative effects within the US are not to suggest that the US' ascension to the Berne Convention was a failed endeavor. In the context of the technology of that time, a good argument can be made that it was a wise decision in order to protect the US' content exports. Nor, is this an argument that any legal regime or tradition of copyright protection is superior to another. This GST analysis has shown, rather, that each system is built upon certain premises and that, if the systems continue to function, they need to operate in accordance to their own internal order. This work's proposed abandonment of the Berne Convention would act to unravel the systematic incompatibilities that the Berne Convention has imposed on American publishing and permit the US system of copyright to be readjusted back to its underlying public benefit tradition through appropriate domestic laws.

This dissertation looked intensively into the university and copyright law systems to formulate a better understanding of their inner workings and interactions. Such an in-depth observation and synthesis of these systems was indeed necessary. This work has presented them in a new light. Throughout my research, though, it became clear that the study on many systems and sub-systems periphery to the ones observed here is also lacking. For example, since technology allows for the instant flow of information and knowledge across political boundaries, an international approach to the questions presented here would provide quite a bit of insight into how these issues unfold globally. All countries around the world face the same difficulty of balancing numerous rights and objectives within their traditions of authors' rights or promoting the public benefit. Their form of protection, if any at all, inevitably causes friction when works are being used in other jurisdictions that are premised on other legal traditions. Further, an international study of this sort could be helpful to study the intersection between copyright limitations and free expression. Freedom of expression is what enables the robust debate of ideas, functioning democracy and innovative progress in the sciences, but is subject to the culture, constitutional principles and circumstances of every country where such a right exists. Digital communications have overreached most political boarders, thus requiring nuanced international leadership on, first and foremost, principles of free expression and, secondly, responsible policies encouraging knowledge dissemination.

Since this dissertation has focused intensively on academic works, further research would also be very valuable to better understand works made for entertainment. The current copyright regime is clearly entertainment-oriented, so further study can inquire into whether it is functioning in line with its legal and social purposes. Moreover, many economic historians have also gone to great lengths to draw connections between industrialization and innovation, but the many working parts of an industrial society can also be looked at more carefully. How has the spread of knowledge been affected by planes, trains and automobiles? How have patents and trade secrets contributed as knowledge systems? What types of institutions are best suited to create and implement these forms of IP? These are, of course, just a few of the many questions that can be further explored to understand our systems of knowledge creation and dissemination.

This work was written primarily in the time leading up to the Covid-19 crisis, so no attempt is made to predict how private, nonprofit universities and copyright law will be affected. Currently, the virus continues to spread, to claim its victims, and to exert stress on every social institution in every country of the world. It appears that the dust from this cataclysmic event may not settle for years to come, obfuscating how the systems discussed in this work will be affected. On the other hand, it is safe to acknowledge that the numerous Covid-19 vaccines, which are based on new methods and were developed in record time, are a testament to the systems discussed in this work. Paradoxically, the same bodies of knowledge that lie behind the creation of these miraculous vaccines remain locked away from most of the people who will need to be vaccinated. Just as important as having an effective and safe vaccine, is having a public that is willing to take it. At this critical juncture, universities are faced with lagging enrollment, threatening their longevity, students are faced with increasing tuition fees, leading them to consider alternative routes, and the public remains in a disadvantaged position in terms of accessing knowledge. If potential students forego enrolling in higher education, they, like the rest of the population, will be reliant on second-class works to access knowledge regarding vaccines, nutrition, and public health. Consequently, the lessons brought up throughout this dissertation, especially those regarding longevity, improving access and the proper functioning of systems, are now more vital than ever before.

Decades ago, the developer of GST observed that the understanding of our own social systems is inadequate as compared to our expanding understanding of the natural sciences.[1179] His pessimism was well founded in the middle of the twentieth century when technology and the natural sciences were being harnessed to wage war and annihilate human life *en masse*. Without the constraint of wisdom, values and morals, people and the knowledge that they had to share were eradicated. We will never know the extent of the knowledge and human potential that was lost in book burnings, wars and other unspeakable atrocities in which our advanced technological abilities, unrestrained by our social systems, were applied for destructive ends or, out of neglect, were not used to help our fellow people. His remarks are as relevant today as they were then. Just as scientific progress can be used both for both good and evil, social systems aided by scientific or technological advances are no different; Orwell's book *1984* all but laid out the dystopian blueprints for today's techno-totalitarians.[1180]

Although, despite these shortcomings, it is only fair to marvel at the instances in which things have gone right, the systems succeeded, and innovation took root. Some of the lessons from this work could act to guide us going into the future. We must trust and support the very best of our systems: constitutional democracy, the checks and balances on governmental powers, equal protection under the law, the robust system of freedom of speech, modern science and our social systems for knowledge proliferation. These are invariably compatible with the creation and disper-

1179 Bertalanffy, *supra* note 52, at 51.

1180 *Ibid.* at 52; *See* Orwell, George. *Nineteen Eighty-Four*. Penguin Books, 2008. Originally published 1949 (stating that, he "who controls the past controls the future.").

sion of knowledge. Some of our systems that are struggling, such as the universities that have buried younger Americans in tens- or hundreds of thousands of dollars of crushing debt, cannot be ignored. With an intricate understanding of the systemic shortcomings that were addressed in this work, we can strive to make these systems better for everybody's sake. Our tremendously complex society is reliant on the welfare of each individual and their contributions in return. In our attempt to further serve the public, though, we must turn the key to unlock our collective patrimony.

Works Cited

International Legal Sources

Agreement on Trade-Related Aspects of Intellectual Property Rights (TRIPS), Articles 12, 14, Apr. 15, 1994.

Berne Convention for the Protection of Literary and Artistic Works, Article 7, Sep. 9, 1886.

Berne Convention for the Protection of Literary and Artistic Works, Article 9, Nov. 13, 1908.

Berne Convention for the Protection of Literary and Artistic Works, Article 10(2), July 24, 1971.

Berne Convention for the Protection of Literary and Artistic Works, Article 7, Sep. 28, 1979.

WIPO Copyright Treaty (WCT), Dec. 20, 1996.

Non-US Legal Sources

An Act for the Encouragement of Learning 1710, 8 Anne, ch. 19 (Gr. Brit.).

Carey v. Kearsley (1803) (UK) 170 Eng. Rep. 679, 681; 4 Esp. 168, 170.

Directive 96/9/EC of the European Parliament and of the Council of 11 March 1996 on the Legal Protection of Databases.

Statute of Charitable Uses 1601, 43 Eliz. I, c. 4 (Eng.).

US Legal Sources

"Berne Notification No. 121 Berne Convention for the Protection of Literary and Artistic Works." Treaty/BerneE/121: [Berne Convention] Accession by the United States of America, 17 Nov. 1988, www.wipo.int/treaties/en/notifications/berne/treaty_berne_121.html.

H.R. Rep. No. 94–1476, at 65 (1976).

U.S. Const. amend. I.

U.S. Const. amend. XVI.

U.S. Const. art. I, § 8, cl. 3.

U.S. Const. art. I, § 8, cl. 8.

U.S. Const. art. VI, cl. 2.

US Federal Legislation

2 Stat. 171 (1802).

4 Stat. 36 (1831).

2 U.S.C. § 17 (1958).
17 U.S.C. § 101 (2012).
17 U.S.C § 201 et seq. (2002).
17 U.S.C. § 302 (2011).
17 U.S.C. § 500 et seq. (2011).
17 U.S.C. § 1201 et seq. (2011).
26 U.S.C. § 4960 (2017).
28 U.S.C. § 1000 et seq. (2011).
28 U.S.C. § 4001 (1998).
35 U.S.C. § 212 (1984).
58 Stat. 268 (1944); (codified as amended at 38 U.S.C. §§ 34, 37 (2011)).
Copyright Act of 1790, 1 Stat. 124 (1790).
Consolidated Appropriations Act, 2008, 218 Stat. 110–161 (2008).
Open Licensing Requirement for Competitive Grant Programs, 2 CFR Part 3474, RIN 1894-AA07 (2017).
P. L. 92–318, title I, § 133(a), 86 Stat. 265 (1972); (codified as amended at 20 U.S.C. § 1087 (2006)).

US Federal Case Law

AIME v. Regents of the University of California, No. 2:10-cv-09378-CBM (D. Ca. 2012).
Authors Guild v. Google Inc., 804 F.3 d 202, 215 (2 d Cir. 2015).
Authors Guild v. HathiTrust, 755 F.3 d 87 (2 d Cir. 2014).
Basic Books, Inc. v. Kinko's Graphics Corp., 758 F. Supp. 1522 (S.D.N.Y. 1991).
Benny v. Loew's, Inc., 239 F.2 d 532 (9th Cir. 1956).
Better Business Bureau of Washington D.C. v. U.S. 326 U.S. 279 (1945).
Burrow-Giles Lithographic Company v. Sarony, 111 U.S. 53 (1884).
Cambridge University Press v. Patton, 16-15726 (11th Cir. 2018).
Campbell v. Acuff-Rose Music, Inc., 510 U.S. 569, 590 (1994).
C.F. Mueller Co., v. Commissioner of Internal Revenue, 190 F.2 d 120 (3 d Cir. 1951).
Community for Creative Non-Violence v. Reid, 490 U.S. 730 (1989).
Eldred v. Ashcroft, 537 U.S. 186 (2003).
Eldred v. Reno, 239 F.3 d 372 (D.C. Cir. 2001).
Elsevier Inc. v. Sci-Hub, No. 1:15-CV-04282-RWS, 4 (S.D.N.Y. 2015).
Family Trust of Massachusetts, Inc. v. U.S., 892 F. Supp. 2 d 149 (D.D.C. 2012).
Feist v. Rural Tel. Serv., 499 U.S. 340 (1991).
Garcia v. Google, no. 12-57302 (9th Cir. Feb. 26, 2014) (order).
Garcia v. Google, no. 12-57302 (9th Cir. May 18, 2015) (en banc).

Golan v. Holder, 565 U.S. 302 (2012).

Harper & Row v. Nation Enterprises, 471 U.S. 539 (1985).

Kirtsaeng v. John Wiley & Sons, Inc., 568 U.S. 519 (2013).

Knight First Amendment Inst. at Columbia Univ. v. Trump, 302 F. Supp. 3d 541 (S.D.N.Y. 2018), aff'd, 928 F.3d 226 (2d Cir. 2019).

Marcus v. Rowley, 695 F.2d. 1171 (9th Cir. 1983).

Miller v. Universal City Studios, Inc., 650 F.2d 1365 (5th Cir. 1981).

Montgomery v. Noga, 168 F.3d 1282 (11th Cir. 1999).

Network LP v. CSC Holdings, Inc., 536 F.3d 121 (2d Cir. 2008).

Orange County Agr. Soc. v. C.I.R. 893 F.2d 529 (2d Cir. 1990).

Rameses School of San Antonio, Texas v. Commissioner, T.C. Memo 2007-85 WL 1061871 (T.C. 2007).

Redlands Surgical v. Commissioner, 113 T.C. 47, 1999 WL 513862 (T.C. 1999), affd., 242 F.3d 904 (9th Cir. 2001).

Scripture Press v. U.S. 285 F.2d 800 (Ct. Cl. 1961).

Sheldon v. Metro-Goldwyn Pictures Corp., 81 F.2d 49 (2d Cir. 1936).

Sherrill v. Grieves, 57 Wash. L. Rep. 286 (D.C. 1929).

Sony Corp. of America v. Universal City Studios, Inc., 464 U.S. 417 (1984).

Stewart v. Abend, 495 U.S. 207 (1990).

Trademark Cases, 100 U.S. 82 (1879).

Triangle Publications, Inc. v. Knight-Ridder Newspapers, Inc. 626 F.2d 1171 (5th Cir. 1980).

Trinidad v. Sagrada, 163 U.S. 578 (1924).

Trustees of Dartmouth College v. Woodward, 17 U.S. (4 Wheat.) 518 (1819).

Vidal v. Executors of Girad, 43 U.S. (2 How.) 127 (1844).

State Case Law

City of Washington v. Washington & Jefferson College, 550 Pa. 175 (1997).

Emerson v. Davies, 8 F. Cas. 615 (C.C.Mass. 1845).

Folsom v. Marsh, 9 F. Cas. 342 (C.C.D. Mass. 1841).

State of New York v. Coalition Against Breast Cancer, Inc., 2013 WL 4283360 (May 2, 2013); *affirmed*, People v. Coalition Against Breast Cancer, Inc., 134 A.D.3d 1081 (N.Y. App. Div. 2015).

Secondary Works Cited

Note: All online sources were last accessed on 7.1.2021

AAUP, "1940 Statement of Principles on Academic Freedom and Tenure with 1970 Interpretive Comments," in *Policy Documents and Reports* (Washington, D.C.: AAUP, 2006).

"About Form 990, Return of Organization Exempt from Income Tax." *IRS*, 5 Nov. 2019, https://www.irs.gov/forms-pubs/about-form-990.

Abrams, Howard B., and Tyler T. Ochoa. *The Law of Copyright*. West, 2018.

Adams, William D. "Not by Earnings Alone: A New Report on Humanities Graduates in the Workforce and Beyond." *American Academy of Arts & Sciences*, 29 Jan. 2018, www.amacad.org/news/not-earnings-alone-new-report-humanities-graduates-workforce-and-beyond.

Altbach, Philip G., Patricia J. Gumport, and D. Bruce Johnstone, editors. *In Defense of American Higher Education*. Johns Hopkins University Press, 2001.

"American Time Use Survey--2018 Results." *Bureau of Labor Statistics*, U.S. Dep. of Labor, 2019, https://www.bls.gov/news.release/pdf/atus.pdf.

Andrezejewski, Adam. "Heaven Helps Notre Dame Football While Taxpayers Subsidize Alabama, Clemson, Oklahoma." *Forbes*, 27 Dec. 2018, www.forbes.com/si tes/adamandrzejewski/2018/12/27/heaven-helps-notre-dame-football-while-taxpa yers-subsidize-alabama-clemson-oklahoma/#20bd19a775ae.

Angulo, A.J. Diploma Mills: How For-Profit Colleges Stiff Students, Taxpayers, and the American Dream. Johns Hopkins University Press, 2016.

"Annual Report 2018." *Max-Planck-Gesellschaft*, www.mpg.de/13594766/annual-report-2018.pdf.

Armstrong, Elizabeth A., and Laura T. Hamilton. *Paying for the Party How College Maintains Inequality*. Harvard University Press, 2013.

"Association of American Universities – Nonprofit Explorer." *ProPublica*, 9 May 2013, projects.propublica.org/nonprofits/organizations/521947112.

"Average Estimated Undergraduate Budgets, 2019-20- Research – College Board." *Research*, 1 Nov. 2019, research.collegeboard.org/trends/college-pricing/figures-tables/average-estimated-undergraduate-budgets-sector-2019-20.

Baldwin, Peter. *The Copyright Wars Three Centuries of Trans-Atlantic Battle*. Princeton University Press, 2016.

Bannerman, Sara. *International Copyright and Access to Knowledge*. Cambridge University Press, 2016.

Bartow, Ann. "The Hegemony of the Copyright Treatise." *University of Cincinnati Law Review*, vol. 73, 2004, pp. 581–644.

Baum, Sandy, Michael McPherson, and Patricia Steele, editors. *The Effectiveness of Student Aid Policies: What the Research Tells Us*. The College Board, 2008.

Beaulieu, Luc, and Parminder Basran. "How Many Citations Are Actually a Lot of Citations?" *Ruminating...*, 28 Dec. 2018, https://lucbeaulieu.com/2015/11/19/how-many-citations-are-actually-a-lot-of-citations/.

Bebchuk, Lucian Arye, and Jesse M Fried. "Executive Compensation as an Agency Problem." *Journal of Economic Perspectives*, vol. 17, no. 3, 2003, pp. 71–92.

Bebchuk, Lucian Arye, Jesse M. Fried, and David I. Walker. "Managerial Power and Rent Extraction in the Design of Executive Compensation." *The University of Chicago Law Review*, vol. 69, no. 3, 2002, pp. 751–846.

Bell, Tom W. "Copyright as Intellectual (Property) Privilege." *Syracuse Law Review*, vol. 58, 2008, pp. 523–46.

Bell, Abraham, and Gideon Parchomovsky. "The Dual-Grant Theory of Fair Use." *University of Chicago Law Review*, vol. 83, no. 3, 2016, pp. 1051–1118.

Benkler, Yochai. *The Wealth of Networks: How Social Production Transforms Markets and Freedom*. Yale University Press, 2007.

Bentley, Peter James, Magnus Gulbrandsen, and Svein Kyvik. "The Relationship between Basic and Applied Research in Universities." *Higher Education*, vol. 70, no. 4, 2015, pp. 689–709.

Bergstrom, Carl T. "The Economics of Ecology Journals." *Frontiers in Ecology and the Environment*, vol. 4, no. 9, Nov. 2006, pp. 488–95.

—, "Free Labor for Costly Journals?" *Journal of Economic Perspectives*, vol. 15, no. 3, 2001, pp. 183–98.

"Berne Notification No. 121 Berne Convention for the Protection of Literary and Artistic Works." *Treaty/BerneE/121: [Berne Convention] Accession by the United States of America*, 17 Nov. 1988, www.wipo.int/treaties/en/notifications/berne/treaty_berne_121.html.

Bertalanffy, Ludwig von. *General System Theory: Foundations, Development, Applications*. Penguin, 1969.

Best, Joel, and Eric Best. *The Student Loan Mess: How Good Intentions Created a Trillion-Dollar Problem*. University of California Press, 2014.

Bezanson, Randall P., and Joseph M. Miller. "Scholarship and Fair Use." *Columbia Journal of Law & the Arts*, vol. 33, no. 4, 2010, pp. 409–70.

Bizjak, John M. & Lemmon, Michael L. & Naveen, Lalitha, *Does the Use of Peer Groups Contribute to Higher Pay and Less Efficient Compensation?*, 90(2) Journal of Financial Economics, 152, 153 (2008).

Bovens, Mark, Robert E. Goodin, and Thomas Schillemans, editors. "Accountability and the Nonprofit Sector." *The Oxford Handbook of Public Accountability*, Aug. 2014.

Boyle, James. *The Public Domain: Enclosing the Commons of the Mind*. Yale University Press, 2009.

Bracha, Oren. "Early American Printing Privileges." In *Privilege and Property, Essays on the History of Copyright*, edited by Ronan Deazley, Martin Kretschmer, and Lionel Bently, Open Book Publishers, 2010.

Brannon, Valerie C. "Free Speech and the Regulation of Social Media Content." *Congressional Research Service, Free Speech and the Regulation of Social Media Content*, 27 Mar. 2019. https://fas.org/sgp/crs/misc/R45650.pdf.

Breneman, David W., Brian Pusser, and Sarah E. Turner, editors. *Earnings from Learning: the Rise of for-Profit Universities*. State University of New York Press, 2006.

Brint, Steven, and Jerome Karabel. *Diverted Dream Community Colleges and the Promise of Educational Opportunity in America, 1900-1985*. Oxford University Press, 1989.

Brint, Steven. *Two Cheers for Higher Education: Why American Universities Are Stronger than Ever, and How to Meet the Challenges They Face*. Princeton University Press, 2018.

Brooks, John R. "Don't Let the G.O.P. Dismantle Obama's Student Loan Reforms." *The New York Times*, 9 Apr. 2018, www.nytimes.com/2018/04/09/opinion/student-loan-reform-prosper-act.html.

Burrell, Thomas H. "A Story of Privileges and Immunities: From Medieval Concept to the Colonies and United States Constitution." *Campbell Law Review*, vol. 34, no. 1, 2011, pp. 7–120.

Cafardi, Nicholas P., and Jaclyn Fabean Cherry. *Understanding Nonprofit and Tax Exempt Organizations*. Carolina Academic Press, 2012.

Carlisle, Stephen. "Why Reducing Current Copyright Terms Would Be Unwise... And Unconstitutional." *Office of Copyright*, 26 Feb. 2016, http://copyright.nova.edu/copyright-terms/.

Carnevale, Anthony P., and Jeff Strohl. "Separate & Unequal How Higher Education Reinforces the Intergenerational Reproduction of White Racial Privilege." *Georgetown University Center on Education and the Workforce*, 2013.

"CC Licenses and Examples." *Creative Commons*, creativecommons.org/share-your-work/licensing-types-examples/.

Clark, Ann Marie. "A Social Scientist Uses E-Books for Research and in the Classroom." *Academic E-Books Publishers, Librarians, and Users*, edited by Suzanne M. Ward, Robert S. Freeman, and Judith M. Nixon Purdue, University Press, 2016.

Cobban, Alan B. "Medieval Student Power." *Past & Present*, no. 53, 1971, pp. 28–66.

Cole, Jonathan R. *Toward a More Perfect University*. Public Affairs, 2016.

---, *Who's Afraid of Academic Freedom?* Columbia University Press, 2015.

Coleman, Nicole, and Stanford University. "Mapping the Republic of Letters." *Mapping the Republic of Letters*, 2013, http://republicofletters.stanford.edu/.

"Compensation for Nonprofit Employees." *National Council of Nonprofits*, 23 July 2019, https://www.councilofnonprofits.org/tools-resources/compensation-nonprofit-employees.

Conklin, Justin, Carter Coudriet, and Caroline Howard, editors. "America's Top Colleges 2019." *Forbes*, 15 Aug. 2019, www.forbes.com/top-colleges/list/#tab:rank.

"Copyright in the Classroom." *Copyright in the Classroom | UC Copyright*, copyright.universityofcalifornia.edu/use/teaching.html.

Coudriet, Carter. "Top Colleges 2018: The Methodology." *Forbes*, 23 Aug. 2018, www.forbes.com/sites/cartercoudriet/2018/08/20/top-colleges-2018-the-methodology/#40b889ee3098.

Cowley, Stacy, and Erica L. Green. "A College Chain Crumbles, and Millions in Student Loan Cash Disappears." *The New York Times*, The New York Times, 8 Mar. 2019, www.nytimes.com/2019/03/07/business/argosy-college-art-insititutes-south-university.html.

Crews, Kenneth D. *Copyright, Fair Use, and the Challenge for Universities: Promoting the Progress of Higher Education*. University of Chicago Press, 1993.

—, *Copyright Law for Librarians and Educators: Creative Strategies and Practical Solutions*. ALA Editions, 2006.

Crow, Michael M., and William B. Dabars. *Designing the New American University*. Johns Hopkins University Press, 2015.

Dallon, Craig W. "The Problem with Congress and Copyright Law: Forgetting the Past and Ignoring the Public Interest." *Santa Clara Law Review*, vol. 44, no. 1, 2004, pp. 365–455.

Darnton, Robert. *The Case for Books*. PublicAffairs, 2009.

Deazley, Ronan. *On the Origin of the Right to Copy: Charting the Movement of Copyright Law in Eighteenth-Century Britain (1695-1775)*. Hart Publishing, 2004.

Denicola, Robert C. "Copyright and Open Access: Reconsidering University Ownership of Faculty Research." *Nebraska Law Review*, vol. 85, 2006, pp. 351–82.

Dickinson, Tim. "Obama's Real Reform." *Rolling Stone*, 6 Aug. 2009, pp. 41–43.

"Directory of Open Access Journals." *Directory of Open Access Journals*, 2020, doaj.org/about.

"Division II Partial-Scholarship Model." *NCAA*, 2019, Division II partial-scholarship model.

Dorta-González, Pablo, Sara M. González-Betancor, and Maria Isabel Dorta-González. "Reconsidering the Gold Open Access Citation Advantage Postulate in a Multidisciplinary Context: an Analysis of the Subject Categories in the Web of Science Database 2009-2014." *Scientometrics*, vol. 112, no. 2, 2017, pp. 877–901.

Drahos, Peter. *A Philosophy of Intellectual Property*. ANU EText, 2016, e-booksdirectory.com/details.php?ebook=11824.

Drake, Stillman. "Early Science and the Printed Book: The Spread of Science Beyond the University." *Renaissance and Reformation*, vol. 6, no. 3, 1970, pp. 43–52.

Dwyer, Philip. "Whitewashing History." *Historical Reflections/Réflexions Historiques*, vol. 44, no. 1, 1 Mar. 2018, pp. 54–65.

Edelstein, Dan, Paula Findlen, Giovanna Ceserani, Caroline Winterer, and Nicole Coleman. "Historical Research in a Digital Age: Reflections from the Mapping the Republic of Letters Project." *The American Historical Review*, vol. 122, no. 2, 2017, pp. 400–24.

Elson, Charles M., and Ferrere, Craig, Executive Superstars, Peer Groups and Overcompensation: Cause, Effect and Solution p. 9 (August 7, 2012). https://lerner.udel.edu/sites/default/files/pdfs/Elson_Ferrere_Paper.pdf.

Elkin-Koren, Niva. "The New Frontiers of User Rights." *American University International Law Review*, vol. 32, no. 1, 2016, pp. 1–42.

Feldmann, Horst. "The Long Shadows of Spanish and French Colonial Education." *Kyklos*, vol. 69, no. 1, 2016, pp. 32–64.

Fielding, David, and Shef Rogers. "Monopoly Power in the Eighteenth-Century British Book Trade." *European Review of Economic History*, vol. 21, no. 4, 12 May 2017, pp. 393–413.

"50 Universities with the Most Nobel Prize Winners." *BestMastersPrograms.org*, 5 Oct. 2018, www.bestmastersprograms.org/50-universities-with-the-most-nobel-prize-winners/.

Fishman, James J. "Improving Charitable Accountability." *Maryland Law Review*, vol. 62, 2003, pp. 218–87.

---, "Standards of Conduct for Directors of Nonprofit Corporations." *Pace Law Review*, vol. 7, 1987, pp. 389–462.

"Freedom on the Net 2018." The Rise of Digital Authoritarianism, Freedom House, Oct. 2018, https://freedomhouse.org/sites/default/files/FOTN_2018_Final Booklet_11_1_2018.pdf.

Fremont-Smith, Marion R. *Governing Nonprofit Organizations: Federal and State Law and Regulation*. Belknap, 2008.

---, *The Nonprofit Sector: a Research Handbook*. edited by Walter W. Powell and Richard Steinberg, Yale University Press, 2006.

Friedman, Zack. "75 Colleges with Free or Reduced Tuition." *Forbes*, 27 Nov. 2018, www.forbes.com/sites/zackfriedman/2018/11/27/colleges-no-student-loans/#37e51ece6156.

---, "Trump's New Plan to Make Student Loans Great Again." *Forbes*, Forbes Magazine, 21 Dec. 2019, www.forbes.com/sites/zackfriedman/2019/12/21/trump-plan-student-loans-great-again/#5763208b4c0 c.

Frijhoff, Willem. "Patterns." In *A History of the University in Europe: Volume II, Universities in Early Modern Europe*, edited by Walter Rüegg, Cambridge University Press, 1996.

Fromer, Jeanne C., and Christopher Jon Sprigman. "Copyright Law: Cases and Materials." *Copyright Law: Cases and Materials*, www.copyrightbook.org/about.

Frumkin, Peter and Elizabeth Keating. "The Price of Doing Good: Executive Compensation in Nonprofit Organizations." *Hauser Center Working Paper*, 2001.

Frumkin, Peter. *On Being Nonprofit: A Conceptual and Policy Primer*. Harvard University Press, 2009.

Fuchs, Christian, and Marisol Sandoval. "The Diamond Model of Open Access Publishing: Why Policy Makers, Scholars, Universities, Libraries, Labour Unions and the Publishing World Need to Take Non-Commercial, Non-Profit Open Access Serious." *TripleC*, 11(2), Sept. 2013, pp. 428–43.

Fulton, JF. "The Rise of the Experimental Method: Bacon and the Royal Society of London." *The Yale Journal of Biology and Medicine*, vol. 3, no. 4, 1931, pp. 299–320.

Galle, Brian D., and David I. Walker. "The Problem of Nonprofit Executive Pay?: Evidence from U.S. Colleges and Universities." *Boston College Law School Faculty Papers*, 2015, pp. 2–42.

Gelbgiser, Dafna. "College for All, Degrees for Few: For-Profit Colleges and Socioeconomic Differences in Degree Attainment." *Social Forces*, vol. 96, no. 4, 2018, pp. 1785–1824.

Ginsburg, Jane C. "Creation and Commercial Value: Copyright Protection of Works of Information." *Columbia Law Review*, vol. 90, no. 7, 1990, pp. 1865–1938.

"Goal 1: End Poverty in All Its Forms Everywhere – United Nations Sustainable Development." *United Nations*, https://www.un.org/sustainabledevelopment/poverty/.

Gordon, Wendy J. "Fair Use as Market Failure: A Structural and Economic Analysis of the Betamax Case and Its Predecessors." *Columbia Law Review*, vol. 82, 1982, pp. 1600–57.

"Governance of Charitable Organizations and Related Topics." *IRS*, 4 Feb. 2008, www.irs.gov/pub/irs-tege/governance_practices.pdf.

Graber-Stiehl, Ian. "Meet the Pirate Queen Making Academic Papers Free Online." *The Verge*, 8 Feb. 2018, www.theverge.com/2018/2/8/16985666/alexandra-elbakyan-sci-hub-open-access-science-papers-lawsuit.

Greenwood, Brian. "The Contribution of Vaccination to Global Health: Past, Present and Future." *Philosophical Transactions: Biological Sciences*, vol. 369, no. 1645, 19 June 2014, pp. 1–9.

Gumport, Patricia J. *Academic Pathfinders: Knowledge Creation and Feminist Scholarship*. Greenwood Press, 2002.

Günther, Karl-Heinz. "Profiles of Educators: Wilhelm Von Humboldt (1767–1835)." *Prospects-Quarterly Rev. of Edu.*, Translated by Karl-Heinz Günther, vol. 18, no. 65, 1988, pp. 127–36.

Hagemann, Melissa. "Overview of Open Access." *Budapest Open Access Initiative | Overview of Open Access*, 16 Jan. 2003, www.budapestopenaccessinitiative.org/pdf/Melissa_Hagemann.pdf/view.

Haidt, Jonathan. *Coddling of the American Mind: How Good Intentions and Bad Ideas Are Setting up a Generation for Failure*. Penguin Publishing Group, 2018.

Hall, Peter Dobkin. *The Jossey-Bass Handbook of Nonprofit Leadership and Management*. Edited by Robert D. Herman and David O. Renz, Jossey-Bass, 2010.

Hammerstein, Notker. "Universities and War in the Twentieth Century." In *A History of the University in Europe: Volume III, Universities in The Nineteenth and Early Twentieth Centuries*, edited by Walter Rüegg, Cambridge University Press, 2004.

Hansmann, Henry B. "The Evolving Economic Structure of Higher Education." *The University of Chicago Law Review*, vol. 79, 2012, pp. 159–83.

--, "The Role of the Nonprofit Enterprise." *Yale Law Journal*, vol. 89, no. 5, 1980, pp. 835–901.

--, "Why Are Colleges and Universities Exempt From Taxes?" *25th Annual Conference, Colleges and Universities: Legal Issues in the Halls of Ivy*, 2013.

"History and Mission." *Harvard Divinity School*, https://hds.harvard.edu/about/history-and-mission.

Holowchak, Mark. *Thomas Jeffersons Philosophy of Education: a Utopian Dream*. Routledge, 2014.

Hobbes, Thomas. *Leviathan, or, The Matter, Forme and Power of a Commonwealth Ecclesiasticall and Civill*. Green Dragon in St. Paul's Churchyard, 1651.

Holdsworth, W. S. "Press Control and Copyright in the 16th and 17th Centuries." *Yale Law Journal*, vol. 19, 1920, pp. 841–58.

Honorof, Marshall. "Best Streaming Video Services 2019." *Tom's Guide*, Tom's Guide, 9 Sept. 2019, https://www.tomsguide.com/us/best-streaming-video-servic es,review-2625.html.

Hoxby, Caroline. "The Changing Selectivity of American Colleges." *Journal of Economic Perspectives*, vol. 23, no. 4, Oct. 2009, pp. 1–34.

"Humanities Bachelor's Degrees as a Percentage of All Bachelor's Degrees Awarded by Public versus Private Institutions, 1987–2015." *Humanities Indicators*, American Academy of Arts & Sciences, 2017, https://www.humanitiesindicators.org/c ontent/indicatordoc.aspx?i=201.

Hwang, Hokyu, and Walter W. Powell. "The Rationalization of Charity: The Influences of Professionalism in the Nonprofit Sector." *Administrative Science Quarterly*, vol. 54, no. 2, 2009, pp. 268–98.

"Ivy League Schools." *U.S. News*, 23 Sept. 2019, https://www.usnews.com/educatio n/best-colleges/ivy-league-schools.

Jade, Olivia. "Basically All the Tea You Need to Know about Me (Boys, College, Youtubers) – Dailymotion Video." *Dailymotion*, 15 Aug. 2018, www.dailymotio n.com/video/x6s0tqn.

Jenkins, Garry. "Incorporation Choice, Uniformity, and the Reform of Nonprofit State Law." *Georgia Law Review*, vol. 41, no. 4, 2007, pp. 1113–80.

"The Joe Rogan Experience #1139 Interview with Jordan Peterson, Prof. of Psychology, University of Toronto." *YouTube*, 2 July 2018, www.youtube.com/watch?ti me_continue=1&v=9Xc7DN-noAc.

Johnson, Daniel M. *The Uncertain Future of American Public Higher Education: Student-Centered Strategies for Sustainability*. Palgrave Macmillan, 2019.

Johnson, Danné L. "Seeking Meaningful Nonprofit Reform in a Post Sarbanes-Oxley World." *Saint Louis University Law Journal*, vol. 54, no. 1, 2009, pp. 187–240.

Johnson, Rob. "The STM Report: An Overview of Scientific and Scholarly Publishing." *STM*, Oct. 2018, www.stm-assoc.org/2018_10_04_STM_Report_2018.pdf.

Johnstone, Bruce. "Higher Education and Those Out-of-Control Costs." In *In Defense of American Higher Education*. Johns Hopkins University Press, 2001.

Junker, Kirk W. *Legal Culture in the United States: an Introduction*. Routledge, 2016.

Kamenetz, Anya. "More College Presidents Join The Millionaires' Club." *NPR*, 13 Dec. 2017, www.npr.org/sections/ed/2017/12/13/569943593/more-college-presid ents-join-the-millionaires-club.

Kant, Immanuel. "Von Der Unrechtmassigkeit Des Buchernachdruckes." In *Immanuel Kants Werke*, edited by Ernst Cassirer, Berlin: B. Cassirer 1913.

Karabel, Jerome. *The Chosen: the Hidden History of Admission and Exclusion at Harvard, Yale, and Princeton*. Houghton Mifflin Company, 2014.

Kelchen, Robert. "How Much do for-Profit Colleges Rely on Federal Funds?" *Brookings*, 10 Jan. 2017, www.brookings.edu/blog/brown-center-chalkboard/2017/01/11/how-much-do-for-profit-colleges-rely-on-federal-funds/.

Kemp, Deborah. "Copyright on Steroids: In Search of an End to over Protection." *McGeorge Law Review*, vol. 41, 2017, pp. 795–842.

Keohane, Nannerl. "The Liberal Arts and the Role of Elite Higher Education." In *In Defense of American Higher Education*. Johns Hopkins University Press, 2001.

Kerker, Milton. "Science and the Steam Engine." *Technology and Culture*, vol. 2, no. 4, 1961, pp. 381–90.

Kerr, Clark. *The Uses of the University*. Harvard University Press, 2001.

Keyes, A.A. *Fair Use and Free Inquiry: Copyright Law and the New Media*. Ablex, 1980.

Kirp, David L. *Shakespeare, Einstein and the Bottom Line: the Marketing of Higher Education*. Harvard University Press, 2004.

Knaplund, Kristine S. "Charity for the Death Tax: The Impact of Legislation on Charitable Bequests." *Gonzaga Law Review*, vol. 45, 2010, pp. 713–44.

Kosturakis, Irene. "Intellectual Property 101." *Texas Journal of Business Law*, vol. 46, no. 1, 2014, pp. 37–65.

Kostylo, Joanna. "From Gunpowder to Print: The Common Origins of Copyright and Patent." In *Privilege and Property, Essays on the History of Copyright*, edited by Ronan Deazley, Martin Kretschmer, and Lionel Bently, Open Book Publishers, 2010.

Kretschmer, Martin, Lionel Bently, and Ronan Deazley. "The History of Copyright History: Notes from an Emerging Discipline." In *Privilege and Property, Essays on the History of Copyright*, edited by Ronan Deazley, Martin Kretschmer, and Lionel Bently, Open Book Publishers, 2010.

Kwon, Diana. "Sci-Hub Loses Domains and Access to Some Web Services." *The Scientist Magazine®*, 25 Oct. 2018, www.the-scientist.com/daily-news/sci-hub-loses-domains-and-access-to-some-web-services-30264.

Lash, Kurt T. *The Lost History of the Ninth Amendment*. Oxford University Press, 2009.

Lawrence, John Shelton., and Bernard Timberg. *Fair Use and Free Inquiry: Copyright Law and the New Media*. Ablex, 1980.

Lerg, Charlotte A. "Academic Freedom In America: Gilded Age Beginnings And World War I Legacies." *The Journal of the Gilded Age and Progressive Era*, vol. 17, no. 4, 2018, pp. 691–703.

Lessig, Lawrence. *Free Culture: the Nature and Future of Creativity*. Penguin, 2004.

–, *The Future of Ideas: the Fate of the Commons in a Connected World*. Random House, 2003.

Letter from Internal Revenue Service to President and Fellows of Harvard College (Dec. 28, 2011), http://internal.procurement.harvard.edu/files/procurement/files/certificate_501.pdf.

"List of Predatory Journals." *List of Predatory Journals | Stop Predatory Journals*, predatoryjournals.com/journals/.

Litman, Jessica. "The Public Domain." *Emory Law Journal*, vol. 39, no. 4, 1990, pp. 965–1023.

Liu, Joseph P. "The New Public Domain." *University of Illinois Law Review*, vol. 1, no. 4, 2013, pp. 1395–1456.

Liu, Nian Cai., Qi Wang, and Ying Cheng, editors. *Paths to a World-Class University: Lessons from Practices and Experiences*. Sense Publishers, 2011.

Locke, John. "Second Treatise on Government, Chapter V of Property" *John Locke – Second Treatise on Government*, 1690, http://libertyonline.hypermall.com/Locke/second/second-frame.html.

Loren, Lydia Pallas. "Fixation as Notice in Copyright." *Boston University Law Review*, vol. 96, 2016, pp. 939–66.

Lucca, David O., Taylor Nadauld, and Karen Shen. *Credit Supply and the Rise in College Tuition: Evidence from the Expansion in Federal Student Aid Programs*. Vol. G28, I22, Federal Reserve Bank of New York Staff Reports, 2017, pp. 1–31.

Madison, James. "The Federalist Papers: No. 43." *The Avalon Project*, 2008, avalon.law.yale.edu/18th_century/fed43.asp.

---, "Memorial and Remonstrance against Religious Assessments." *National Archives and Records Administration*, 20 June 1785, founders.archives.gov/documents/Madison/01-08-02-0163.

Magraner Rullan, Jp, and R. Martinez-Val. "The Birth of Airplane Stability Theory." *Proceedings of the Institution of Mechanical Engineers, Part G: Journal of Aerospace Engineering*, vol. 228, no. 9, 2013, pp. 1498–1506.

Marciani, Dante. "Boycott of Elsevier Journals: Can New Ideas Reduce the Cost for Scientific Publications?" *Enago Academy*, 23 May 2018, www.enago.com/academy/boycott-of-elsevier-journals-brings-new-ideas-about-cost-for-scientific-publications/.

Marginson, Simon. "The New World Order in Higher Education." In *Questioning Excellence in Higher Education: Policies, Experiences and Challenges in National and Comparative Perspective*. Sense Publishers, 2011.

May, James R., and Erin Daly. *Global Environmental Constitutionalism*. Cambridge University Press, 2015.

Mayer, Lloyd Hitoshi. "Fragmented Oversight of Nonprofits in the United States: Does It Work – Can It Work." *Chicago-Kent Law Review*, vol. 91, 2016, pp. 937–63.

McCullough, David. *The Wright Brothers*. Simon & Schuster, 2015.

McGreal, Chris. "Pentagon Tries to Buy Entire Print Run of US Spy Expose Operation Dark Heart." *The Guardian*, 13 Sept. 2010, www.theguardian.com/world/2010/sep/13/pentagon-afghanistan-spy-book-pulp.

Mcintire, Mike. "The College Sports Tax Dodge." *The New York Times*, 28 Dec. 2017, www.nytimes.com/2017/12/28/sunday-review/college-sports-tax-dodge.html.

McLuhan, Marshall, and Quentin Fiore. *The Medium Is the Massage*. Random House, 1967.

McSherry, Corynne. *Who Owns Academic Work?: Battling for Control of Intellectual Property*. Harvard University Press, 2001.

Meer, Jonathan, and Harvey S. Rosen. "Altruism and the Child Cycle of Alumni Donations." *American Economic Journal, Economic Policy*, vol. 1, 2009, pp. 258–86.

"Membership Policy." *Association of American Universities (AAU)*, Oct. 2016, www.aau.edu/who-we-are/membership-policy.

Mohrman, Kathryn. "Excellence and Mass Higher Education in China and the United States." In *Questioning Excellence in Higher Education: Policies, Experiences and Challenges in National and Comparative Perspective*. Sense Publishers, 2011.

Mokyr, Joel. *A Culture of Growth: the Origins of the Modern Economy*. Princeton University Press, 2017.

--, *The Gifts of Athena: Historical Origins of the Knowledge Economy*. Princeton University Press, 2004.

Morison, Samuel Eliot. *Three Centuries of Harvard, 1636-1936*. Harvard University Press, 1986.

Morse, Robert. "U.S. News Best Colleges Rankings Turn 30 Years Old." *U.S. News & World Report*, 27 Nov. 2013, www.usnews.com/education/blogs/college-rankings-blog/2013/11/27/us-news-best-colleges-rankings-turn-30-years-old.

Nardi, Paolo. "Relations with Authority." In *A History of the University in Europe: Volume I, Universities in The Middle Ages*, edited by Hilde De Ridder-Symoens, Cambridge University Press, 1992.

"National Collegiate Athletic Association – Nonprofit Explorer." *ProPublica*, 9 May 2013, projects.propublica.org/nonprofits/organizations/440567264.

"National Federal Student Loan Cohort Default Rate Continues to Decline." *National Federal Student Loan Cohort Default Rate Continues to Decline | U.S. Department of Education*, U.S. Department of Education, 25 Sept. 2019, www.ed.gov/news/press-releases/national-federal-student-loan-cohort-default-rate-continues-decline.

Netanel, Neil W. *Copyright's Paradox*. Oxford University Press, 2010.

--, *Copyright: What Everyone Needs to Know*. Oxford University Press, 2018.

Nguyen, Nicole A. "Not All Textbooks Are Created Equal: Copyright, Fair Use, and Open Access in the Open College Textbook Act of 2010." *DePaul Journal of Art, Technology and Intellectual Property*, vol. 21, 2010, pp. 105–130.

Nimmer, David and Melville Nimmer. *Nimmer on Copyright*. Matthew Bender Elite Products, 2019.

Nimmer, David. "Access Denied." *Utah Law Review*, no. 3, 2007, pp. 769–88.

---, "Innocence of Copyright: An Inquiry into the Public Interest." *Journal of the Copyright Society of the USA*, vol. 63, no. 3, Summer 2016, pp. 367–410.

---, "Nimmer on Copyright." *LexisNexis Store*, Matthew Bender Elite Products, https://store.lexisnexis.com/products/nimmer-on-copyright-skuusSku10441.

Nimmer, Melville. "Does Copyright Abridge the First Amendment Guarantees of Free Speech and Press." *UCLA Law Review*, vol. 17, no. 6, June 1970, pp. 1180–1204.

Novy-Williams, Eben. "College Football Teams Are Risky and Expensive—and Schools Keep Adding Them." *Bloomberg*, 6 Jan. 2017, www.bloomberg.com/news/features/2017-01-06/college-football-teams-are-risky-and-expensive-and-schools-keep-adding-them.

Nuzhat, Malik. "Charity and Charitable Purposes in the United Kingdom." *The International Journal of Not-for-Profit Law*, vol. 11, no. 1, Nov. 2008, pp. 31–75.

O'Brien, Rebecca Davis. "Ex-Adidas Executive Gets 9-Month Sentence in Basketball Bribery Case." *The Wall Street Journal*, 5 Mar. 2019, www.wsj.com/articles/adidas-executive-gets-9-month-sentence-in-college-basketball-bribery-case-11551821093.

Ochoa, Tyler T. "Origins and Meanings of the Public Domain." *University of Dayton Law Review*, vol. 28, no. 2, 2002, pp. 215–67.

Orwell, George. *Nineteen Eighty-Four*. Penguin Books, 2008. Originally published 1949.

Ovink, Sarah, Demetra Kalogrides, Megan Nanney, and Patrick Delaney. "College Match and Undermatch: Assessing Student Preferences, College Proximity, and Inequality in Post-College Outcomes." *Research in Higher Education*, vol. 59, no. 5, 10 Nov. 2017, pp. 553–90.

Parker, Jacob. "The Best Audiobook Sites 2020: Easy Listening Anywhere." *TechRadar*, 3 Feb. 2020, www.techradar.com/best/the-best-audio-book-sites#4-kobo-audiobooks.

Parker, Kim, and Renee Stepler. "As U.S. Marriage Rate Hovers at 50%, Education Gap in Marital Status Widens." *Pew Research Center*, 14 Sept. 2017, www.pewresearch.org/fact-tank/2017/09/14/as-u-s-marriage-rate-hovers-at-50-education-gap-in-marital-status-widens/.

Parkinson, Robert G. "Print, the Press, and the American Revolution." *Oxford Research Encyclopedia of American History*, 3 Sept. 2015, pp. 1–18.

Peifer, Karl-Nikolaus. "The Return of the Commons – Copyright History as a Common Source." In *Privilege and Property, Essays on the History of Copyright*, edited by Ronan Deazley, Martin Kretschmer, and Lionel Bently, Open Book Publishers, 2010.

"Percentage of All U.S. Doctorates in the Humanities Awarded by Public versus Private Institutions, 1987–2013." *Humanities Indicators*, American Academy of the Arts & Sciences, 2015, https://www.humanitiesindicators.org/content/indicatordoc.aspx?i=10846.

"Percentage of Bachelor's Degrees Awarded to Members of Traditionally Underrepresented Racial/Ethnic Groups,* Selected Academic Fields, 1995–2015." *Humanities Indicators*, American Academy of Arts & Sciences, 2017, https://www.humanitiesindicators.org/content/indicatordoc.aspx?i=38.

Pinker, Steven. *Enlightenment Now the Case for Reason, Science, Humanism, and Progress*. Viking, 2018.

Porter, Roy. "The Scientific Revolution and Universities." In *A History of the University in Europe: Volume II, Universities in Early Modern Europe*, edited by Walter Rüegg, Cambridge University Press, 1996.

Posner, Richard A. *Economic Analysis of Law*. 7th ed., Wolters Kluwer Law & Business, 2007.

Post, Robert. "Academic Freedom and the Constitution." In *Who's Afraid of Academic Freedom?* Columbia University Press, 2015.

Priest, Eric. "Copyright and the Harvard Open Access Mandate." *Northwestern Journal of Technology and Intellectual Property*, vol. 10, no. 7, 2012, pp. 377–440.

"Principprogram." *Piratpartiet*, 2020, piratpartiet.se/principprogram/.

"Privilegium." *Black's Law Dictionary*, edited by Bryan Garner, 9th ed., West Group, 2009.

"Public Catalog." *WebVoyage*, United States Copyright Office, 2020, cocatalog.loc.gov/cgi-bin/Pwebrecon.cgi?DB=local&PAGE=First.

Pugatch, Meir, Rachel Chu, and David Torstensson. "U.S. Chamber International IP Index, 6th Ed." *U.S. Chamber International IP Index, 6th Ed.*, Global Innovation Policy Center, 2018, https://www.uschamber.com/sites/default/files/023331_gipc_ip_index_2018_opt.pdf.

Putnam, R.D. *Bowling Alone: The Collapse and Renewal of American Community*. New York: Simon & Schuster, 2000.

"Rebuttable Presumption – Intermediate Sanctions." *IRS*, 8 Jan. 2020, https://www.irs.gov/charities-non-profits/charitable-organizations/rebuttable-presumption-intermediate-sanctions.

"Research and Reference Services: Frequently Asked Questions." *Library of Congress*, www.loc.gov/rr/res-faq.html.

"Research Guides: Copyright and Fair Use: Copyright in the Classroom." *Copyright in the Classroom – Copyright and Fair Use – Research Guides at Texas A&M University – Central Texas*, tamuct.libguides.com/copyright.

De Ridder-Symoens, Hilde. "Management and Resources." In *A History of the University in Europe: Volume II, Universities in Early Modern Europe*, edited by Walter Rüegg, Cambridge University Press, 1996.

"Right." *Black's Law Dictionary*, edited by Bryan Garner, 9th ed., West Group, 2009.

Roberts, John, Agueda M Rodriguez Cruz, and Jürgen Herbst. "Exporting Models." In *A History of the University in Europe: Volume II, Universities in Early Modern Europe*, edited by Walter Rüegg, Cambridge University Press, 1996.

Roche, Mark. *Was Deutsche von der amerikanischen Universität lernen können und was sie vermeiden sollten*. Translated by Christiana Goldmann, Meiner Felix Verlag, 2014.

Roden, Robert F. *The Cambridge Press, 1638-1692; a History of the First Printing Press Established in English America, Together with a Bibliographical List of the Issues of the Press*. Dodd, Mead, and Company, 1905.

Rooksby, Jacob H. *The Branding of the American Mind: How Universities Capture, Manage, and Monetize Intellectual Property and Why It Matters*. Johns Hopkins University Press, 2016.

—, "Copyright in Higher Education: A Review of Modern Scholarship." *Duquesne University Law Review*, vol. 54, no. 1, 2016, pp. 197–221.

Roomkin, Myron J., Burton A. Weisbrod. "Managerial Compensation and Incentives in For-Profit and Nonprofit Hospitals." *Journal of Law, Economics and Organization*, vol. 15, 1999, p. 750–81.

Rose, Mark. "The Public Sphere and the Emergence of Copyright." In *Privilege and Property, Essays on the History of Copyright*, edited by Ronan Deazley, Martin Kretschmer, and Lionel Bently, Open Book Publishers, 2010.

Rose-Ackerman, Susan. "Unfair Competition and Corporate Income Taxation." *Stanford Law Review*, vol. 34, May 1982, pp. 1017–39.

Rosenfield, Harry N. "The American Constitution, Free Inquiry, and the Law." *Fair Use and Free Inquiry: Copyright Law and the New Media*, edited by John Shelton. Lawrence and Bernard Timberg, Ablex, 1980.

Rostan, Michele, and Massimiliano Vaira. *Questioning Excellence in Higher Education: Policies, Experiences and Challenges in National and Comparative Perspective*. Sense Publishers, 2011.

Roser, Max, Esteban Ortiz-Ospina, and Hannah Ritchie. "Life Expectancy." *Our World in Data*, Oct 2019, https://ourworldindata.org/life-expectancy#citation.

Roth, Gary. "The New Underemployed, Educated Working Class." *New Labor Forum*, vol. 28, no. 3, 18 July 2019, pp. 88–91.

Rounce, Adam. *Authorship in the Eighteenth Century*. Oxford Handbooks, 2015.

Rubin, Eric. "Knowing an 'Educational Institution' When You See One: Applying the Commerciality Approach to Tax Exemptions for Universities Under § 501 (c)(3)." *Washington Law Review*, vol. 92, 2015, pp. 1055–81.

Rüegg, Walter. "The Rise of Humanism." In *A History of the University in Europe: Volume I, Universities in The Middle Ages*, edited by Hilde De Ridder-Symoens, Cambridge University Press, 1992.

—, "Themes." In *A History of the University in Europe: Volume I, Universities in The Middle Ages*, edited by Hilde De Ridder-Symoens, Cambridge University Press, 1992.

—, "Themes." In *A History of the University in Europe: Volume III, Universities in The Nineteenth and Early Twentieth Centuries*, edited by Walter Rüegg, Cambridge University Press, 2004.

—, "Themes." In *A History of the University in Europe: Volume IV, Universities Since 1945*, edited by Walter Rüegg, Cambridge University Press, 2011.

Russo, Ralph D. "Wave of Concussion Lawsuits to Test NCAA's Liability." *USA Today*, 7 Feb. 2019, eu.usatoday.com/story/sports/ncaaf/2019/02/07/wave-of-concussion-lawsuits-to-test-ncaas-liability/39022587/.

Salamon, Lester M. *Partners in Public Service Government-Nonprofit Relations in the Modern Welfare State*. The Johns Hopkins University Press, 1996.

Salamon, Lester M., and Stefan Toepler. "The Impact of Law on Nonprofit Development: A Framework for Analysis." In *Met Recht Betrokken: Opstellen Aangeboden Aan Prof. Mr. T.J. Van Der Ploeg*. Edited by C. H. C. Overes and T. J. van der Ploeg, Kluwer, 2012.

Salmi, Jamil. "Paths to a World-Class University." In *Paths to a World-Class University: Lessons from Practices and Experiences*. Sense Publishers, 2011.

Samuels, Edward B. *The Illustrated Story of Copyright*. Thomas Dunne Books/St. Martins Griffin, 2000.

Saul, Stephanie. "Endowments Boom as Colleges Bury Earnings Overseas." *The New York Times*, The New York Times, 8 Nov. 2017, https://www.nytimes.com/2017/11/08/world/universities-offshore-investments.html.

Scott, W. Richard. *Organizations: Rational, Natural and Open Systems*. 5th ed., Prentice Hall, 2003.

Schrum, Ethan D. *The Instrumental University: Education in Service of the National Agenda after World War II*. Cornell University Press, 2019.

Schuessler, Jennifer. "Hoaxers Slip Breastaurants and Dog-Park Sex Into Journals." *The New York Times*, The New York Times, 5 Oct. 2018, www.nytimes.com/2018/10/04/arts/academic-journals-hoax.html.

Serena, Jeff, editor. *The Autobiography of Benjamin Franklin the Complete Illustrated History*. Zenith Press, 2016.

Shapiro, Harold T. *A Larger Sense of Purpose: Higher Education and Society: Non Nobis Solum*. Princeton University Press, 2005.

Shahbaz, Adrian. "The Rise of Digital Authoritarianism." *Freedom on the Net 2018*, Oct. 2018, freedomhouse.org/sites/default/files/FOTN_2018_Final Booklet_11_1_2018.pdf.

"Share Your Work." *Creative Commons*, creativecommons.org/share-your-work/.

Shils, Edward, and John Roberts. "The Diffusion of European Models Outside Europe." In *A History of the University in Europe: Volume III, Universities in The Nineteenth and Early Twentieth Centuries*, edited by Walter Rüegg, Cambridge University Press, 2004.

Sidel, Mark. "The Nonprofit Sector and the New State Activism." *Michigan Law Review*, vol. 100, no. 6, 2002, pp. 1312–35.

Siegmund-Schultze, Reinhard. *Mathematicians Fleeing from Nazi Germany Individual Fates and Global Impact*. Princeton University Press, 2009.

Sites, Brian. "Fair Use and the New Transformative." *Columbia Journal of Law and the Arts*, vol. 39, no. 4, 2016, pp. 513–50.

Smith, Adam. *An Inquiry into the Nature and Causes of the Wealth of Nations*, edited by S.M. Soares. MetaLibri Digital Library 2007, original published in 1776, p. 48.

Smith, Chris. "College Football's Most Valuable Teams: Texas A&M Jumps To No. 1." *Forbes*, 11 Sept. 2018, www.forbes.com/sites/chrissmith/2018/09/11/college-footballs-most-valuable-teams/#4c1eb8906c64.

Smith, Steven Carl. *An Empire of Print: the New York Publishing Trade in the Early American Republic*. The Pennsylvania State University Press, 2017.

Smith, Steven Rathgeb, and Michael Lipsky, *Nonprofits for Hire: The Welfare State in the Age of Contracting* 26 Cambridge, MA: Harvard University Press (1993).

Snyder, Thomas D., Cristobal de Brey, and Sally A. Dillow. "Digest of Education Statistics, 2017." 53rd ed., National Center for Education Statistics, 2019, pp. 1–854.

Spann, Girardeau. "Constitutionalization." *St. Louis University Law Journal*, vol. 49, 2005, pp. 709–47.

"Spotlight on Speech Codes 2019." *FIRE*, 2019, www.thefire.org/resources/spotlight/reports/spotlight-on-speech-codes-2019/.

"The State of the Humanities 2018: Graduates in the Workforce & Beyond." *Humanities Indicators*, American Academy of Arts & Sciences, Feb. 2018, www.amacad.org/publication/state-humanities-2018-graduates-workforce-beyond.

Stone, Geoffrey R. "A Brief History of Academic Freedom." In *Who's Afraid of Academic Freedom?* Columbia University Press, 2015.

Strauss, Karsten. "The Highest-Paid Private College Presidents." *Forbes*, 13 Dec. 2017, www.forbes.com/sites/karstenstrauss/2017/12/13/the-highest-paid-private-college-presidents-2/#eec628f6e67 b.

Sugin, Linda. "Strengthening Charity Law: Replacing Media Oversight with Advance Rulings for Nonprofit Fiduciaries." *Tulane Law Review*, vol. 89, 2015, pp. 869–907.

Sullivan, Neil J. *The Prometheus Bomb the Manhattan Project and Government in the Dark*. Potomac Books, an Imprint of the University of Nebraska Press, 2016.

Tarr, G. Alan., Robert F. Williams, and Josef Marko, editors. *Federalism, Subnational Constitutions, and Minority Rights*. Praeger, 2004.

"These Law Schools Leave Students with the Most Debt." *U.S. News & World Report*, www.usnews.com/best-graduate-schools/top-law-schools/grad-debt-rankings?name=Wake Forest University.

"This Information Wants to Be Free: Casebooks by NYU Law IP Professors Are Available at No Charge." *NYU School of Law*, 5 Sept. 2019, www.law.nyu.edu/news/ideas/Fromer-Sprigman-Beebe-copyright-trademark-casebooks.

Trow, Martin. "From Mass Higher Education to Universal Access, the American Advantage." In *In Defense of American Higher Education*. Johns Hopkins University Press, 2001.

"The Ultimate Admissions Guide: 75 Steps For Getting Into Your Dream College." *YesCollege*, yescollege.com/guides/get-into-your-dream-school/.

"Understanding College and University Endowments." *American Council on Education*, 2014, www.acenet.edu/Documents/Understanding-Endowments-White-Paper.pdf.

"Use & Remix." *Creative Commons*, creativecommons.org/use-remix/.

"Using Content ID – YouTube Help." Google, Google, https://support.google.com/youtube/answer/3244015?hl=en.

Vance, J. D. *Hillbilly Elegy*. HarperCollins Books, 2016.

Van der Wende, Marijk. "Towards a European Approach to Ranking." In *Paths to a World-Class University: Lessons from Practices and Experiences*. Sense Publishers, 2011.

Veblen, Thorstein. *Higher Learning in America: a Memorandum on the Conduct of Universities by Business Men*. Nabu Press, 2010.

Vedder, Richard K. *Restoring the Promise: Higher Education in America*. Independent Institute, 2019.

---, "There Are Really Almost No Truly Private Universities." *Forbes*, 8 Apr. 2018, https://www.forbes.com/sites/richardvedder/2018/04/08/there-are-really-almost-no-truly-private-universities/#a61d0c757bc5.

Verger, Jacques. "Patterns." In *A History of the University in Europe: Volume I, Universities in The Middle Ages*, edited by Hilde De Ridder-Symoens, Cambridge University Press, 1992.

Vest, Charles M. *The American Research University from World War II to World Wide Web: Governments, the Private Sector, and the Emerging Meta-University*. University of California Press, 2007.

Wade, James B., Joseph F. Porac, and Timothy G. Pollock. "Worth, Words, and the Justification of Executive Pay." *Journal of Organizational Behavior*, vol. 18, 1997, pp. 641–64.

Wagner, Bettina, and Marcia Reed. *Early Printed Books as Material Objects: Proceedings of the Conference Organized by the IFLA Rare Books and Manuscripts Section, Munich, 19–21 August 2009*. International Federation of Library Associations, 2010.

"Wake Forest University 2019 Tuition." *Univstats*, www.univstats.com/colleges/wake-forest-university/cost-of-attendance.

"Wake Forest University Is #98 on MONEY's 2019-20 #BestColleges List." *#98 In MONEY's 2019-20 Best Colleges Ranking*, money.com/best-colleges/profile/wake-forest-university/.

Walshok, Mary Lindenstein., and Daniel Yankelovich. *Knowledge without Boundaries: What Americas Research Universities Can Do for the Economy, the Workplace, and the Community*. Jossey-Bass, 1995.

Weisbrod, Burton Allen. *The Nonprofit Economy*. Harvard University Press, 1988.

Wenger, Mark R. "Thomas Jefferson, the College of William and Mary, and the University of Virginia." *The Virginia Magazine of History and Biography*, vol. 103, no. 3, July 1995, pp. 339–74.

Westerheijden, Don, et.al. “Ranking Goes International.” In *Questioning Excellence in Higher Education: Policies, Experiences and Challenges in National and Comparative Perspective*. Sense Publishers, 2011.

“What Is Fair Use?” *YouTube*, YouTube, https://www.youtube.com/about/copyright/fair-use/#yt-copyright-protection.

“Who We Are.” *Association of American Universities (AAU)*, www.aau.edu/who-we-are.

Willinsky, John. *The Access Principle: the Case for Open Access to Research and Scholarship*. MIT Press, 2006.

Wilson, Helen. “Retracted Article: Human Reactions to Rape Culture and Queer Performativity at Urban Dog Parks in Portland, Oregon.” *Gender, Place & Culture*, 22 May 2018, pp. 1–20. doi:https://doi.org/10.1080/0966369X.2018.1475346.

Winther, Rasmus Grønfeldt. “Systemic Darwinism.” *PNAS*, vol. 105, no. 33, 2018, pp. 11833–38.

“World Happiness Report 2019.” edited by John F. Helliwell, Richard Layard and Jeffrey D. Sachs, *World Happiness Report*, United Nations, 2019, s3.amazonaws.com/happiness-report/2019/WHR19.pdf.

Zetter, Kim. “Pirate Bay Has Been Raided and Taken Down: Here's What We Know.” *Wired*, Conde Nast, 3 June 2017, www.wired.com/2014/12/pirate-bay-raided-taken-down/.

Miscellaneous Sources

ABA Model Nonprofit Corporation Act, Third Edition § 6.40. (2008).

ABA Model Nonprofit Corporation Act, Third Edition § 6.41. (2008).

Interview with Professor from India (name withheld) (Nov. 13, 2018).

Telephone interview with Paul S. McGrath Esq., Business and Legal Affairs Coordinator, Skydance Media (Feb. 26, 2019).

Telephone interview with Richard Allen, Mechanical Engineer, Perryman Company (Mar. 26, 2019).

Telephone interview with Sarah Pearson, Senior Counsel Creative Commons (Nov. 14, 2018).